Chemical Muscle Enhancement
(The BDR)
By Author L. Rea

TABLE OF CONTENTS

WARNING: READ FIRST

OVER 20 YEARS AGO...

Over 2o years ago I was an avid martial arts competitor and power lifter, weighing 135 pounds. I had a goal of becoming a doctor with a degree in biochemistry. Obviously sports medicine was my dream, but something changed this: I became a bodybuilder. I read every magazine (between studies) available concerning bodybuilding and trained exactly as outlined. I ate what the magazines said I should; I used the supplements they promised would "add 20 pounds of muscle in only 10 days" and gained about 10 LBS... eventually. Something was really wrong. First, I began my quest for mass by researching every known available paper on training, nutrition, and yes...anabolic/androgenic steroids (AAS). Next I did a survey of a profound number of bodybuilders and athletes. 30 months later I weighed 230LBS with 9 % body fat and had not yet administered a single AAS. Not bad, I suppose, for 5'7'. But genetics are merely "accepted" (unnecessarily) limitations. Science has answers for all those who will learn. There is unlimited scientific research available. But putting the complete maximum-results-puzzle together took time.

My next project was to learn the growth mechanisms beginning at the cellular level, and yes, anabolic chemistry. Next stop 270 LBS at 10% body fat. However, this took far too much time in my opinion. To cut the story short, I can now manipulate my body weight 30 LBS in 60 days, or less. I am not claiming that this was the healthiest approach, nor am I endorsing the use of any drug by any stretch of the imagination. I am merely reporting upon the facts derived from several athletes personal experiences as well as my own.

I started a professional training and sports rehab company and did part time research and development for various supplement companies. This added nicely to my bank account but failed to be interesting or progressive. Most supplement companies want cheap, not effective, products.

Training and writing became the primary outlet for knowledge gathered through studies, research, and at times from rather bizarre sources. To say I truly love the human body as the supreme expression of art is simplistic at best.

WHY STEROIDS AND WHAT IS POSSIBLE ?

The body is in a constant state of "protein turn over". Two terms the reader should be very familiar with are catabolic (catabolism) and anabolic (anabolism). Catabolism is a tissue wasting state and anabolism is a tissue rebuilding or growth state. The "protein turn over" is a balance between the two. Many scientists believe that a 154 LB adult turns over about 280 g of protein daily. Of course not all of this is muscle protein, but some where around 30% is the general accepted amount. Guess what? This figure group is for a sedentary adult, not an athlete, and refers to basal protein anabolism/catabolism. Using 30 % as a qualified representation of the amount of muscle proteins turned over, we see about 77 LBS of the amount of muscle was both gained and lost in one year. This means that this sedentary adult could have actually gained half again his body weight in lean mass tissue without a single work out all year. Also a note of interest is the fact that he actually gained and lost a total of 225 LBS in lean protein tissue in one year. By the way, this is all fact established by research done **by W.E. Mitch and published in the New England Journal of Medicine (96-335:1897)**. To find your own daily protein turn over rate (PTOR), simply multiply your body weight in pounds by 1.818. (154lbs x 1.818 = 279.972g). This is your potential daily mass gain! (What?) Yes, if you could control all metabolic factors this is the amount of protein based tissue you could gain in one day. But being cheesy is not always easy.

Anabolic and catabolic hormones control the body's PTOR. The balance between gain and loss is called homeostasis and basal. If our adult reduced catabolism by 50% without altering the anabolic rate, our 154LB adult would gain 38 LBS of lean muscle in a single year. Weight training accelerates both anabolism and catabolism. If he trains in a manner which accelerates catabolism more than anabolism he loses muscle. This is over training. If he trains in a manner which accelerates anabolism more than catabolism then he gains muscle. Studies have established that training induced catabolism destroys 80% of the training induced anabolism. This leaves us with about a 20% growth differential. Most bodybuilders actually reach a point very quickly where anabolism is equal to catabolism and they stagnate. Now you know why you are stuck in your training efforts so often. You lose what you gain.

Let's take a look at the actual break down of a 20% differential using a 200 LB bodybuilder who trained properly, ate properly, and maintained this 20% anabolism differential for a year:
**Protein tissue gains from basal (normal resting) protein synthesis = 100 LBS
**Protein tissue gains induced by training = 55 LBS. Total muscle gain =155 LBS
**Protein tissue lost due to basal muscle catabolism =100 LBS
**Protein tissue lost due to training induced protein catabolism =44 LBS
**Total muscle lost yearly = 144 LBS
**Total muscle gained yearly = 11 LBS.
Our bodybuilder beat homeostasis by 11 LBS!

Any questions about *why* athletes reported use of anabolic chemistry or anti-catabolic chemistry should be clearer by now.

I have utilized pretty much every available chemical muscle enhancing technique there is at one time or another on myself or monitored the results upon those who (of their own volition) did so. This would of course traumatize many of my peers, but so what. Mine is not to judge others who make informed choices of their own. Many of these so-called peers have or will die from alcohol and tobacco. Sad, but their choice. My blood tests always look far better than most of these peers... and I am pretty cheesy! The reader should again note that this is not an endorsement of such practices. It is simply a fact.

I once personally (once? Ya right!) pushed the envelope to see how much of this scientific data (most of which was available 15 years ago) could be validated in the real world. I suppressed my cortisol (chemically), increased anabolism (also chemically) and increased metabolism (of course chemically) for 30 days. I ingested protein (complete) levels based upon basal plus 20%, and ate 2.5g of carbs (mostly maltodextrin and veggies) per LB of bodyweight while allowing fats to fall where they may. 30 days later I was 33 LBS heavier with a slightly lower body fat level. Ya pretty cheesy, huh?

So, though I seldom directly quote research, I do have a great deal of personal interest in the subjects which follow as well as anecdotal information collected from literally hundreds of athletes over the years. This of course would mean nothing if not for clinical information for validation as well. At least to me! And it pays the bills.

Explanations of abbreviated terms utilized in The Drug Descriptions section:

-AMP Ampule
-CAP Capsule
-INJ Injection
-I.U. International Units
-MCG Microgram (1/1000 of a milligram)
-MG Milligram (1/1000 of a gram)
-GM/gm Gram (1/1000 of a Kilogram)
-50MG/ml The product provides 50 mg of substance contained in one milliliter of injection fluid.
- 3mg 2xd (or) 3mg 2XD 3 milligrams two times daily

WHAT ARE STEROIDS ?

Before reading the following chapters it is vital the reader has a basic understanding of natural testosterone production and its actions. I realize that it is probably pretty boring for many readers but I have also found it is quite necessary foundational knowledge. Besides the obvious, it is kind of fun to find out what else "the boys" can do anyway. I wish to warn any sensitive readers about my writing style: Though some may take offense at my candidness concerning any topic including sexuality (yes, I said the "S" word) I apologize to no one who chooses to read beyond this point. Simply stated, it is my right to freedom of expression and your right to choose not to read on or agree. (Yes, I once received a letter declaring me "perverse" for the words…"the boys became raisins no sun could shrink worse".)

There are several sex hormones. Some such as estradiol, estrone, and progesterone are sex hormones referred to as estrogens. Androstenedione, androstenediol, and testosterone are referred to as naturally occurring endogenous (made inside the body) androgens. The former group is the prominent hormones in females responsible for the formation of female pattern fat deposits such as in breast, hips, and buttock areas as well as the formation and maturation of the female sex organs. The latter group, Androgens, are the prominent hormones in males that are responsible for characteristics such as a deeper voice, increased muscle and bone mass, facial hair, increased body hair, male sex organ formation and development, and aggressiveness.

*You would think that last characteristic was true of estrogens too, since PMS is a defense for murder! (It is)

Both men and women produce androgens and estrogens. Women's dominant production is estrogens, and men's dominant production is androgens. Reverse this and each will take on their counter-parts characteristic to quite some extent. Our main focus for the following chapters is the male androgen testosterone and its almost endless derivatives and esters.

On average, men produce 4-10 mg of testosterone daily. This means that an average male can synthesize 28-70mg of endogenous testosterone weekly. However, before we go on, a basic understanding of other hormones is necessary also.

FEMALE HORMONE SYNTHESIS

(And hormones men share with them)

Women produce testosterone without testicles. (DUH!) A woman's sex hormones are produced starting at the adrenal glands and ovaries. Through a series of conversion enzyme pathways (chemicals that alter the molecular structure of other chemicals) their bodies synthesize the necessary sex, Glucocorticoid, and Mineralocorticoid steroids.

Mineralocorticoid hormones like Aldosterone regulate mineral balances such as electrolytes and their corresponding water retention and release. Aldosterone is responsible to a great extent for the bloated look and edemas women experience during menstruation. Aldosterone release is significantly affected by other hormones such as estrogens. High estrogen levels result in high aldosterone levels, which in turn result in high water retention.

Glucocorticoid steroids are catabolic (tissue wasting) steroids which break down predominantly damaged tissues for repair and subsequent reuse. The catabolized tissues can be reused as an energy source, or as a source of amino acids (proteins) for assimilation into new tissue. Yes, this Borg-like hormone class will assimilate healthy muscle tissue also to maintain homeostasis (a balance between building and tearing down). The main glucocorticoid steroid hormone focused upon for this book long discussion is cortisol due to the fact that it has a profound catabolic effect upon muscle tissue. Before you think, "Why don't muscleheads just stop all cortisol synthesis somehow and be the next Mr. or Ms. Olympia ?", let me explain. Their intent is to regulate, not stop, cortisol production. Tissue can not be rebuilt or made bigger and stronger unless it is first damaged and cleared of the waste products created. Cortisol aids in this metabolic process. Without it, anabolic (tissue building) hormones and chemicals would greatly lose their effects (and immune systems would fail to work adequately). So their goal is to allow enough cortisol for proper catabolism and immune function, but not so much as to allow catabolism to become dominant over anabolism. Cortisol activity can also be controlled site-specifically, but that is a complete different issue. Both men and women endogenously (naturally occurring in the body) synthesize mineralocorticoid and glucocorticoid steroids.

MALE HORMONE SYNTHESIS

Males synthesize androgens at a much higher level than females because they have testicles. Testicles are referred to as "testes" and are located in the scrotum. (Hey, I once received a letter asking how to get "testes" and where do they come from. So stop with the "hey stupid" comments) They also produce androgens through biosynthesis due to enzymatic pathways starting from the adrenal glands which are located near the kidneys. Predominantly, the adrenal glands (there are two) produce epinephrine, which is also called adrenaline, but also produce other hormones commonly referred to as pro-hormones through a biosynthesis processes and due to conversion enzymes. The lion's share of a male's androgens are produced by the Leydig's cells located in the testes. The most active and dominant androgen is testosterone, which is of course the main focus of this discussion.

Testosterone production is governed by the hypothalamus- pituitary -testes -axis referred to hereafter as the "HPTA". The HPTA has a series of checks and balances all influenced by serum (the fluid part of the blood containing the active hormones which circulate through the body) levels of several hormones and pro-hormones. If testosterone production is too low, the testes signal the hypothalamus to release more leutenizing-hormone-releasing- hormone (LHRH). The circulating LHRH tells the pituitary to release more leutenizing- hormone (LH) and follicle-stimulating-hormone (FSH). When the circulating FSH and LH reach the testes, they signal the Leydig's cells to produce more sperm and testosterone.

When testosterone levels are too high the testes signal the hypothalamus to release less LHRH…and then "the boy's" production process decreases or stops. It is quite interesting that elevated estrogen levels can signal a production decrease for androgens, such as testosterone, far more significantly than any androgen. Please, read that again to be sure you understand the basic HPTA function. It does relate heavily to the effects and effectiveness of exogenous (occurring outside the body) AAS use by athletes. THIS IS AN IMPORTANT FUNCTION TO PROTECT!

TESTOSTERONE... WHAT DOES IT DO ?

The main androgen focused upon for this discussion is testosterone. But please realize that almost all synthetic AAS are chemical variants of testosterone and therefore much of the characteristics apply to them as well. (But not all!) Testosterone has two distinct characteristics or effects.

First, its anabolic characteristics (tissue building) which express themselves as increased and accelerated muscle tissue build-up which leads to faster recovery time after training, illness, and injuries, and to a quicker "regeneration" (I hate that word!) of the entire body. This is because an anabolic response leads to the promotion of protein synthesis and tissue repair or increase.

Secondly, androgenic characteristics or effects which are commonly referred to as secondary male characteristics that promote sexual behavior, libido, development and maturing of the penis, body hair, beard growth, deeper voice, aggressiveness, and formation and maturation of sperm. And of course, as any pubescent boy will tell you, increased production of the sebaceous gland and pimples.

As mentioned before, circulatory levels of testosterone also effect HPTA function, so I should not list it as a characteristic unless I also list pretty much every other sex-hormone as well.

When discussing the characteristics of testosterone or its androgen cousins and synthetic AAS relatives, it is important to understand the difference between free (or active) testosterone and bound (or inactive) testosterone/AAS (Anabolic/Androgenic Steroids). Bound testosterone is inactive because it is bound to SHBG (Sex Hormone Binding Globulin) and to a lesser degree, albumin. The sex-steroid molecules are bound by SHBG contained in the blood, which prevents them from fitting into their receptors. That will be explained later. Free (unbound/active) testosterone is able to transmit its characteristics because it fits into receptors. Bound testosterone equals about 97-99% of total testosterone circulation while free testosterone equals 1-3% of total testosterone.

That probably does not sound like much, but even 0.1-0.3 mg of free testosterone has a whole lot of individual separate molecules. And 1 molecule can activate every receptor-site it binds to.

Males have a total testosterone reference range of 225-950 ng/dl (nanograms per decaliter). And a free testosterone reference range for males is 1-3% of the total testosterone reference range. Females have a total testosterone reference range of 14-76 ng/dl and a free testosterone reference range of 0.5-1.8 ng/dl.

Bound testosterone can be unbound due to metabolic requirements and different steroid molecules. And both endogenous and exogenous AAS can react differently to **SHBG**. For this reason some synthetic AAS can alter the ratio for any other free and/or bound androgenic levels.

*As can prohormones and some minerals such as zinc, copper, and magnesium.

Most steroid molecules are specific to their respective cell receptors. This means only testosterone/androgen/AAS molecules can fit into (and transmit their respective message) testosterone/androgen receptor-sites. This is due to shape and size much like a key and a lock: Some keys can fit into other locks, but only the right key can fit in *and activate* the mechanism. Steroid molecules travel through the blood stream and lymphatic system. This means that everywhere blood goes, the molecules are sure to follow. Using muscle cells as an example, testosterone molecules circulate until they come into contact with testosterone/androgen receptor-sites on the muscle cell. Then they lock together and they form a complex called (what else?) a steroid / receptor complex. Now the complex travels to the cell nucleus where it can bond to specific sequences on the nucleic acid sections of desoxyribonucleic acid (DNA). Here is where a transcription happens and a template of the DNA is created, resulting in messenger ribonucleic acid (mRNA). The mRNA exits the cell nucleus and bonds to/with RNA in the liquid part of the cell called the cytoplasm. Here a translation of the message takes place and an increase in protein synthesis occurs. There is a correlating decrease in catabolism as well. This is because testosterone molecules can occupy cortisol receptor-sites and block them. Therefore cortisol can not get in to transmit its message. The results are growth! A simple way of looking at this is… you go to someone's house to deliver a message and their mom relays it exactly so the job gets done. Sorry about the techno-geek info, but it helps later.

*It should be noted that different labs in different places use slightly different reference ranges. As example 300-1000ng/dl is a common male reference range used by my local lab.

AAS INCREASE PHOSPHOCREATINE SYNTHESIS

Those who have used creatine products such as creatine monohydrate or creatine phosphate realize the effects that more creatine can provide. When anabolic/androgenic steroids (AAS) are administered they cause an increase in Phosphocreatine (CP) synthesis. Let me explain why this creatine stuff is such a cool thing.

ATP (Adenosine Triphosphate) is the fuel that your muscles use to actuate contractions. For this to happen ATP must be changed into ADP (Adenosine Diphosphate) so that energy can be released. This in turn allows for muscular contractions. In order to convert ADP back into the energy source ATP phospcreatine (CP) is needed. So the more CP that is available, the greater the regeneration of ADP to ATP and the greater the work capacity of the muscle at an accelerated rate. There was once a belief that elevated cellular CP levels added strength but not size. Obviously this belief was crushed when creatine products hit the supplement market. Increased CP levels also increase cellular glycogen and protein stores (amino acids) in muscle tissue. This action of course AAS do quite well and so do creatine products. So CP also increases cellular size, due to an increase in intercellular nutrient volume.

*Phosphocreatine is the endogenously produced form of creatine, and is often referred to as creatine phosphate or CP.

AAS POSITIVELY EFFECT FAT

AAS have a positive effect upon fat distribution and storage. There are 3 reasons for this. The first reason is that AAS reduce the amount of insulin released in response to nutrient intake and improved insulin sensitivity. This is in part due to an improved CP synthesis rate and other metabolic factors resulting in an athlete's muscle cells becoming better able to absorb nutrients such as carbohydrates in the form of glucose and glycogen and proteins in the form of amino acids. Insulin is anti-catabolic and anabolic. Great for muscle cells, but it also causes the conversion of glucose into glycerol and then into triglycerides. Insulin can therefore increase fat stores and growth of fat cells. A decrease in insulin release and an increase in insulin sensitivity means better utilization of nutrients for muscle growth.

The second reason AAS effect fat is because testosterone blocks the activity of a fat-synthesizing hormone called lipoprotein lipase. Since lipoprotein lipase is blocked, less can be produced and stored. GH also has this effect.

The third way testosterone affects fat synthesis is not positive. When testosterone levels are elevated, more is converted into estrogens by way of the conversion enzyme aromatase. This is called aromatization, an important word to understand before reading the rest of this book! Estrogen in turn increases female pattern fat deposits and suppresses HPTA function. Atleast estrogen can increase GH production.

AAS EFFECT BLOOD VOLUME

Anyone who has used AAS (anabolic/androgenic steroids) in the past has noted the increased "muscle pump" effect. This is partly due to elevated phosphocreatine (CP) synthesis explained earlier, but also due to an increase in blood volume. Testosterone increases red blood cell production and count by stimulating the red bone marrow. This also up-regulates hemoglobin production. Hemoglobin is an iron containing compound found in the blood that carries oxygen from the lungs to body tissues such as muscle. This results in a larger appearing, more vascular, harder muscle that receives more oxygen and nutrients. This is a potentially a positive aspect to a point since the result is greater training capacity and improved tissue regeneration. Unfortunately excessive increases in red blood cell count can lead to platelet aggregation and blood clots.

*A note of interest here is that a circulatory chemical called fibrinogen causes blood clotting. There is a great deal of evidence supporting the belief that beer and red wine inhibit this chemical. This is not an excuse to get plowed, but moderate ingestion may be a consideration. A common OTC (over the counter) drug utilized as a so-called blood thinner is Asprin. Asprin is a non-specific COX inhibitor (See Prostaglandins for more info) which may also have some negative effects upon PGE-1 and PGF-2. Prostaglandins are important growth factors in the muscle building process.

WHAT HAPPENS AFTER TESTOSTERONE MOLECULES LEAVE RECEPTORS?

After a testosterone (or AAS) molecule has bonded with an androgen receptor-site and delivered its message, it returns to the blood stream. It can either contact other receptor-sites and do it all again, or it can be changed by enzymic reactions into other compounds such as estrogen, androstenediol, etc., or converted into ineffective molecules which are then excreted though urine. The testosterone molecule can also be converted into DHT (dihydrotestosterone). DHT has a higher affinity (attraction) to receptor-sites than testosterone. DHT has strong androgenic characteristics and weak anabolic qualities for the most part. In fact, DHT is about 5-times as androgenic as testosterone. It also loves sebaceous glands, hair follicles, and prostate tissue. This means more acne and oily skin, hair loss on the scalp, and potential growth of prostate tissue if there is an excess of estrogen and the 5-LO enzyme present. The good news is that DHT improves muscle hardness and cannot be aromatized to estrogen. Regardless of type or derivative, all steroid molecules are processed by the liver and hit the toilet eventually.

STEROIDS: GROWTH ON THE CELLULAR LEVEL

Only a few years ago, scientists claimed that all muscular size increases realized from AAS use was due to nothing more than increased water retention. Part of the reason for such idiotic beliefs was the obvious size and strength losses that occurred after AAS were discontinued.

Muscle growth happens by way of 2 mechanisms:

(1) The enlargement of individual muscle cells and muscle fibers via elevated protein synthesis caused by anabolic substances. This is the first growth mechanism and its called hypertrophy. Androgens such as testosterone (endogenous or exogenous) and all AAS have the greatest effect at this level.

(2) The second is called hyperplasia which involves the formation of new muscle cells and fibers. Though hyperplasia has not been proven in humans, there is a great deal of research creating great doubt that it does not. As example…a study involving a group of college students that were untrained, and a group of competitive bodybuilders that were. Obviously the bodybuilders had much larger arm measurements, yet when muscle biopsies were performed on both groups the individual muscle fibers were identical. Since the bodybuilders had significantly "more" fibers, the researchers theorized that they must have experienced hyperplasia.

Another study on power lifters told the story much more clearly. Two groups of highly trained power lifters were divided in two (groups that is). One group had trained life-long steroid free while the other group had an average of 9 years of steroid use. The steroid group had cycled Anadrol-50, Winstrol-V, Primobolan, Deca Durabolin, Masteron, and Proviron off and on in various combinations for that period. The steroid group showed a significant increase in the "number" of muscle fibers when compared to the drug free power lifters. In the steroid group, researchers also noted an increase in the number of muscle cell nuclei and an enhanced proportion of newly formed muscle fibers. These new fibers with more nuclei were formed from satellite-cells. Satellite cells are immature muscle cells. That is HYPERPLASIA.

Another finding that is equally amazing is that the satellite-cells were found to have a higher number of androgen receptors. This means that the new cells/fibers have a greater capacity to use androgens such as AAS. This study showed that the size of the muscle cell reflects the number of cell nuclei. This study also showed that there was an increase in satellite-cell numbers in the steroid group significantly higher when compared to the drug free group.. So what does this all mean?

Intense training with heavy weights creates a stress on muscle fibers and cells high enough to cause hyperplasia and cellular growth. Those who utilize AAS as part of their training protocol accelerate these responses to the training stimuli. The newly formed muscle cells and fibers have a higher content of androgen receptors so AAS work better on these new cells. Since AAS cause an increase in muscle cell DNA and therefore increases protein synthesis with no increase in catabolism, (actually AAS decrease the normal rate of catabolism) the formation of new cells and fibers is accelerated. Bigger muscles! An important point to add is that years of training intensely can pay off for those who do not give up training without AAS. New fibers added to existing fibers means more fibers that can grow. In theory, this suggests AAS, which are highly anabolic, (protein synthesis) would be advantageous over those providing higher androgen qualities for long term gains. This is, in part, why more lean mass has been retained post-cycle when high anabolic/ low-moderate androgenic steroids were utilized.

* Satellite-cell production and subsequent fiber inclusion are predominantly stimulated by IGF-1 and FGF (See IGF-1 and FGF for more info).

DRUG
REFERENCES

&

DESCRIPTIONS

It should be noted by the reader that this section is based upon clinical research information, personal experiences, and returns from surveys of athlete's whom have used the drugs listed. In the **Drug References & Descriptions** section under **"Reported Characteristics"** listings such as "Average Reported Dosages" are based upon interviews with athlete's and the survey returns from polled athletes and are *not in any way meant as a recommendation or advise.*

ORAL ANABOLIC/ANDROGENIC STEROIDS

Many Anabolic/Androgenic Steroids (AAS) are available in an oral form. Unfortunately some are also quite toxic to the liver. Orally administered AAS are very susceptible to first pass liver deactivation unless chemical molecular structures are altered to make them harder to deactivate. When an oral AAS is swallowed it enters the stomach where it is partially broken down and passed to the small intestines. The small intestines contain a group of enzymes called CYP-450's. These enzymes begin to break down the AAS further in an attempt to deactivate it. The AAS is then absorbed through intestinal mucosa cells and transferred to the liver portal vein for further deactivation into inactive chemicals such as etiocholanone. These chemicals are then conjugated with glucuronic acid and excreted in urine. Up to 100% of the original compound can be deactivated in this process which is known as first pass deactivation.

By altering the steroid molecule structures deactivation can be greatly reduced. Some AAS are made orally active by adding an alkyl (methyl or ethyl) chemical group to the alfa position of the 17th carbon. These are commonly called c17 alfa-alkylated or methylated AAS. This creates a heavy load upon the liver and will alter or affect enzyme and other chemical levels. This is why orals, particularly methyltestosterone and Anadrol-50, are so harmful if administered for prolonged periods and in high dosages. The reason that this alteration is done is that more of the AAS enters the blood stream and remains active for a prolonged period. The reader should note that it is these c17 alfa-alkylated alterations that cause the possible liver dysfunction and not the original testosterone molecule. For this reason Andriol orals are reasonably liver friendly due to the fact that it is not altered in this way.

Like their injectable cousins, oral steroids are also altered for higher or lower ratios of anabolic and androgenic effects. As an example, injectable testosterone is highly androgenic and highly anabolic. By altering the testosterone molecule structure, nortestosterones such as nandrolones are created. This shifts the ratio in favor of anabolic qualities with less androgenic effects. It is true that the higher the androgenic and potential aromatization quality an AAS possesses, the higher the number of negative side effects possible. But the reader should realize that this is not necessarily due to the androgenic quality itself. This is more so due to aromatization to estrogens and its effects upon HPTA function. For this reason, it would seem that a total anabolic steroid with no androgenic effects would be highly effective with an absence of possible negative side effects.

When androgenic qualities/effects are reduced, so are the anabolic qualities/effects reduced. When an AAS is listed as high anabolic or a high androgenic it simply means the ratio has shifted in favor of these qualities due to structural modifications. This is true for both oral and injectable AAS.

ANADROL-50
(OXYMETHOLONE)

Reported Characteristics
Active - Life: Less than 16 hours
Drug Class: Highly Androgenic / Anabolic Steroid (Oral)
Average Reported Dosage: Men 50-400 mg daily. Women 25-mg daily
Acne: Yes
Water Retention: Yes, high
High Blood Pressure: Yes
Liver Toxic: Yes, very high
DHT Conversions: This is a derivative of DHT
Decreases HPTA Function: Yes, severe
Aromatization: Debatable

This is an oral 17-alfa-alkylated steroid that is highly androgenic and highly anabolic. Reported gains in body weight of up to 20 LBS in the first 3 weeks of use were not uncommon. Athletes using this drug experienced remarkable strength and recovery elevations. Users noted a distinct increase in aggressiveness, (which if focused on training only was noted as positive) excessive water retention, and muscular size. Oxymetholone is commonly used as an off season mass building drug, though some mass monsters have used it up to 7-10 days before competition by stacking antagonist anti-estrogens and diuretics.

Unfortunately this drug is probably the most dangerous of all AAS when abused and utilized when not under a physician's care. Users get huge but often feel flu-like symptoms during use. Oxymetholone abuse is linked to prostate and liver cancer, liver disease, thyroid dysfunction, leukemia, and heart disorders. Even hepatic coma can result from abuse. Not uncommon side effects included: sensitivity to anti-coagulants (the stuff that regulates bleeding internally and externally) hair loss, prostate enlargement, severe suppressions of the HPTA resulting in low sperm and endogenous (natural) androgen production, nausea, stomach aches, diarrhea, and throwing up on occasion. Women can add possible virilizing symptoms such as clitoral enlargement, facial hair growth, deeper voice, missed periods, and other androgenic linked side-effects.

Oxymetholone negatively effects liver function such as an increase in SGPT and SGOT enzymes which are indications of hepatitis (liver infections) which can manifest itself as yellowing of the eyes and finger nails because of an increase in biliburin in the liver. Another liver enzyme, gamma -GT, is sensitive to Oxymetholone, and alkaline phosphatase is altered as well. I can not stress the importance of monitoring by a doctor.

Oxymetholone is a derivative of DHT. Many report gyno from use but this is unlikely due to this drug aromatizing because DHT does not aromatize to estrogen. The more likely reason is they purchased bogus oxymetholone from a black market dealer that actually contained methyltestosterone. There is another reason gyno is possible, but we will discuss that in a moment. Oxymetholone does cause high water retention due to electrolyte retention thus creating a massive but puffy appearance to muscles. For the same reason, the drug causes water retention and fluid build up in joints. This manifests itself in joint pain-free training for most users. In medicine Oxymetholone is used to treat low red blood cell production which means during administration red blood cell count is stimulated. For this reason the drug increases oxygen transport to the muscles resulting in an incredible muscle pump after only a few sets of training. I have often noted those who used oxymetholone recovered between sets, exercises, and work-outs at a remarkable rate. So the drug does protect against overtraining quite well, thus when it was stacked with anti-estrogen such as Nolvadex and a diuretic to cut electrolyte (aldosterone) caused water retention, and a high anabolic drug such as Deca Durabolin, quality, quantitative, muscle gain resulted. The fact that this drug's water retention side effect responds to antagonist type anti-estrogens is interesting since, from a chemical structure stand-point, it should not aromatize to estrogen. Even the insert states edemas (water retention) may occur but does not list elevated estrogen levels under "side effects". However, readers should realize Oxymetholone itself can merge with Progesterone receptors and may act as an estrogen in this manner.

As to dosages, advanced bodybuilders and power lifers usually reported excellent results with 50-200 mg daily divided in 2-3 dosages. Since results begin to decline after the first 2 weeks it some reported that their protocols were more productive (and safer) when they started at 50mg daily and increase by one tab weekly until a total of 150-200 mg daily was reached at week 3. They then maintained that dosage for a total of 2-3 additional weeks. Some reported a following protocol that allowed reduced dosages by one tab weekly. My personal experience has been that liver stress becomes an issue after the 4th week of administration and as such did not personally exceed this time period for use. Replacing Oxymetholone with a high anabolic such as Deca Durabolin or Equipoise during the transitional phase was quite effective for maintaining a greater amount of the oxymetholone induced lean mass. Many reported exceptional results with a stack consisting of 50-100 mg oxymetholone daily, 152-228 mg of Parabolon weekly, and 200-500 mg of testosterone enethate weekly.

*Women should not use oxymetholone, but of course some hard core types did report self administration. Novice steroid users should never use oxymetholone without a doctors supervision.

In most cases users reported that liver values returned to normal after 1-2 months of discontinued. This seems to be supported by the available medical literature on oxymetholone. High blood pressure was common during use. High blood pressure should never go untreated. The hair loss does not reverse by the way. Post-cycle the administration of HCG and Clomid was used to return normal HPTA function in all but very rare cases. "The boys" normally began to produce normal sperm and testosterone levels after 2-3 weeks of discontinuance. Can you tell that I did not like Oxymetholone for long term personal use? Post-cycle, without the layering of a transitional phase replacement AAS such as nandrolones, Primobolan Depot, Equipoise or Winstrol Depot, gains made with Oxymetholone alone soon disappear in most cases. (See "Max Androgen Phases" in "Building The Perfect Beast" for a discussion of solutions some hard core types have utilized)

TRADE NAMES

ANADROL-50 50 MG TABS
ANAPOLON 5, 50 MG TABS
HEMOGENIN 50 MG TABS
SYNASTERON 50 MG TABS
OXYMETHOLONE USP XXII 50 MG TABS

* A note of interest: There is not a "legit" injectable form of Oxymetholone. However, it would be very physiologically active as is the 25mg sublingual form. I have used a MEGA-MIX product that contained Oxymetholone in a 3 oil mix injectable that was a black-market product with excellent results and fewer negative side effects. However, black market manufactured AAS are often dangerous and unlikely legal anywhere.

ANDRIOL
(TESTOSTERONE UNDECANOATE)

Reported Characteristics

Active -Life: Less than 8 hours

Drug Class: Androgenic/Anabolic Steroid (Oral)

Average Reported Dosage: Men 240-320 mg daily (Women experienced serious VIRILIZTION)

Acne: Low except if used by androgen sensitive athletes

Water Retention: Yes, higher in dosages of 280-400mg daily

High Blood Pressure: Rare (Dosage related)

Liver Toxic: Low

DHT Conversion: Significant in higher dosage administration

Decreases HPTA functions: Low, except in higher reported dosages (above 320mg)

Aromatization: Low-moderate.

Andriol is an orally active testosterone. The only other orally active testosterone is methyltestosterone. But unlike its counterpart, Andriol has a unique absorption method. When ingested with or after meals it is reabsorbed through the mucosal cells in the small intestine via the lymphatic system. This ester therefore avoids absorption through the portal vein in the liver and subsequent first pass deactivation. This means that a much higher level of Andriol enters the blood stream. Some of the drug is then converted into DHT (dihydrotestosterone) which has a high affinity for androgen receptors. Due to higher DHT conversion, Andriol does not aromatize (transform) into estrogen at a high rate like other testosterone. For this reason, water retention is much lower while gyno and female pattern fat deposits are far less likely. This drug has a reported low negative effect on the HTPA (hypothalamic pituitary testes axis) and therefore does not suppress natural (endogenous) androgen production to a significant degree in the lower reported dosages. For the most part it is due to estrogen's negative influences that HPTA function is decreased. However, estrogen must be present in lower levels for any steroid to reach its full potential effects. Kind of a paradox huh?

When stacked with other AAS, Andriol has provided a mild androgenic/anabolic synergistic effect at dosages of 200 mg daily. However, if this drug was administered alone, this dosage did not provide much in the way of results when compared to injectable testosterone. To rival its injectable cousins, daily dosages would need to be in the above 290-320 mg range minimum. This dosage would not only be quite expensive, it also would reach a level where suppression of the HPTA would increase a great deal due to elevated aromatization. This also increases water retention significantly. Since Andriol is quickly excreted through urine release, the drug was be taken 3-6 times daily to maintain adequate circulatory levels.

All in all Andriol was reported as a mildly Androgenic / Anabolic steroid that was best used in stacks for its excellent compatibility at dosages of 240-320 mg daily. For novice steroid users, older athletes, and safety conscience individuals, a stack of 200-240 mg Andriol daily, 200 mg of Primobolan depot (or 200-400 mg Anadur or Deca Durabolin) weekly, and 20 mg of Oxandrolone daily was reported to provide excellent lean mass and good strength gains with minimal suppression of the HPTA and other negative side effects. The good news was that athletes retained the gains quite well after use was discontinued. (Unless they were highly psychologically influenced by off periods!)

TRADE NAMES

ANDRIOL 40-MG GEL CAPS
ANDROGEN 40 MG CAPS
PANTESTON 40 MG CAPS
RESTANDOL 40 MG CAPS
UNDESTOR 40 MG CAPS
VIRIGEN 40 MG CAPS

ANDROSTANOLONE
(SAME CHEMICAL NAME)

Reported Characteristics

Active-Life: About 1.5 days for injection product and 4-6 hours for oral

Drug Class: Androgenic steroid similar to DHT, very low anabolic quality at listed dosages.

Average Reported Dosage: Men 5-25mg daily (women did not report use of this product).

Acne: With higher long term dosages, yes.

Water Retention: None, due to nonaromatization

Frequent Comments: High Androgenic /Very low anabolic at listed dosages

Aromatization: None

Liver Toxic: None

DHT Conversion: DHT derivative

Decreases HPTA Function: Very little

This was a rarely used or available drug. Since it is almost identical to DHT, it cannot convert to estrogen. Water retention is rare for the same reason. As a strength or weight gain drug, androstanolone is of no value unless dosages are increased significantly. In this case the individuals whom have used larger dosages have reported significant increases in strength and muscle quality similar to those realized during utilization of so-called contest prep drugs like trenbolones and Masteron. (Both will be reported upon later in this text)

This has not been a commonly used drug simply due to cost. If the economic issues had been resolved some reported the drug would be a common replacement for so-called hardening AAS. However, some women have replied that they have used it with moderate success as a pre-contest hardening drug in the listed average reported dosages. For this to be successful, a very low body fat level was achieved first.

TRADE NAMES

ANDRACTIM   2.5% GEL

APETON   5MG, 25MG TABS

APETON DEPOT   2%, 5 X INJ. SOLUTION

* There is an OTC product available in the United States that is chemically almost identical to the oral androstanolone. It is called Hyroxy-Bolasterone. Interestingly enough, it is my personal opinion from experience that it is a more effective product with fewer potential negative side effects.

DIANABOL
(METHANDROSTENOLONE or METHANDIENONE)

Reported Characteristics
Active-Life: 6-8 hours (Injection product remains active for about 60-72 hours)
Drug Class: Anabolic/androgenic steroid
Average Reported Dosage: Men 15-50 mg daily Women 5-10 mg daily
Acne: Yes, especially in higher dosages.
Water Retention: Yes, similar to testosterone
High Blood Pressure: Yes, due to water retention, some experience elevated heart rate
Aromatization: Yes, strongly
Liver Toxic: Yes, 17-alfa alkylated oral
DHT conversion: No
High anabolic/high androgenic
Decreases HPTA function: Yes, dose and administration period dependent

Oral Dianabol was reported to be a highly effective mass AAS which provided impressive weight and strength gains. Most users experienced a 2-4 LB bodyweight increase per week with heavy water retention. With higher dosages gynecomastia (bitch tits) was a common negative side effect. Obviously much of this was avoided by those who reported co-addministration of Proviron and/or Novladex. When stacked with a nandrolone, some gyno problems seemed to lessen. This was probably due to Nandrolones aromatization to a weaker estrogen called Norestrogen and the resulting mild anti-estrogenic effect that results in moderate dosage administration. Methandrostenlone becomes active in 1-3 hours with a half-life of about 3.5-4.5 hours. For this reason, dosages were spread through out the day to maintain blood serum concentrations at an elevated state. Massive dosages just were not necessary since a single 10-mg dose has increase androgen anabolic activity 5 times over normal with a correlating reduction in natural cortisol activity of 50-70%. Males using 5mg per 25-LBS of body weight broken into 3-5 equal dosages throughout the day have experienced impressive results. At dosages above 50 mg per day, results were not progressively quantitative. Most first time AAS users who used a daily dosage of 20-30mg daily experience significant results over a 4-6 week period. Women should not utilize Methandrostenolone but a surprising number did report the inclusion of the drug in AAS protocols. For those who insisted, no more than 10-mg daily for 3-4 weeks stacked with a very low androgenic product minimized masculization type negative side effects.

Side effects such as increased liver values (toxicity) "usually" returned to normal within a short period of time after use was discontinued. High blood pressure, elevated heart rates, gyno, heavy water retention, and acne were all frequent reported negative side effects of Methandrostenlone use. Some literature on this drug supports DHT- like activity. Finasteride "usually" prevented this effect as well as possible prostate enlargement. Dianabol heavily suppresses natural testosterone production within only 10 days after continuous administration begins (dose dependent). Most note a sense of well being during use of this drug. Significant strength and weight loss follows discontinued use due to the loss of excessive water and HPTA suppression. So retained gains were only fair post-cycle.

My personal experiences with this drug have led me to believe that no athlete should have ever stacked high dosage protocols of Dianabol with Anadrol-50 or Methyltestosterone. It is a liver killer combo. A last note: Injectable Dianabol did not have anywhere near as dramatic effects when utilized in its intended method. However, the injectable is orally active and as such was reported to be commonly used in this manner by filling gel-caps with the desired amount/dosage and subsequent ingestion. This is probably due to oral administration of a c17-alkylated AAS results in increased liver production of IGF-1. I have also learned that it was best to avoid Russian Methandrostenlone. It commonly contains a large amount of unconverted methyltestosterone.

TRADE NAMES

ANABOL TABS   5MG TABS
ANABOLIN   5MG TABS
ANDOREDAN   5MG TABS
BIONABOL   2,5MG TABS
DIALONE   5MG TABS
DIANABOL   5MG
ENCEPHAN   5MG TABS
METANABOL   1,5MG TABS
METHANDROSTENOLONUM   5MG TABS
NEROBOL   5MG TABS
PRONABOL-5   5MG TABS
STENOLON   1,5MG TABS
TRENERGIC   5MG CAPS
NAPOSIM   5MG TABS
D-BOL   10MG CAPS

VETERINARY:

ANABOLIKUM 2.5%   25MG/ML;50ML
METANDIOBOL   25MG/ML;50ML
D-BOL INJECTION 25MG/ML

HALOTESTIN
(FLUOXYMESTERONE)

Reported Characteristics

Active-Life: 6-8 hours
Drug Class: High androgenic/anabolic steroid (Oral)
Average Dosage: Men 20-40-mg daily   Women: none
Acne: Common
Water Retention: None
High Blood Pressure: Rare
Liver Toxic: Very
Aromatization: Unlikely
DHT Conversion: Does not apply
Decreases HPTA function: Yes, moderately

Haltestin is an oral 17-alfa-alkylated AAS that provided good strength gains and low-moderate anabolic qualities. This means that the drug alone failed to provide significant muscle mass gains. Obviously power lifters seeking improved strength while maintaining a certain body weight liked this drug. Bodybuilders used Haltestin to improve muscle hardness during the last 4-6 weeks of dieting before competition. Since this drug does not aromatize and water retention seldom results from its use, this drug worked quite well for this purpose. However, when stacked with an injectable anabolic prone drug such as EQUIPOISE, DECA, or ANADUR, for example, the high increase in strength gains realized from Halotestin were well transformed into quite respectable lean muscle mass gains.   Normally males ingested 20-40 mg daily divided into 2-3 even dosages for 3-6 weeks.

Though gyno or water retention is unlikely to occur from the use of Halotestin, there are several side effects. Since this drug is an alteration of Methyltestosterone (with a higher androgenic/lower anabolic effect) and a c17-alkylated steroid, it is quite hard on the liver. Nose bleeds, headaches, stomach aches, and acne are some of the reported side effects. Users seldom reported profitable use that extended beyond 4-6 weeks.

TRADE NAMES

ANDROID –F 10-MG TABS	HALOTESTIN 2MG TABS
HALOTESTIN 5MG TABS	HALTESTIN 10MG TABS
HYSTERONE TABS 20MG TABS	ORA-TESTRYL 5MG TABS
STENOX 2.5MG TABS	

METHYLTESTOSTERONE

Reported Characteristics

Active Life: 6 -8 hours
Drug Class: Androgenic/Anabolic Steroid (Oral)
Average Reported Dosage: Men-25-200 mg daily Women mostly avoided this drug
Acne: Yes
Water Retention: Yes
High Blood Pressure: Yes
Liver Toxic: Very
Aromatization: High
DHT Conversion: Yes, high
Decreases HPTA function: Yes, severe

Methyl testosterone is an orally active high androgenic steroid with a very short active life of about 6-8 hours. It is a c17-Alfa alkylated steroid molecule. This means a methyl group has been added to the c-17-Alfa position of the testosterone molecule to slow deactivation of the active substance by the liver. This makes methyltestosterone highly live toxic. This testosterone aromatizes more easily to estrogens than its injection form cousins due to P-450 enzyme activity that occurs during intestinal and liver metabolism. Most of the initial weight gained from the use of this drug was water weight. Though a quick (an hour!) increase in strength and confidence was often realized by athletes during administration the gains were very short term as they disappeared soon after use was discontinued. High blood pressure, nose bleeds, seriously aggressive behavior, gyno, and sodium retention are common. I could not think of any good use for this drug in bodybuilding.

Unfortunately, methyltest is the most common used substitution drug in bogus oral steroids. (Perhaps this explains all the gyno from even low dosage use of Anadrol-50 reported) Serious aggression results in some users (most).

*I once stood in a Department of Motor Vehicles (DMV) line with a heavy user. To say the least, no one deserves him more than the DMV, IRS, and bank employees. I actually enjoyed the department of motor vehicles for once.

Methyltestosterone was reported used commonly by strength oriented athletes and usually with co-committent administration of a high anabolic/low or moderate androgenic drug such as a nandrolone.

TRADE NAMES

ANDRO 25-MG TABS   METHYLTESTOSTERONE 10-MG TABS
ANDROID 10,25-MG TABS   MESTERON 10-MG TABS

THERE ARE SEVERAL OTHER MANUFACTURER NOT LISTED, (BUT WHY BOTHER)

NILEVAR
(NORETHANDROLONE)

Reported Characteristics
Active Life: 12-16 hours
Drug Class: Androgenic/Anabolic Steroid (Oral)
Average Reported Dosage: 20-40-mg daily take in 2-3 divided dosages
Acne: Yes
Water Retention: Yes
High Blood Pressure: Yes
Liver Toxic: Yes, 17-alfa-alkylated Oral Steroid
Aromatization: Moderate-High
Decreases HPTA function: Moderate-High
DHT conversion: Moderate reduction to less active nor-DHT

Nilevar is an oral AAS that is a derivative of nortestosterone. Many assume Nilevar is similar to Anavar. Like Anavar, the drug has a reported mild anabolic effect. However, unlike Anavar, Nilevar has a distinct androgenic quality. Good strength gains were realized by users although much of this was due to the high water retention side effect. Used alone, Nilevar did not provide good retention of weight or strength gains post-cycle. Being an oral 17-alfa-alkylated oral steroid, liver toxicity was high in those whom reported high dosage protocols above those listed under **Reported Characteristics**. Polled users were wise to avoid cycles containing this drug lasting longer than 4 weeks and seldom stacked other 17-Alfa -Alkylated drugs with it. Due to Nilevar's moderate-high rate of suppression upon the body's natural testosterone production, HCG and Clomid were reported to be necessary to restart the Hypothalamic-pituitary -testes- axis (HPTA) post-cycle within an adequate time frame.

*Many athletes who have used high aromatizing AAS have reported a delayed period of HPTA regeneration. As such post-cycle lean mass tissue retention suffers as a negative reaction to suppressed endogenous androgen production. If "the boy's" are shrunken so is the athlete they are attached to.

TRADE NAME

NILEVAR   10-MG TABS

ORABOLIN
(ETHYLESTRENOL)

Reported Characteristics

Active-Life: 8-12 hours
Drug Class: Anabolic /Androgenic steroid (Oral)
Average Reported Dosage: Men 20-40mg daily Women 10-16mg daily
Acne: Rare
Water Retention: Low
High Blood Pressure: Rare
Liver Toxic: High
Aromatization: Low
Moderate anabolic/Low Androgenic
Decreases HPTA function: Low-moderate

This is an oral AAS once popular with female athletes known under the trade name Maxibolin. (Now discontinued under this name) The substance is an alteration of the estrogenic/androgenic hormone Progesterone and is a 19-Nortestosterone (Nandrolone) derivative as well. Since Orabolin is a weak anabolic/very low androgenic steroid, most athletes erroneously dismissed its value. Orabolin does not have a high affinity (attraction/absorption) for androgen receptors. So used alone in the average reported administered dosages the drug did not provide much in the way of results. However, when it was combined with other steroids such as Deca Durabolin (or other Nandrolones), Parabolan, and/or Winstrol, the results were of a high quality muscle which was well retained after use was discontinued.

Women reported a high quality lean muscle mass augmentation resulted when 10-16mg of Orabolin (divided into 2-3 equal daily dosages) was stacked with 50-100-mg Durabolin or Deca Durabolin weekly. Males reported requiring as much as 60-100 mg daily of Orabolin to achieve good results. Unfortunately that high of a dosage would create several negative side effects including bankruptcy.

TRADE NAMES

ORABOLIN   2-MG TABS
ORGABOLIN   2-MG TABS
ORGABOLIN DROPS   2MG

OXANDROLONE SPA
(OXANDROLONE)

Reported Characteristics
Active-Life: 8-12 hours
Drug Class: Anabolic/Androgenic Steroid (Oral)
Average Reported Dosage: Men 20-50mg daily Women 10-15mg daily
Acne: Only when administered in high dosages
Water Retention: Rare
High Blood Pressure: Rare
Liver Toxic: Yes, c17-alfa-alkylated steroid. Due to low dosages toxicity is low-moderate
Aromatization: None
DHT conversion: Quite low
Decreases HPTA function: Unlikely even in high dosage use

Oxandrolone was often refereed to as an all purpose oral AAS. This drug was once marketed under the product name (still commonly used trade name) of Anavar. It has the unique quality of significantly stimulating (more than other AAS) the synthesis of phosphocreatine in muscle cells which in turn provides faster regeneration of, and a distinct elevation in, ATP. Of course all AAS have this effect to some extent. Oxandrolone is simply unmatched in this aspect.
(See Creatine for more info) Due to this quality, a rapid build- up in strength was frequently reported and an obvious distinct hardness in muscle was obtained with little weight gain and no aromatization.

Though it is a common belief that Oxandrolone is not very anabolic, a clinical study showed a 44% increase in muscle cell protein synthesis after only 5 days of administration. Since Oxandrolone does not aromatize to estrogen, water retention is reported as quite low and gyno was of no concern. Also, for the same reason, during dieting phases fat deposits were said to be "burned away" more quickly. (Especially when the drug was co-administered with Clenbuterol).

Oxandrolone was reported to stack well with so -called mass steroids such as testosterone or with high anabolic/moderate androgenic steroids such as Equipoise or Nandrolones. Persons over 40 have reported excellent results by stacking 15-25 mg of Oxandrolone daily with 200-400 mg of Deca.

A very hard pre-contest appearance has been achieved by males when stacked with Oxandrolone and Halotestin if a estrogen/progesterone receptor antagonist (*See Nolvadex) had been utilized as well. As I said: "all purpose" was commonly the term of choice.

The drug Oxandrolone was originally manufactured to be used by women to prevent osteoporosis and for children as a cure for stunted growth. The low androgenic quality prevents almost all virilization for women in dosages of 15-mg daily or less. And for the same reason does not cause closure of the epiphysial plates prematurely. An interesting note: Oxandrolone does not suppress any part of the HYPOTHALAMUS-PITUITARY-TESTES AXIS (HPTA). This means Oxandrolone by itself will not significantly suppress natural testosterone production. Therefore it was not uncommon for some athletes to report post-cycle HPTA regeneration protocols that included this drug. The result was prominent lean mass retention.

TRADE NAMES

LIPIDEX 2.5-MG
LONAVAR 2-MG TABS
VASOROME 0.5-2MG TABS
OXANDROLONE SPA 2.5-MG

PRIMOBOLAN TABLETS
(METHENOLONE ACETATE)

Reported Characteristics

Active-Life: 4-6 hours
Drug Class: Anabolic/Androgenic Steroid (Oral)
Average Reported Dosage: Men-50-200-mg daily Women 50-100-mg daily
Acne: Rare
Water Retention: None
High Blood Pressure: Rare
Liver Toxic: Very low and only in _very_ high dosages
Aromatization: None
Moderate Anabolic/ Low Androgenic
DHT Conversion: No
Decreases HPTA function: Low

Primobolan tablets are a moderately anabolic and low androgenic oral steroid that was reported as limited in use by most bodybuilders. This was likely simply because alone and when it was administered in listed dosages the drug was not very effective. However, gains were made in muscle mass and strength were consistently reported to be of a very high quality and were mostly retained post-cycle. Acetates are "said" to aid in fat burning, so this drug was mostly used in a stack pre-contest.

The problem _in effectiveness_ lies in the fact that PRIMOBOLAN ACETATE is not a c17-ALFA-ALKYLATED steroid and is therefore mostly deactivated during the first pass through the liver. As the reader is aware, oral AAS are commonly altered to decrease liver deactivation. The most common alteration is called a c-17 alfa-alkylated drug. This alteration makes the liver work over-time to deactivate it and is therefore said to be highly liver toxic. (But so are most oral birth control drugs) But another alteration in structure allows Primobolan orals to be somewhat resistant to liver deactivation. It is referred to as unsaturation in the 1-position.This alteration allows the compound to resist metabolic deactivation by significantly shifting the 17-Keto redox potential toward creation of active 17-beta hydroxyl AAS. The result is an active oral AAS that is not liver toxic except in very high dosages.

Some have recalled the injectable form of Primobolan acetate with great fondness for its supposed fat burning/lean mass building qualities. The vials contained only 20-mg of METHENOLONE ACETATE (MA) yet it was reported far more effective than 150-mg of the oral. A commonly reported method to obtain greater blood circulatory levels of the oral form was to mix 20-25-mg of the ground tables with either DMSO gel or a 50/50 solution of DMSO and water. Users then simply applied the mixture to their skin (especially in areas of stubborn fat deposits). 10-20% absorbed and passed directly into the blood stream thus avoiding first pass liver deactivation. This was done 1-5 times daily.

DMSO is a solvent that carries smaller molecule structures mixed with it directly through the skin. It is said to be found at some health food stores and chemical supply warehouses.

Another reported method was mixing ground Primobolan tabs with Vitamin-E oil. The users then ingested it orally. This caused a great deal of the active steroid to be absorbed through the lymph system like Andriol and therefore avoid first pass deactivation.

*There is a great deal of research under way in the OTC supplement industry that employs a similar pharmacological solution to liver destruction of micronutrients.

Back to reported tablet use...

Primobolan tabs were reportedly used most by women and steroid novices because they do not aromatize or cause water retention. Women who utilized 50-100mg daily of this drug seldom noted virilizing side effects. Most report a distinct harder look and a 3-4 LB muscle mass gain in 6-8 weeks. Obviously many females also stacked Primobolan tabs with other drugs to heighten results. Males normally ingested 100-200 mg daily in 2-4 divided doses (due to short half-life 4-6 daily divided dosages were more effective at maintaining plasma concentrations of the active drug) and report fair gains. Stacked with more androgenic steroids such as testosterone, Parabolan, or even moderate androgenics such as Deca Durabolin or Equipoise, males made high quality muscle mass and strength gains with safer low side effect results.

*Since Primobolan is a derivative of dihydrotestosterone (DHT) an acceleration in hair loss can occur in those with genetic receding hair lines (but was rarely noted).

TRADE NAMES

PRIMOBOLAN-S 5, 25 & 50 MG TABS
PRIMOBOLAN TABLETS 25 & 50 MG TABS

WINSTROL TABS
(STANOZOLOL TABLETS)

Reported Characteristics

Active-Life: About 8 hours
Drug Class: Anabolic/Androgenic steroid (Oral)
Average Reported Dosage: Males 20-50-mg daily Women 10-15-mg daily
Acne: Rare
Water Retention: Rare
High Blood Pressure: Rare
Liver Toxic: High in high oral dosages
DHT Conversion: None, DHT derivative
Decreases HPTA Function: Low

Pretty much everything written thus far about Stanozolol injectable (*See "Winstrol Depot" under "Injectable Anabolic Androgenic Steroids" for more info) was also attributed also to the oral form. It was often said that the oral form is less effective than the injectable. In truth, it was usually due to dosages, and this in turn was due to price. Athletes usually administered a lower dosage orally because it seemed like 25 pills daily was mega dosing. In my personal opinion this was true to a point. Oral use of any 17-alfa-alkylated steroid is hard on the liver. This is because it is difficult for the liver to deactivate these modified testosterone and derivatives. Let me make it clear. Milligram for milligram oral administration of Stanozolol was reported significantly more potent than the injection product (but it is more liver toxic). Oral dosages were commonly broken into 2-3 daily dosages to maintain circulatory androgen elevation. An effective reported daily oral dosage for women was 10-15mg and for men 20-30. However, this listed male dosage was not as effective (or as toxic) as the 30-50mg daily dose range.

Male athletes reported the practice of stacking 40-50mg of Stanozolol daily with 300-400mg weekly of a nandrolone provided significant lean muscle tissue augmentation with good post-cycle retention. For "bulking" purposes many reported the use of this drug with a testosterone at an average reported dosage of 200-600mg weekly resulted in "amazing strength and weight gains" and improved post-cycle lean mass retention.

Women athletes commonly reported the use of Stanozolol at a dosage of 10-15mg daily with 50-100mg of a nandrolone weekly resulted in a rapid increase in quality lean mass tissue with low water retention and rare virilizing negative side effects.

TRADE NAMES

STANOZOLOL   5-MG TABS
STANAZOLIC   6-MG CAPS

INJECTABLE ANABOLIC/ANDROGENIC STEROIDS

AAS also are manufactured in an injectable form. Most are used as deep intra muscular injections containing various oils and, in a few cases, sterile water. The active ingredient is suspended in the oil or water solution.

Injectable AAS have 2 distinct advantages over their oral cousins. First, due to structure and the method in which they are administered they have much longer active-lives (the period in which the AAS remains active start to finish). Injectables usually range in active-life from 1 day to 4 weeks, depending on their chemical structure and in which form the drug is manufactured in. Orals usually have an active-life of 4-16 hours depending on structure and alterations in its molecule. Second, injectables avoid first pass deactivation in the small intestines and liver, but are eventually deactivated by the liver as well. So an oral dosage is based upon what makes it past the stomach, small intestines, and liver. And an injected dosage is what is drawn into a syringe and injected. Since few injectable AAS are methylated or 17-alfa-alkylated, it should be noted that they are much easier on the liver even in much higher dosages.

EQUIPOISE
(BOLDENONE UNDECYLENATE INJECTION)

Reported Characteristics

Active-Life: 7-9 days
Drug Class: Anabolic /Androgenic steroid (for injection)
Average Reported Dosage: Men 150-500mg weekly   Women 50-150mg weekly
Acne: Rare
Water Retention: Low
High Blood Pressure: Rare
Aromatization: About 50% less than testosterone
Liver Toxic: None
Noted comments: High anabolic/moderate androgenic
DHT Conversion: Low
Decreases HPTA function: Moderately (Dose dependent)

Boldenone is available as a veterinary steroid under various trade names and was commonly refereed to as EQ by athletes polled. However, the quality is normally quite high due to its use in million dollar race horses. Boldenone was reported as one of the safest and most effective anabolic / androgenic injectable steroids used by both power lifters and bodybuilders. This drug brought slow but continuous muscle mass and strength gains over a prolonged period. Gains were mostly of a high quality lean mass nature and were maintained for several weeks after use was discontinued. Improved pumps and vascularity were normal are common attributes while low aromatization brought an improved hardness to users musculature.

Males normally reported a dosage range of 150-500mg weekly total, usually utilizing an every other day (EOD) injection schedule. Women made excellent progress with dosages of 50-150mg total weekly with a 1-2 injections weekly schedule. In this dose range, women seldom reported virilizing side effects. Most experienced an elevate libido (cool) with few other negative side effects reported. But in some cases, increased hair growth on face and legs were noted. This was usually due to higher dosages however and predominantly limited to existing hair (not new hair growth).

Due to Boldenone's reported "non-toxic to the liver" structure, most users experienced great gains with none or few negative side effects. The appetite and red blood cell production stimulating effects of Equipoise marked this drug as a standard for those who sought few negative side effects with quality muscle mass gains. Obviously with increased red blood cell count an increase in oxygen transport was also realized, as was improved nutrient transport.

Due to a double carbon bond between carbons one and two, boldenone experiences only slight DHT conversion by the 5-alfa-reductase enzyme and is fairly resistant to aromatization to estrogens.

Male athletes commonly stacked Boldenone with testosterone and/or Anadrol-50 for mass and strength cycles. Pre-contest cycles utilizing this drug often included Trenbolones, Winstrol, and anti-estrogens to create the ultra hard and vascular look.

*Personal experiences with Boldenone have resulted in very high quality lean tissue and freaky vascularity. This quite beneficial from a competitive appearance stand-point but long term use resulted in an unfavorable CBC result. I believe my error was in protocol length.

TRADE NAMES
ULTRAGAN 100   100MG/ML
BOLDEBAL-H   50MG/ML
EQUIPOISE   25MG,50MG, /ML
ULTRAGAN 50   50MG/ML
GANABOL   25MG, 50MG/ML
PACE   25MG/ML
VENBOL   25MG/ML

VIAL SIZE RANGES: 10,50,100,250 ML (No joke, 250ml vials)

ESICLENE
(FORMEBOLONE PLUS 20MG LIDOCAINE PER VIAL)

Reported Characteristics
Active-Life: 1 day
Drug Class: Anabolic/inflammatory steroid (For injection)
Average Reported Dosage: 1-2 ampules per muscle per day
Acne: None
Water Retention: Site-specific
High Blood Pressure: None
Aromatization: None
Liver Toxic: None
DHT Conversion: Unknown

Esiclene was not an anabolic steroid in the conventional sense. The drug was injected directly into a lagging (smaller muscles such as biceps, triceps, calves and delts, usually respond best) body part during the last 7-15 days before a contest. Though Esiclene is anabolic it is the drugs distinct site specific inflammatory /tissue fluid accumulatory effects users pursued. When an injection is administered, the muscle responds by receiving fluid from the lymph system as an inflammatory response. Within 1-2 weeks arm sizes were reported to increase in size by as much as 1.5 inches. This effect was quite temporary as inflammation began to decrease within about 24 hours. Since 20-mg of lidocaine was contained in each vial, the swelling effect it is not a surprise that the injections were not as painful as one may think. Usually a bodybuilder would inject 1-ml into each of 1-2 lagging body parts daily for 4-7 days, then increase to 2-ml per muscle for and additional 3-7 days. Some reported an improved muscle hardness over the whole body during use.

ESTANDRONE
(Contains)

-**TESTOSTERONE PROPIONATE   20-MG**
-**TESTOSTERONE PHENYLPROPIONATE   40-MG**
-**TESTOSTERONE ISCAPRIOATE   40-MG**
-**ESTRADIOL PHENYLPROPIONATE   4MG**
-**ESTRADIOL BENZOATE   1-MG**

Reported Characteristics
Active-Life: Various due to 3 testosterone esters (About 21 days total)
Drug Class: Anabolic/Androgenic steroid (For injection)
Average Reported Dosage: Men-2-6 ml weekly Women 1-2 ml weekly
Acne: Yes
Water Retention: Yes, excessive (did you note the estrogens in its contents?)
High Blood Pressure: Depending on dosage
Aromatization: High
Liver Toxic: Low-moderate
Noted comments: High Anabolic/High Androgenic
Decreases HPTA function: Severely
DHT Conversion: High

This is an interesting drug containing 3 different testosterone esters and 2 estrogen esters. Based upon interviews, males using 2-6 ml weekly divided into 2-3 injections, and women using 1-2 ml weekly experience fast strength and mass weight gains due to Estandrons major anabolic /anti-catabolic properties. Additionally, this drug increased joint lubrication, muscle glycogen/nitrogen storage, and due to its estradiol content, increased calcium storage in bones significantly.

The product was created with the intended use of treatment for various conditions resulting from menopause in women. Female athletes used the product to obtain the effects of testosterone while utilizing the somewhat protective qualities from virilization of estrogens. Males who are prone to prostate problems, hair loss, and serious acne use reported the product allowed them to reap the rapid mass gains of testosterone use while minimizing these effects.

*These individuals (Males) are in error. Estrogens have been shown to have a growth stimulating effect upon prostate tissue also.

The down side was the increased fat deposits the elevated estrogen levels brought. Since estrogen are anabolic in low dosages, some just do not care. Instead they rave about the weight and strength gains while enjoying amazing pumps. Males prone toward gynecomastia should have obviously avoided this drug unless wet T- shirts were the competition plan.

TRADE NAMES
AMBOSEX   105MG/ML   ESTANDRONE   105MG/ML
ESTRANDRONE   105MG/ML

MASTERON
(DROSTANOLONE PROPIONATE)

Reported Characteristics
Active Life: 2-3 days
Drug Class: Androgenic/Anabolic steroid (For injection)
Average Reported Dosage: Men 300-500-mg weekly Women 100-350mg weekly
Acne: Yes
Water Retention: None
High Blood Pressure: Rare
Liver Toxic: None
Aromatization: None
Noted Comments: High Androgenic/Moderate Anabolic/Moderate anti-estrogenic
DHT Conversion: None, DHT derivative
Decreases HPTA Function: Low suppression in most cases

Masteron is a highly androgenic injectable steroid that is a synthetic derivative of DHT (dihydrotestosterone). Since DHT does not aromatize to estrogens, there was no noted water retention during administration. If a bodybuilder had achieved a low body fat level, this drug was reported to dramatically improved shape and hardness in muscle tissue while augmenting the vascular appearance of a contest ready athlete. Normally, Masteron was used only during the last 3-5 weeks before a show as part of a pre-contest stack. In this case, 100-mg was commonly injected every second or third day (2-3 times weekly) by males and at a dosage of 50mg every other day by most women whom reported use. Additionally, according to available literature, Masteron is quite anti-catabolic and anti-estrogenic in nature due to receptor inhibition. So the reported characteristics of this drug do have supportive clinical validation to consider.

Combined with so- called mass steroids, Masteron did aid in a rapid build-up of strength and mass even with its relatively moderate anabolic qualities. However, Masteron was not reported to be the best choice for this purpose by those polled. DHT can promote hair loss and prostate disorders in prone individuals though it is not well documented as to whether or not deviants of the DHT structure can in all case do the same.

Masteron has a receptor binding ability 3-5 times greater than that of testosterone. This means that the drug can hang out longer in androgen receptor-sites and is not easily displaced. The result should be increased AAS activity.

An interesting facet of Masteron is the way it acts as an anti-estrogen. This is due to its ability to compete for the aromatase receptor. As the reader is aware of by now, many AAS are capable of conversion to estrogens. The process is caused by an enzyme called aromatase. (Of course the process of AAS conversion to estrogen is referred to as aromatization) If a drug has the ability to inhibit the enzyme at its own receptor and still act as a powerful non-aromatizing AAS, its interesting and unusual to me.

My personal experiences with this drug have always been favorable with no negative side effects. Additionally I feel that the drug has had value as a sort of AAS moderator. Let me explain this. Masteron has a high SHBG and albumin binding rate. Since these two hormone binding proteins prevent AAS from merging with their receptors, some would assume this is a bad thing. Masteron is 3-5 times more active than testosterone, so the unbound portion circulating in the blood stream goes a long way. Since the drug binds a higher percentage of SHBG and albumin, any other AAS co-administered with it remains in an unbound/active/free state to a greater extent and is able to induce a greater response. This is an example of noted drug synergy common to protocols reported as most effective yet requiring lower dosages to accomplish a specific result. The implication is that lower dosages of co-administered drugs allowed a decrease in negative side effects.

A point of interest is that two OTC prohormones in the United States have similar effects to Masteron (though oral administration is not the most effective delivery method and injection type administration would be illegal in most countries) (1) 5a-androst-1-en-3b,17b- dione (2) 5a-androst-en-3b,17b-diol. My personal research has shown that there is a realistic approach to an orally administered version of the latter of the two drugs that has shown great promise. We will complete the final testing soon before turning the project over to the crazies at Hazardous Materials Supplements. Personally, I am totally stoked about the project due to its vast application potential in the world OTC supplemental industry. The key is a compound from Eastman that allows lipophilic substances to become hydrophilic (Oil soluble to water soluble). This means that the high expense of effective supplements like methoxyisoflavone (and its deviants) to be reduced due to lower dosage requirements.

*Since this drug clears the body quickly, it was a favorite for tested competitors.

TRADE NAMES

MASTERIL   100-MG/2-ML
MASTERON   100-MG/2-ML

MEGAGRISEVIT-MONO
(CLOSTEBOLE ACETATE)

Reported Characteristics

Active Life: 36-48 hours
Drug Class: Anabolic/ Androgenic steroid (For injection)
Average Reported Dosage: Men-20-mg daily; Women-20-mg every other day
Acne: Yes, Rare
Water Retention: None
High Blood Pressure: None
Liver Toxic: No
Aromatization: None
Noted Comments: Anabolic/Very low Androgenic
DHT conversion: Low
Decreases HPTA function: Low with listed dosages

For many whom had used Primabolan acetate injections in the past with good results during dieting, this steroid stacked with a higher androgenic drug such as Parabolan or Masteron was reported to be a great replacement. The drug itself is fairly anabolic and only a small androgenic quality exists. It was not noted as liver toxic nor have any users reported water retention or gyno. This is probably due to low dosages and high prices. However, the brief half- life provided benefits for women and tested events.

    TRADE NAME

    MEGAGRISEVIT-MONO   10MG/1.5ML

METHANDRIOL DIPROPIONATE
(METHYLANDROSTENEDIOL DIPROPIONATE)

Reported Characteristics

Active-Life: 2-3 days injectable/ 4-6 hours orals
Drug Class: Anabolic/Androgenic Steroid
Average Reported Dosage: Tabs- men 40-60mg daily, injectable 100-mg every 2-3 days.
Acne: Yes
Water Retention: High
High Blood Pressure: Yes
Liver Toxic: Injectable- Moderate /Oral-yes due to higher dosage requirements
Noted Comments: Strong Anabolic/Strong Androgenic/Estrogenic activity
DHT Conversion: Unknown
Aromatization: Low-Moderate
Decreases HPTA function: Yes, significantly

MD is a highly Anabolic/Androgenic steroid with unique reported quality of improving receptor affinity for/with other anabolic/androgenic compounds. It provided good muscle mass gains with good strength gains while causing high water retention. While the injection form was "said" to be easy on the liver, the tablet form is highly liver toxic due to its 17-alfa-alkylated structure. Males normally injected 100 mg every second or third day, or ingested 300-600mg in divided daily dosages. Even after only 4 weeks of use the orals can cause liver problems. The injectable form of MD is also available in combination with other steroids. These are the Australian veterinary drugs: Drive, Filibol Forte, Geldabol, and Spectriol.

Something I liked about MD was its noted ability to clean out androgen receptor-sites. Often individuals who had experienced so called receptor burn-out finally utilized an MD product to discover new gains. DNP does this as well, but in a different manner. When utilizing site -injection protocols, MD was an excellent addition for me. Many have obviously reported improved growth stacking MD with other AAS. It should be noted that the drug MD is similar in structure to a weak estrogen. This means higher dosage use can lead to estrogenic side effects.

*Since both oral and injection forms of MD are c17-alkylated it seems obvious that both are potentially liver toxic though the latter possesses a lower potential due to dosage administered in comparison.

TRADE NAMES

ANDRIS 10-MG TABS
METYLANDROSTENDIOL 10,25MG TABS
DENKDIOL 75mg/ml

PACE
(Provides)
BOLDENONE UNDECYLENATE 25 mg/ml
METHANDRIOL DIPROPIONATE 30 mg/ml

Reported Characteristics

Active-Life: Boldenone-7-8 day/Methandriol 2-3 days
Drug Class: Anabolic/Androgenic injectable steroid mixture
Average Reported Dosage: Men: 6-12 ml weekly Women 3-6ml weekly
Acne: Yes (due to Methandriol)
Water Retention: Moderate
High Blood Pressure: Dosage dependent
Aromatization: Moderate
Liver Toxic: Low-moderate (only due to methandriol)
DHT Conversion: Low
Decreases HPTA function: Yes, low to moderately (dose dependent)

This is a veterinary steroid manufactured in Australia containing a mixture of two steroids: Boldenone Undecylenate (Equipoise/EQ) and Methandriol Dipropionate (MD). The combination provided a highly anabolic and androgenic mixture that, due to Methandriol, had a high receptor-site affinity and caused some water retention for users. It was reported as only slightly liver toxic and noted that it decreased HPTA function moderately in higher dosages. The combination was quite effective for building high quality muscle mass while causing continuous gains in strength and weight. The resulting quality "lean tissue" was retained post-cycle reasonably well considering the estrogenic effects of MD. This drug did not cause a rapid build- up in strength or mass like testosterone, but provided long term progress quite well. Males divided injections into 3-7 administrations weekly with reported best results from daily administration. This was likely due to methandriol's relatively short active-life. Like all products containing boldenone or methandriol, Pace was said to stack well with almost any anabolic product.

*Another similar veterinary AAS is Tribolin 75. This is a mixture of Nandrolone Decanoate (Deca) and Methandriol Dipropionate in equal ratios, providing 75mg/ml

PRIMOBOLAN DEPOT
(METHENOLONE ENANTHATE)

Reported Characteristics
Active Life: 10-14 days

Drug Class: Anabolic/Androgenic Steroid (For injection)

Average Reported Dosage: Men 200-400-mg weekly Women 50-150-mg weekly

Acne: Light at dosages of up to 200-mg weekly

Water Retention: Very low

High Blood Pressure: Rare

Liver Toxic: Low

Aromatization: None

DHT Conversion: None

Decreases: HPTA function: Only slightly in dosages over 300mg weekly and due to prolonged periods of use.

Primobolan Depot is similar to the acetate tablets with a few differences. Though it is a predominantly anabolic steroid, being a DHT derivative it also maintains some androgenic qualities. For this reason, it does have virilizing aspects to consider. This explains the improved strength and harder appearance polled users obtained in part. Naturally since it does not convert to estrogens, induced low water retention and a distinct lack of gyno and female pattern fat deposits was noted as avoided. In fact, the drug does theoretically act as an anti-estrogen to a lesser extent.

*Women reported they were able to avoid some virilizing aspects with Proscar.

Most first time male (AAS novices) users reported an 8-16 lb gain after 6-8 weeks of 200mg weekly dosages. The new muscle was of a high quality and usually was retained quite well after discontinuance. This may have been due to Primobolan depot having only a slight negative effect upon the Hypothalamic-Pituitary-Testes-Axis (HPTA). In short, this drug was noted to only slightly shut down natural testosterone production and therefore there was not a significant lack of testosterone or an elevation in circulatory estrogen post- cycle. This was especially true if dosages were kept at 200-300-mg weekly for no more than 6-8 weeks for males. (Women don't have testes, remember?). For this reason, older males made excellent and reasonably permanent gains with little interruption in their already lower natural androgen production. For stacks focusing on this issue, Oxandrolone and Android were said to work very well with Primobolan Depot. Primobolan based stacks containing nandrolones and/or Equipoise were commonly utilized for this purpose also.

*A point of interest: Primobolan Depot (like Winstrol Depot) has been noted to possess excellent site- injection qualities. This means that a lagging body part became the injection site for dosages. Most who used this type of protocol did so after training that body part to avoid bruising.

Women actually should not have used high dosages of any DHT product or derivative. DHT has excellent hardening effects, but also has masculinizing aspects. An often noted as safer method for use of such drugs was to also co-administer a 5-ALFA-REDUCTASE INHIBITOR such as Proscar. Its active ingredient is Finasteride which blocks testosterone's conversion to DHT. Yes, that is the pill guys take to stop their hair - line from receding. 1mg daily was said be enough when women stayed in the 50-200mg weekly dosage range when using Primobolan Depot.

Since Primobolan Depot actually has an active-life of closer to two weeks, injections were commonly administered weekly by those whom reported lower dosage use. But due to predominantly 50-mg/ml ampules being the most available a 4-ml/200mg injection "hurt" to an excessive degree for those whom employed the higher dosage protocols. So twice weekly injections was the normal method chosen.

*It was my experience that Primobolan was one of the few steroids capable of increasing lean mass during calorie restricted periods therefore remaining effective even in calorie deficit induced catabolic environments. This drug is an Enanthate ester and should provide an 8 day active life. Strangely enough it does provide the above listed active-life range though the ester is an enanthate.

TRADE NAMES

PRIMOBOLAN DEPOT   100-MG/ML
PRIMOBOLAN DEPOT-MITE   50MG-ML
PRIMOBOLAN DEPOT   50MG-ML

WINSTROL DEPOT
(STANOZOLOL INJECTION)

Noted Characteristics

Active-Life: About 48 hours
Drug Class: High Anabolic/Androgenic steroid (For injection)
Average Reported Dosage: Men 50-100mg every 1-2 days Women 25-50-mg weekly
Acne: Rare from real Stanozolol
Water Retention: Rare
High Blood Pressure: Rare
Liver Toxic: Yes, moderate when injected
DHT Conversion: None, DHT variant
Decreases HPTA function: Low
Aromatization: No, DHT derivative (Potential for DHT receptor stimulation)

The injection form of stanozolol is a water based injectable steroid that is a derivative of DHT. Both oral and injectable forms are c17-alfa-alkylated chemicals. This of course makes the injectable form moderately liver toxic and the oral form liver toxic in high dosages. Before going on let me make it clear that the injectable form is the same as the oral. For this reason the injectable form has frequently been used as an oral also. Why would anyone have done that? Well, all c17-alfa-alkylated AAS, when passing through the liver for deactivation, cause a distinct elevation in IGF-1 production. (*Please see IGF-1). This is why 30-mg of Dianabol orals daily (210-mg weekly total) has been revered as more effective for mass and strength gains than 400-mg of testosterone enanthate. The injectable stanozolol has been much cheaper than oral stanozolol, so some athletes opted to utilize it as an oral.

Stanozolol is a high anabolic /moderate androgenic that causes a significant elevation in protein synthesis and an improved nitrogen retention. Since it does not aromatize to estrogen, water retention, gyno, and female pattern fat deposits do not occur. A high protein diet of 1.5-2-g of protein per LB of bodyweight daily was necessary to obtain the best results. This was not noted as a steroid for rapid weight gains but was commonly affirmed as ideal for a continuous slow gain in very high quality lean muscle mass that was well retained after discontinuance. Many who compete utilized Winstrol off-season with testosterone in a Max Androgen Phase for its anabolic value.

Many used Winstrol (stanozolol) as a pre-contest drug because it provided a continuously harder appearance. When 50-100mg every 1-2 days was stacked with 76-mg of Parabolan every 2-3 days, the results were quite impressive. Many also added Masteron, Equipoise, or Testosterone Propionate/ Testosterone Suspension with the addition of anti-estrogens for water retention and aromatization control.

43

Women often reported use of Winstrol Depot. "Usually" those who reported 25mg 2-3 times weekly or a single weekly 50-mg injection use reported no virilization effects. (I have known many women who have utilized 50-100mg daily of this drug) Stacked with Oxandrolone and/or Durabolin, women achieved excellent quality lean mass gains.

Winstrol tabs were often thought to be a better choice at a dosage of 10-20-mg daily, or about 1/4 -1/2ml of the injectable taken orally due to results realized. The method often employed for the injection product used as an oral was to mix 1ml of Stanozolol with 9 ml of water. Each ml=5-mg. (Duh!)

Since Stanozolol produced a surprising increase in strength, it has been used as a part of a mass cycle as well. Novices and older males made very impressive "second cycle" gains stacking 50mg of Stanozolol every other day with 50-100mg of Primobolan Depot every 2-3 days, or with 200-400mg of Deca-Durabolin weekly. Many hard-core males reported serious strength and mass gains using 50-100mg stanozolol with 50-100mg Testosterone Suspension daily. This was a fairly high weekly dosage and was hopefully considered for advanced athletes..if at all.

Winstrol is another AAS that was commonly used in a site-injection protocol for lagging body parts.

*I have been impressed with the results I have seen, but this method requires careful location. Hitting a vein would end any Mr. "O" dream real quick. Some black market Winstrol is testosterone suspension, so if gyno was reported…

TRADE NAMES

WINSTROL-V   50-MG/ML
WINSTROL DEPOT   50-MG/ ML
STROMBA   50-MG/ML
STANOZOLOL USP XXII   50-MG/ML
STANAZOLIC 50-MG/ML
STANAZOLIC 100-MG/ML

ZERANABOL
(BETA-RESORCYLIC ACID LACTONE)

Reported Characteristics
Drug Class: Non-steroidal estrogen
Water Retention: High
High Blood Pressure: Yes
DHT Conversion: Does not apply
HPTA Suppression: Severe

Zeranabol is used in research as a means of causing liver damage in test animals. (Cruel but true) In the case of drug treatment research, the drug is utilized for this intent so they can find out if another drug they wish to market will cure the damage they have caused. (Even crueler)

Sometime in the 80's athletes found out Zeranabol had anabolic activity. Since it is actually a form of estrogen, the drug increases nitrogen retention. IGF-1, GH, and Insulin secretion increases are also realized for the same reason. The result is some lean mass gain with high water retention. For the most part, users have realize HPTA function suppression at extreme rates, gyno, fat deposits, and head-aches. Oh, did I mention liver damage?

The reason this non-steroidal estrogenic fungus based drug has been included is simple: Some dealers have claimed it to be a Mexican methandriol. Yes, it would have similar effects such as better androgen receptor-site sensitivity and elevated IGF-1 levels, but so does some oral female contraceptives. Worse yet is the bad bogus versions of Zeranabol that were floating around. Bottom line, do not do it!

TESTOSTERONE AND ITS ESTERS

Testosterone and its esters still produce the greatest over-all mass weight and strength gains on a cost-per-milligram basis. No other AAS is as versatile for use in both off-season mass cycles and pre-contest cycles (when properly applied and utilized).

NOTED POSITIVE EFFECTS OF TESTOSTERONE

*Excellent anabolic qualities and the resulting lean tissue augmentation due to increased protein synthesis.
*Rapid mass weight and strength gains.
*Increased muscle glycogen synthesis.
*Improved muscle insulin sensitivity.
*Equally anabolic and androgenic in activity.
*Increased fat mobilization and decrease fat synthesis.
*Promotes red blood cell count for improved oxygen/nutrient transport and vascularity.
*Increased bone density, formation, and mineral use.
*Increased creatine phosphate (CP) synthesis and storage.
*Good recovery and regenerative qualities.
*Moderate cortisol control and protein sparing qualities.
*Androgenically induced brain function/training intensity.
*Improved immune function/protection against auto immune.
*Increased metabolic rate.
*Increased HDL/decreased LDL and total cholesterol (in reasonable dosage administration situations).
*Significant increase in libido.
*Improved self-confidence and sense of well being.

NOTED SIDE EFFECTS (POTENTIALLY NEGATIVE)

*Aromatization to estrogens at a high rate/high water retention.
*Reduces to dihydrotestosterone (DHT)
*Decreased HDL/increased LDL (Reported due to high dosage prolonged use).
*Increased body hair growth.
*Accelerated genetic predisposition expression of male pattern balding.
*Promotion of platelet aggregation (which can cause blood clots in rare cases).
*Significant HPTA inhibition (due to high aromatization)
*Poor post-cycle mass/weight retention due to HPTA inhibition and loss of estrogen induced water retention.

Testosterone and its various esters was the base of most intermediate and advanced AAS protocols. This was due to very predictable mass weight and strength gains resulting when utilized.

When stacked with Nandrolones, Dianabol, and / or Anadrol-50, testosterone was the base for off-season mass weight gains. On the other side of the coin was the pre-contest stacks with anti-estrogens, Trenbolones, Primobolan, Anavar and/or Winstrol to consider when discussing the versatility of reported testosterone use.

GODZILLABOL
(4 TESTOSTERONE ESTER MIX 300 MG/ML)

Reported Characteristics

Active-Life: (total) 21 days.
Drug Class: Androgenic/Anabolic steroid (For injection)
Average Reported Dosage: 300-1500 MG weekly.
Acne: Yes, high
Water Retention: Yes, high.
Decreases HPTA function: Yes, significantly.
High Blood Pressure: Common with higher dosage use.
Aromatization: Yes, high.
Liver Toxic: Low, except in ridiculous dosages.
DHT Conversion: Yes, high.

An interesting (underground) manufacturer called GAC (Generic Agriculture and Chemical) has created a multiple testosterone ester product aptly called Godzillabol. The product may be available in Mexico and is provided in a 6 milliliter vial. Some would assume this is nothing more than another Sustanon-250 knock-off, but they could not be more wrong.

Each ML (Milliliter) of Godzillabol provides:

Testosterone Acetate-50 MG /48 hour active life.
Testosterone Propionate-50 MG/72 hour active life.
Testosterone Cypionate-150 MG/15-16 day active life.
Testosterone Laurate 50 MG/20-21 day active life. (Traces of laurate ester up to 28 days)
    Total MG/ML. = 300 MG (No Joke)

The timing sequence of the 4 different testosterone esters contained in Godzillabol made the idea of creating a specific blood plasma level quickly a bit difficult for most polled athletes. Since acetates tend to have about a 48 hour active-life, Propionates a 72 hour active-life, and Cypionates a 15-16 day active-life, the addition of 75 MG Testosterone Enanthate to the single 300 MG/ML mixture would have been a plus in my opinion. As the product is provided, utilization in a Max Androgen Phase required the administration of the total dosage intended within the first 8-10 days of the cycle. This of course applies to the intent of allowing the system to adequately clear within 30 days of total AAS activity to reduce HPTA suppression and other negative action/reaction factors. A reasonable constant blood plasma (circulating) androgen level was notably accomplished with twice weekly administration. Most polled reported the theory that once discontinued, the effects of Testosterone Laurate did taper off slowly during the proceeding 3 weeks. This may have been a plus or minus depending on protocol intent.

The structure of this drug allowed for near immediate results due to fast acting Testosterone Acetate and Propionate. Additionally, the slow tapering effect caused by long acting Testosterone Laurate decreased the negative psychological aspects (I'm-shrinking -I-tis) of discontinuance.

As a whole, Godzillabol is a more powerful drug than Sustanon-250, Primoteston, or Testanon-250 and less expensive. Most users realized significant weight and strength gains within the first 7-10 days, though many reported seeing and feeling results by day #2.

OMNADREN 250
(4-TESTOSTERONE ESTER MIXTURE)

Reported Characteristics

Active Life: About 18 days total

Drug Class: Androgenic/Anabolic Steroid (For injection)

Average Reported Dosage: 125-1500MG weekly (males only)

Acne: Yes

Water Retention: Yes

High Blood Pressure: Yes

Liver Toxic: Low, except in high dosages

Aromatization: Yes

DHT Conversion: Yes, high

Decreases HPTA function: Yes, severely

Omnadren is a mixture of 4 Testosterones:

60-mg Testosterone Phenylpropionate

30-mg Testosterone Propionate

60-mg Testosterone Isohexanoate

100-mg Testosterone Hexanoate.

Omnadren is similar to Sustanon only in the fact that each contains four different Testosterone esters. However, they reportedly differed, both in effect and mixture. Both contain Testosterone Propionate and Testosterone Phenylpropionate. But Sustanon contains Testosterone Iscoparoate and Testosterone Decanoate, where as Omnadren contains Testosterone Isohexanoate and Testosterone Hexanoate. This gave Omnadren a distinct higher water retention rating and aromatization factor over Sustanon. (Ester type has an effect upon aromatization rates) Sustanon also remains active a few days longer than Omnadren.

Omnadren provided fast weight and strength build-up. However much of the weight gain was due to water retention from aromatization. This gave users a bloated appearance to the whole body including the face. Most users reported an increased pump, appetite, and training aggressiveness as well as elevate sex drive (duh!).

Though Omnadren remains active for 2-3 weeks, users commonly injected multiple times weekly. The noted range of dosage was quite wide as some individuals actually administered 14,000mg or more weekly. This was an unnecessary practice, though some swear it was the best way. Then again, some once thought Jim Jones made great drinks

*From 250mg every 2 weeks to 2000-mg per day? You read that right, 2000-mg per day. A more reasonable dosage of 250-mg -1000-mg weekly was observed by most users.

As is true with one other eastern European country AAS products, Omnadren is said to be manufactured with less concern for impurities. (You should see some of this stuff under a microscope. You would swear the credo for some manufacturing was *"After we pee in it we are done"*) For this reason, many Omnadren users experienced harsh acne (including small rash like pimples on their arms, chest, back, face, and legs). I have known a couple users who report injection site abscess problems. Surgery will most likely be needed to remove these nasty pus pockets.

So why did athletes use Omnadren? It is cheap and it worked.

Omnadren is very androgenic and anabolic. For this reason, mass and strength build-ups were high and rapid. Unfortunately, maintaining these gains post-cycle were not good. An anti-estrogen was reported as almost a must at any dosage with this product and the shut down of natural testosterone production during use was considered normal. So post-cycle use of HCG, Clomid, Novladex, and Proviron were considered almost a must as well (depending on dosage and cycle length of time). To avoid serious crashing after use, a switch to Nandrolones helped.

*Those who have read the second book in this series know that the excessive HPTA function inhibition and post-cycle lean mass tissue loss was mostly avoided with Max Androgen Phases, Tide-Cycles, Cortisol/Estrogen Suppression Phases, Absolute Anabolic Phases, and others. See "Building The Perfect Beast" Featuring "Frank N. Steroid" for more info.

TRADE NAMES

OMNADREN 250   250-MG/ML

*STEN IS AN AAS FOUND IN MEXICO that was only noted by a few of those polled so a brief note was warranted:

EACH 2ML VIAL PROVIDES:
TESTOSTERONE PROPIONATE-25-MG
TESTOSTERONE CYPIONATE-75MG
DIHYDROTESTOSTEREONE-20MG

Due to STEN containing Dihydrotestosterone (DHT) the drug was utilized pre-contest. This is because DHT increases vascularity and over all hardness. Normally 1 vial every 3 days for 4-6 weeks was added to the pre-contest stack (Also see Proscar)

SUSTANON -250

Reported Characteristics
Active-Life: About 3 weeks
Drug Class: Androgenic/Anabolic steroid (For injection)
Average Reported Dosage: Men 125-2000mg weekly
Acne: Yes
Water Retention: Yes
High Blood Pressure: Yes
Liver Toxic: Low except in high dosages over 1000-mg weekly
DHT Conversion: Yes
Decreases HPTA Function: Significantly after 2 weeks
Aromatization: Yes, somewhat less than testosterone cypionate or enanthate.

Sustanon 250 is a mixture of the 4 testosterone esters:
PROPIONATE-30-MG
PHENYLPROPIONATE-60-MG
ISOCAPROATE-60-MG
DECANOATE-100-MG

This is a well structured product that acts as a well timed time-released high anabolic/high androgenic testosterone. In fact, due to TESTOSTERONE PROPIONATE, this product becomes active after one day, but through the series of the other 3 testosterones, remains active for 3 weeks. This mixture had a reported better over all effect milligram for milligram than any other testosterone alone. Users experienced a rapid increase in strength and an even increase in solid mass during administration. SUSTANON aromatized less and caused less water retention when compared to other single testosterones and much less than OMNADREN. Liver toxicity was low (Except in ridiculous dosages) as the liver metabolizes testosterone very efficiently. Like all testosterones, SUSTANON provided improved muscle pumps, better post-training recuperation, and an elevation in aggressiveness toward training.

SUSTANON significantly suppressed the HPTA so natural testosterone production was significantly decreased as well. For this reason, HCG and CLOMID were considered mandatory after 4-6 weeks of continuous use and after the discontinuance of the drug.

Males normally utilized dosages of 250-1000mg weekly, but some used higher dosages. As a rule, excellent results were realized with a dosage of 250-500mg every 7-10 days. Most novices and women noted that they felt that they should not use testosterone. Novices…because it was not necessary and it will limit later potential progress. Women should not use them (but a few reported doing so) due to virilizing effects.

51

Some woman polled just could not leave testosterones alone. PROSCAR (FINASTERIDE, A DHT BLOCKER) was considered mandatory for co-administration and TESTOSTERONE PROPIONATE 50mg 1 time weekly was noted to cause less virilizing side effects.

TRADE NAMES

SUSTENON 250	250-MG/ML
SUSTANON	250-MG /ML
SUSTANON 250	250-MG/ML
SUSTANON 250	250-MG/ML
SUSTENON 250	250-MG /ML

VERTEINALY DEPOSTERONE   (60-MG MIX PER ML)

TEST 400 (3-TESTOSTERONE ESTER MIX 400 MG/ML)

Reported Characteristics
Active-Life: (total) 16 days.
Drug Class: Androgenic/Anabolic steroid (For injection)
Average Reported Dosage: Men 400-1600mg weekly.
Acne: Yes, High.
Water Retention: Yes, High.
Decreases HPTA function: Yes, significantly.
High Blood Pressure: Common with higher dosage use.
Aromatization: Yes, High.
Liver Toxic: Low.
DHT Conversion: Yes, High.

The Australian veterinary drug company Denkall manufactures a variety of quality AAS. As a rule, the products contain the listed dosages of any given drug plus or minus 1%. In the case of "Test 400" they have created a 3-testosterone ester mix that actually provides 400 MG of testosterone esters per milliliter and comes in 10 ML bottles/vials. This is unusual since 400 MG of any testosterone ester would not be soluble in a single milliliter of any oil. From the injection site irritation users reported it is very likely that the manufacturers have increased the benzyl alcohol content as a means of increasing total testosterone esters possible, dosage wise, for solubility. More bang for your dogy's buck, but more burn also. Athletes who experienced higher sensitivity to injection site irritation from benzyl alcohol usually mixed "Test 400" with Synthol, Protest, or another oil based AAS to reduce irritation. But doing so required a site-injection type protocol.

As said several times prior, testosterone is testosterone regardless of brand or ester the active drug is joined to. The question is a matter of chosen active-life and dispersion profile, with the chosen blood serum or plasma level desired. Sounds confusing but it is not. For example: Testosterone Enanthate and Cypionate are testosterone joined to an ester to create a time-release effect. For this reason, Testosterone Enanthate provides 144 MG of free testosterone per 200 MG dosage and Testosterone Cypionate provides 140 MG of free testosterone per 200 MG dosage. So actually 200 MG of Testosterone Suspension is about 30% more powerful simply due to the fact that suspension is raw free testosterone in sterile water, and 200 MG is 200 MG. The rest is a matter of dividing the active-life by the dosage to decide how many milligrams of free testosterone (or simply use the dosage as a base number for less accuracy) the ester releases or disperses daily. Okay…Testosterone Cypionate has a 16 day active-life, so 200 MG/16=12.5 MG daily (including ester) or 140 MG of "actual" free testosterone released or dispersed daily. Got it? Faster acting testosterone esters such as an Acetate do "seem" to be more potent for the same reason!

Per milliliter Test 400 provides:
Testosterone Cypionate 187 MG /15-16 day active-life.
Testosterone Enanthate 188 MG/7-8 day active-life.   **Total MG per ML= 400 MG**
Testosterone Propionate 25 MG /72 hour active-life.

*Some have stated both cypionate and enanthate have the same actual active-life. My experience with "real" products shows this to be untrue, though some underground drugs are mislabeled. As are some legit products for black market sales purposes. Go figure!

TESTOSTERONE CYPIONATE

Reported Characteristics
Active-Life: 15-16 days
Drug Class: Androgenic/Anabolic Steroid (For injection)
Average Reported Dosage: Men 200-1000mg weekly
Acne: Yes, common
Water Retention: Yes, high
High Blood Pressure: Yes, due to water/electrolyte retention
Liver Toxic: Low, except in absurd dosages
Aromatization: Yes, high
DHT conversion: Yes, high
Decreases HPTA Function: Yes, severely

Pretty much all that was written about TESTOSTERONE ENANTHATE also applies to TESTOSTERONE CYPIONATE. A slight distinction was made in that they each provided a notable different half- and active-life period. For this reason, CYPIONATE injections were reduced to every 8th day by some reported users. Dosages of 200-1000mg weekly were common, but most users experienced excellent results with 200-600mg weekly. Both testosterone preparations stacked well with any other AAS and added a distinct androgenic effect. This meant improved regenerative qualities and greater training intensity with a correlating significant increase in weight-load capacity. For those who wished to use testosterone but were highly sensitive to gyno and water retention, TESTOSTERONE PROPIONATE was commonly reported to be the better choice. Oddly enough, a few of those polled reported more sensitively due to Propionate's fast action. Interesting paradox, huh? The issue was simply a matter of dosage/administration protocols. Since PROPIONATE remained active for about 3 days a weekly administration protocol allowed circulatory clearing of the drug. It should be noted that both TESTOSTERONE ENANTHATE and CYPIONATE were said to be more anabolic and less androgenic then SUSPENSION or PROPIONATE. This is pure imagination. The truth is that suspension actually is a faster acting testosterone and contains more total testosterone per 100mg dosage than any esterfied testosterone.

TRADE NAMES

ANDRÉ-CYP 100,200-MG/ML	TESTA-C 200-MG/ML
DEP ANDRO 100&200 100,200-MG/ML	TESTADIATE-DEPO 200-MG/ML
DEPO TESTOSTERONE 50-MG/ML	DURA TEST 100,200-MG/ML
TESTEX LEO PROLONGATUM 100,200-MG/ML	DEP TEST 100,200-MG/ML
TESTOSTERONE CYPIONATE 100,200-MG/ML	
TESTED CYPIONATE 200-MG/ML	

TESTOSTERONE ENANTHATE

Reported Characteristics
Active-Life: 8 days
Drug Class: Androgenic/Anabolic Steroid (For injection)
Average Reported Dosage: Men 200-1000mg weekly.
Acne: Yes
Water Retention: Yes, high due to estrogen conversion
High Blood Pressure: Yes, normally due to high water /electrolyte retention
Liver Toxic: Low in listed dosages
Aromatization: Yes, high
DHT Conversion: Yes, high
Decreases HPTA Function: Yes, high

Testosterone was generally toted as the big daddy of injectable steroids. No other steroid was consistently reported to bring such high returns as quickly in weight gain and strength increases. Due to its high anabolic/high androgenic effects, many athletes used this drug in an off-season mass cycle. Water retention during administration of ENANTHATE was not reportedly as high as that realized during the use of OMNADREN… but darn close. Like all testosterone esters, Enanthate aromatized easily and has a high conversion rate to DHT. Those with prostate problems or who were sensitive to gyno and female pattern fat deposits, readily agreed that they should have either left it alone or taken steps to suppress estrogenic activity due to aromatization. Drugs such as PROVIRON and NOVLADEX were often utilized for this reason. DHT conversion enzyme blockers such as Proscar were commonly co-administered with testosterones for the former reason.

Testosterone enanthate notably suppressed HPTA function severely. HCG/Clomid were considered almost a must to stimulate normal endogenous (natural) testosterone production within a positive period of time at post use. My personal experience has been that if a cycle containing testosterone enanthate lasted longer than 6 weeks, HCG and usually Clomid were introduced for 10 days beginning at the end of week #4. (5000 i.u. of HCG 3 times in 10 days usually normalized sperm and endogenous testosterone production to a respectable extent) Without the use of HPTA stimulating compounds normalization did occur, only at a much slower rate. For this reason, gains made during "enanthate only" administrations were not well maintained after use was discontinued, and much was lost needlessly by most regardless. Perhaps this was why so many uninformed individuals stayed on the stuff almost year round. (There are several solutions and protocols that prevented excessive post-cycle lean mass tissue loss for the more informed athletes)

Males injected 200-1000mg weekly. Some did use much higher dosages of course. Due to a plasma half-life of 4-5 days, injections were normally administered bi-weekly. Most novice steroid should not use testosterone. Not only was considered unnecessary, it would have been foolish to diminish possible later gains when more gentle AAS were no longer providing results at reasonable dosages. Most users made excellent progress with a total weekly dosage of 200-600mg. Post-cycle use of an anti-catabolic drug was a constant agreed upon factor since it helped to maintain gains. (See Clenbuterol)

The negative side effects reported were mostly water retention and strong androgenic effects. These included gyno, accelerated hair growth, receding hair-lines, aggressiveness, higher blood pressure, acne, and increased fat deposits (due to aromatization). Since testosterones are metabolized by the liver fairly easily, alarming elevated liver enzymes occurred in very high dosages only… usually.

TRADE NAMES

ANDRO LA 200   200-MG/ML
ANDROTARDYL   250-MG/ML
DELATESTRYL   200-MG/ML
DURATHATE 200 INJ.   200-MG/ML
EVERONE   100,200-MG/ML.
PRIMOTESTON DEPOT   250-MG / ML
TESTOSTERON DEPOT   250-MG/ML

VETERINARY**

TESTOSTERONA 200   200-MG/ML

TESTOSTERONE PROPIONATE

Reported Characteristics
Active-life: 2-3 days
Drug class: Anabolic/Androgenic steroid (For injection)
Average Reported Dosage: Male 50-200mg daily
Acne: Yes
Water Retention: Yes
High Blood Pressure: Yes
Liver Toxic: Low
Aromatization: Yes, high
DHT Conversion: Yes, high
Decreases HPTA Function: Yes, severely

Due to Testosterone Propionate possessing a brief active-life of 2-3 days, many athletes involved in tested competitions liked the stuff...a lot. Testing is usually based upon testosterone /Epitestosterone levels. Though most individuals have a much lower ratio, athletes can have natural ratios of up to 6:1. This is considered a negative test for steroids… usually. By injecting Propionate up to 36 hours before competition, plasma Testosterone levels remained elevated while urine concentrations usually fell within the 6:1 levels. Of course IOC testing protocols would detect any plant origin AAS today. But several groups still simply test for the ratio only.

Testosterone Propionate is considered a fast acting testosterone due to effects beginning in about 1 day. The drug reportedly has all the benefits of other testosterones (quick strength and muscle mass increases, increased training aggressiveness, fast post-training recovery) but caused a distinctly lower level of water retention. Users noted an improved muscle pump and increased appetite after one to two days of administration. Even with a high rate of aromatization, propionate did not cause gyno as often as other testosterone esters. Users who realize this normally did so due to less frequent injections: Not due to some special quality of the drug. I liked propionate because an increase in IGF-1 was common during liver deactivation. Also because use could be discontinued at the first sign of overt side effects (thus allowing the chemical to no longer be the cause after 2-3 days post-discontinuance).

A high quality muscle gain has been achieved with 50-100mg Testosterone propionate every 1-2 days, 50mg Winstrol Depot every 2nd day, and 20-25mg of Oxandrolone daily. If Parabolan (76mg every other day) was substituted for Winstrol and Proviron is utilized as an anti-estrogen, this became an excellent pre-contest cycle providing superior hardness. Those who had used Primobolan only and no longer made progress at 200-400 mg weekly made consider progress by stacking 200-400mg Primobolan Depot weekly with 50-100mg of Testosterone Propionate every second day. Improved vascularity was common due to increased in red blood cell count as well.

Women who did use testosterones considered propionate to be the superior choice over any other. 25-50mg of Propionate every 5-7 days stacked with any high anabolic such as Anadur, or especially Durabolin caused a dramatic result with less virilizing characteristics. As always, women who are extremely sensitive to androgens reported the use of 1mg Finasteride daily lowered DHT conversion of Propionate.

*It should be noted: Propionate also severely suppresses HPTA function and HCG/Clomid have been considered post administration stables.

TRADE NAMES

AGOVIRIN   25-MG/ML
NEO-HOMBREOL   50-MG/ML
TESTEX LEO   25-MG/ML
TESTOSTERONE PROPIONCUM   10,25-MG/ML
TESTOSTERONE PROPIONATE   100-MG/ML.
TESTO VIRON   10,25,50-MG/ML
VIRORMONE   25,50,100-MG/ML

VETERINARY

ARA-TEST   25-MG/ML, 10-ML
TESTOGAN   25-MG/ML, 50-ML
TESTOSTERONA- 50   50-MG/ML, 10-ML

TESTOSTERONE BERCO SUPPOSITORIES   40-MG, 18 SUPP. (RECTAL USE)

TESTOSTERONE SUSPENSION
(AQUEOUS TESTOSTERONE SUSPENSION)

Reported Characteristics
Active-Life: About one day.
Drug Class: Androgenic/Anabolic Steroid (For injection)
Average Reported Dosage: Men 150-1400mg weekly Women 25-50mg weekly
Acne: Yes, high
Water Retention: Yes, high
High blood Pressure: Often in higher dosages
Liver Toxic: Low
Aromatization: Yes, high
DHT Conversion: Yes-high
Decreases HPTA function: Yes, significantly

Testosterone suspension is Testosterone crystals suspended in sterile water. The product becomes active about 1 hour after injection. Those who used suspension noted an unbelievable elevation in strength and aggression coupled with a rapid build-up in muscle mass. Women bodybuilders commonly reported the use of use 25-50mg daily during the last 1-4 days before competition to cause a rapid increase in androgens to over ride high estrogen levels and the resulting aldosterone levels. Since Aldosterone is the body's water regulating hormone this method improved hardness significantly.

Males usually administered 50-200mg daily for the same purpose. Testosterone suspension significantly boosts glycogen storage in muscle tissue. After carb depletion and during a 2-4 carb-loading phase, the results of suspension use have been amazing: Increased muscle striation and separation combined with a fall hard look to the tissue. Suspension was rarely reported to be used by novice testosterone users even during mass gaining cycles simply because it "hurt like hell" and maintained plasma levels required daily administrations. (But it actually produced better results than other testosterones). As with other testosterones, prolonged use led to a serious decrease in natural androgen production.

*Suspension is more androgenic and anabolic than either Enanthate or Cypionate only because it is not testosterone joined to an ester. This simply means 100mg of suspension actually has 100mg of active testosterone that enters the circulatory system at a fairly rapid rate. (More testosterone = more activity!)

TRADE NAMES

AGOVIRIN DEPOT   50-MG / 2 ML
HISTERONE INJ.   100-MG / 1ML
TESTOSTERONE-AQUEOUS 50,100-MG/ 1ML

TESTOVIRON DEPOT 50, 100, 135, 250
(TESTOSTERONE PROPIONATE/ENANTHATE MIXTURE)

Reported Characteristics
Active-Life: Propionate-3 days/Enanthate- 8 days
Drug Class: Androgenic/Anabolic Steroid (For injection)
Average Reported Dosage: Men 250-1000mg weekly
Acne: Yes
Water Retention: Yes
High Blood Pressure: Yes
Liver Toxic: Low
Aromatization: Yes, high
DHT conversion: Yes, high
Decreases HPTA function: Yes, severely

This is a mixture of a fast acting testosterone propionate and a slower acting Testosterone enanthate. The benefit of this mixture was a noted quicker metabolic reaction to the propionate with a longer effect realize from the enanthate. (*Please see "Testosterone Propionate" and "Testosterone Enanthate" for more info) When combined the two drugs created a slightly more effective compound due to synergistic effects. To maintain plasma levels it was necessary to administer this drug every 2-3 days. All side effects and qualities pertaining to the two testosterones have been listed in their respective sections. So I will not make you read it here again

TRADE NAMES

TESTOVIRON DEPOT 50   20-MG PROP.; 55-MG ENAN/ML
TESTOVIRON DEPOT 100   25-MG PROP.; 110-MG ENAN./ML
TESTOVIRON DEPOT 250   50-MG PROP.; 200-MG ENAN.; /ML

*THERE IS A   TESTOVIRON 135. HOWEVER I WAS   UNABLE TO OBTAIN CLARIFICATION ON THE CONTENTS AT THIS TIME

THERAMEX
(TESTOSTERONE HEPTYLATE)

Reported Characteristics

Active-Life: 20 days
Drug Class: Androgenic /Anabolic Steroid (For injection)
Average Reported Dosage: Men 250-1500mg weekly
Acne: Yes
Water Retention: High
High Blood Pressure: Yes, due to water retention
Liver Toxic: Low
Aromatization: Yes, high
DHT Conversion: Yes
Decreases HPTA Function: Yes, severe

Milligram for milligram the French manufactured testosterone heptylate was often said to be stronger than any other testosterone ester. Again, testosterone is testosterone and activity is a factor of the actual parent drug content of an ester as well as dispersion rate (active -life). Like all testosterones, this drug is a high androgen/high anabolic substance that provided a serious build-up in size and strength. Water retention was lower than with cypionate. This may be due to a slightly lower level of aromatization. (Some esters also effect the rate of conversion to estrogens slightly) Severe suppression of the HPTA was common and HCG/Clomid administration was considered mandatory after 4-6 weeks of use and at the end of the cycle. DHT conversion is high so androgen sensitive athletes opted to either not use testosterone or utilize a conversion inhibitor such as Finasteride. Anti-estrogens such as Novladex or Teslac were reported as necessary for sensitive individuals and higher dosage use. Most athletes seemed to experience fewer side effects with Testosterones Heptylate than with Cypionate.

Gains were of a higher quality nature. Due to lower water retention, the musculature's had a somewhat less smooth appearance than what is common with some other testosterones. Excellent muscle pumps and an improved appetite were also common after only a few days of use. Like most Testosterones, a quicker recovery / regeneration quality existed.

Men commonly used a weekly dosage of 250-1000mg. However, excellent results were realized by novice testosterone users at a dosage of 250-mg every 5-7 days. Women do not seem to suffer virilization symptoms at dosages of 25-50mg weekly, but women and testosterone use is/are always a crap shoot! Even though Testosterone Heptylate remains active for about 20 days, it was necessary to use injections every 10 days to avoid a roller coaster effect in plasma androgen levels.

TRADE NAME

TESTOSTERONE HEPTYLATE THERAMEX   50,100,250-MG/ML

NORTESTOSTERONE (NANDROLONE) AND ITS ESTERS

Nortestosterone, or Nandrolone as it is more commonly known, is a deviation of the testosterone molecule that results in a highly anabolic/moderately androgenic AAS. Additionally, Nandrolone is very protein sparing and liver friendly according to the drug insert literature.

NOTED POSITIVE EFFECTS OF NORTESTOSTERONE (NANDROLONE)

*Significant anabolic qualities.
*High quality (but slow) lean tissue gains.
*Excellent post-cycle lean mass retention.
*Low-moderate water retention.
*Low aromatization to estrogens.
*Does not negatively effect HDL.
*Moderate strength and weight gain.
*Noted improvement in joint/soft tissue function.
*Excellent protein sparing /anti-catabolic qualities.
*Inhibition of fat synthesis.
*Increased metabolic rate.
*Does not reduce to DHT (Dihydrotestosterone)
*Very low-moderate HPTA function inhibition. (Dose Dependent)
*Increased muscle glycogen synthesis.
*Increased Creatine Phosphate (CP) synthesis.
*Reduction in total triglyceride and cholesterol levels.
*Beneficial/improved insulin metabolism.

POSSIBLE NEGATIVE EFFECTS OF NORTESTOSTERONE (NANDROLONE)

*Poor protection from over training.
*Some males experienced decreased libido (Not true for women)
*Inhibition of HPTA function at dosages in excess of 400 MG weekly.

There are distinct qualities not commonly listed under "nortestosterone effects". A few examples are:

*Nandrolones aromatize to estrogen (as a NOR-ESTROGEN) at about 20% (1/5) of the rate that testosterone does. This results in little or no estrogenic side effects or reduction in HPTA function at a dosage of 1MG/KG of bodyweight weekly.
*Nandrolone reduces to Nor-dihydrotestosterone (Nor -DHT) instead of Dihydrotestosterone (DHT) via the enzyme 5-Alfa-reductase. The resulting Nor-DHT actually decreases negative androgenic activity upon sex-specific tissues. (Prostate gland/hair follicles)
*Nandrolones possess a very high affinity for androgen receptor-sites and bind more effectively than testosterone. This results in a significant increase in receptor-site binding time and greater activity.

ANADUR
(NANDROLONE HEXYLOCY PHENYLPROPIONATE)

Reported Characteristics
Active-Life: About 4 weeks
Drug Class: Anabolic /Androgenic Steroid (For injection)
Average Reported Dosage: Men 150-450mg every 10-14 days Women 50-100 mg every 10-14 days
Acne: Rare liver toxic: none
Water Retention: Low; less than Deca Durabolin
High Blood Pressure: Rare due to low water retention
High Anabolic/ low androgenic
Decreases HPTA function: Low
Aromatization: Low, and conversion product is NORESTROGEN
DHT Conversion: No, NOR-DHT only.

Anadur is the longest lasting injectable Nandrolone. The use of this drug provided results similar to Deca Durabolin. Like all Nandrolones, a very high protein intake was needed during cycles as a fundamental fact. This is due to Nandrolones high anabolic effect which stimulates protein synthesis at an impressive rate. 1-2 gm of protein per LB of body weight daily was considered a good guideline.

This is a very slow acting anabolic that provided slow but steady lean mass gains and some strength gains. Others (and myself) had noted that gains that were made on cycles utilizing this product tended to be retained quite well after cycles were discontinued. Another noted plus was the lack of DHT activity for those whom reported prior prostate concerns. The use of HCG or Clomid to stimulate natural testosterone production post-cycle was rare if reasonable dosages and/or short term cycles were employed. Being a Nortestosterone product, Anadur aromatizes only slightly to a less active estrogen by-product called Norestrogen. The use of anti-estrogens was seldom employed for this reason unless the drug was utilized during pre-contest protocols. If Anadur was used during a diet phase it was considered highly effective and important that an androgenic was also stacked with it due to its inability to protect against muscle loss as a normal result of restricted calories and over training. To date, I have not seen virilization effects with women athletes whom have not exceed the reported upper average dosage even after several months of use.   However, any derivative of testosterone has the potential to induce virilization. Liver damage, even in high dosages, was very unlikely. In fact the product was often taken by those with liver disease.

TRADE NAMES

ANADOR   50 MG/ML
ANADUR   50 MG/ML
ANADURIN   50MG/ML

63

DECA-DURABOLIN
(NANDROLONE DECANOATE)

Reported Characteristics
Active-Life: 14-16 days
Drug Class: Anabolic/Androgenic steroid (For Injection)
Average Reported Dosage: Men 200-600mg weekly Women 50-100mg weekly
Acne: Yes, in higher dosages in androgen sensitive individuals
Water Retention: Some, much less than testosterone.
Decreases HPTA function moderately
High Blood Pressure: Rare (When used in dosages over 600-mg weekly)
Aromatization: Low, converts to less active norestrogens
Liver Toxic: None.
 DHT Conversion: No, converts to NOR- DHT with low activity
Noted Comments: Highly anabolic/moderate androgenic effects

Nandrolone Decanoate is a very anabolic, moderate androgenic form of nortestosterone that was the most commonly used drug to create a rapid build-up of lean muscle mass or as a diet "protein- sparing" drug by athletes of all kinds. This is a longer lasting nandrolone than Durabolin so some water retention resulted with long term administration (especially in higher dosages). A prominent positive nitrogen balance occurs with the use of nandrolones and therefore a high protein intake was a must for all reported users. If you read the section on protein, you know that nitrogen in its bonded form is a part of protein/amino acids. Since nandrolone promotes nitrogen storage in muscle cells (a positive nitrogen balance) then the cell contains more protein for growth and repair than normal. Remember: This could only happen if above normal calories (with a focus on protein) were ingested. Since nandrolone is moderately androgenic, good strength gains also resulted. Another plus for nandrolone was that most users experienced a joint healing effect during cycles and a suppressed cortisol/cortisone activity due to nandrolones ability to long-term block cortisol receptors. Since aromatization was low, in 200-400-mg weekly dosages, anti-estrogens were not commonly necessary to avoid gyno and estrogenic induced side effects. Based upon available research and information available it seems liver toxicity is unknown with nandrolone. So it was not a surprise to find that even those with liver disease have used this drug with great success.

Common dosages for men were 200 600mg weekly. Though dosages over 400 mg weekly caused more water retention. For first time use of dosages over 400 mg weekly, I preferred to add 50-100mg Durabolin to each of the 2 weekly injections. This was because Durabolin is much faster acting and therefore creates chance for water retention and gyno. (This applied to first -time users only)

An added benefit of this method was that nandrolone decanoate begins significant activity at 6 days and peaks at about 8 days after administration. The faster acting durabolin "kicks in" after about 1 day. This also resulted in higher "quality" muscle tissue gain.

Women seemed to do very well with nandrolones due to the lower androgenic/masculining effect. Women consistently reported excellent lean mass and strength gains at dosages of 50-100 mg weekly. Masculine effects usually were avoided by single weekly injections of 25-50 mg nandrolone decanoate and 25-50 mg of Durabolin (nandrolone phenylpropionate). In both men and women, this method seemed to result in more "quality" muscle, less water retention, less gyno for males, and good retention of gains after the cycle ends.

*Metabolites can be found in urine or blood tests for 12-18 months after use of nandrolone is discontinued.

TRADE NAMES

ANABOLINE   50-MG/ML
ANDROLONE- D 200   200-MG/ML
DECA DURABOLIN   25-MG/ML   DECA DURABOLIN   50-MG/ML
DECA DURABOLIN "100" 100-MG/ML
DECA DURABOLIN   200-MG/ML
ELPIHORM   50MG/ML
EXTRABOLINE   50MG/ML
HYBOLIN DECANOATE   50,100MG/ML
JEBOLAN   50MG/ML
NANDROLONE DECANOATE   50,100, 200MG /ML
NANDROBOLIC L.A. 100MG/ML
NEO-DURABOLIC 100,200,/ML
NUREZAN   50MG/ML
RETABOLIL   25MG/ML   RETABOLIL   50MG /ML
DECANANDROLEN 200   200MG/ML
STEROBOLIN   50MG/ML
TURINABOL DEPOT   50MG/ML

VETERINARY

ANABOLICAN   25ML/ML 10, 50ML
NORANDREN 50   50MG/ML 10,50ML

DURABOLIN
(NANDROLONE PHENYLPROPIONATE)

Reported Characteristics

Active-Life: 2-3 days

Drug Class: Anabolic/androgenic steroid (indictable)

Average Reported Dosage: Men 150-600 mg weekly Women 50-100 mg weekly

Acne: Rare, except with high dosages

Water Retention: Low, much less than nandrolone decanoate

High Blood Pressure: Rare, except with high dosages

Aromatization: low (Aromatizes to nor-estrogen)

Decreases HPTA function: Moderately, except high dosages

Liver Toxic: None

DHT Conversion: No, converts to less active NOR-DHT

Highly anabolic/moderately androgenic

Durabolin is a fast acting nandrolone with an active-life of 2-3 days as compared to Deca Durabolin's 14-16 day active-life. For this reason, males injected Durabolin every 2-3 days and women reportedly avoided virilization effects with injections every 5-7 days (while still enjoying a very high quality but slow lean mass gain). For more rapid strength and mass gains, Deca Durabolin was noted as a better choice of nandrolone. Post-cycle retention of lean muscle mass gains were somewhat better with Durabolin however. This was mostly due to the fact that most individuals used lower dosages of Durabolin and therefore experience less HPTA suppression. Durabolin is highly anabolic, which means a quick build-up of proteins stored intracellularly in muscle tissue, and a positive nitrogen balance. For this reason, as with all nandrolones, a high protein diet was a must. Since Durabolin caused much less water retention than Deca Durabolin (again due to lower dosages), it was an excellent addition to pre-contest stacks. Also due to a shorter active-life, Durabolin appears to aromatize less than Deca.

This drug has no reported negative effect on the liver but will decrease natural androgen production in higher long-term dosages. Durbolin was considered the safest AAS. I have utilized Durabolin's fast acting highly anabolic qualities as part of a site-injection protocol (stacked with testosterone propionate and Primobolan Depot with methandriol deipropionate) with great results.

TRADE NAMES

ANABOLIN 50MG / ML
ANABOLIN-IM 50MG/ML
ANABOLIN LA-100 100MG/ML
ANDROLONE 50MG/ML
DURABOLIN 25MG/ML
DURABOLIN 50MG/ML,
DURABOLIN 100MG/2ML.
EQUIBOLON 100MG/2ML
FHERBOLICE 50MG/ML
HYBOLIN IMPROVED 25,50 MG/ML
NANDROBOLIC 25MG/ML
NANDROLONE PHEYLPROPIONATE 50MG/ML.
NEROBOLIL 25MG/ML
NU-BOLIC 25MG/ML
SUPERANABOLON 25MG/ML
TURINABOL 25MG/ML

DYNABOLIN
(NANDROLONE UNDECANOATE)

Reported Characteristics
Active-Life: 8-10 days
Drug Class: Anabolic/Androgenic injectable steroid
Average Reported Dosages: Men 161mg-402.5mg weekly Women 80.5mg-161mg weekly
Acne: Low except in higher dosages
Water Retention: Medium
High Blood Pressure: Rare
Decreases HPTA function: Low to moderate
Aromatization: Low; higher in dosages of over 322 mg weekly
Liver Toxic: Low
Noted Comments: Should not be used by those with liver dysfunction
High anabolic/moderate androgenic (More androgenic than Deca Durabolin)
DHT conversion: no, Low conversion to less active NOR-DHT

This is a nandrolone drug with a noted higher androgenic effect than Deca. Due to this, Dynabolin was considered to be a stronger drug than Durabolin or Deca milligram for milligram. Therefore it was commonly believed to bring a quicker and larger build-up of strength and muscle mass. Gains were usually very solid and water retention was slightly higher than Deca. Dynabolin also aromatizes more than Deca so the slight increase in reported estrogenic negative side effects was not surprising. According to the available literature, Dynabolin is well tolerated by the liver well. But in some cases liver markers did charge. High blood pressure and elevated cholesterol levels can occur in some individuals due to higher dosages, but most recent research suggests nandrolones positively effect the HDL (Good) to LDL (Bad) ratio. All in all most of these possible side effects disappeared after usage stooped.

Males made fair progress with a dosage of 161-322-mg (2-4-ml) per week divided into two equal injections such as Mon. & Thurs. Based upon reports, women should not use more than 80.5 mg (1-ML) once weekly.

Some women noted virilization effects with even this dosage when the cycle lasted more than 30-42 days. Since Dynabolin is actually a shorter lasting injectable nandrolone, injections for males were administered twice weekly to maintain serum levels.

This drugs active-life falls between Durabolin and Deca in fact. This drug causes a high nitrogen retention and increases protein synthesis dramatically. So higher protein intake was a must if athletes wanted to utilize its full potential. It was rare that anti-estrogen drugs were necessary when using this drug except in dosages of well over 402.5 mg weekly.

Due to low-to-moderate aromatization and high anabolic properties, this drug induced quality lean muscle tissue gains with little increase in the body's water retention extracellularly (outside of cells). The result was a reasonable lean appearance during use.

TRADE NAMES

DYNABOLIN   80.5MG/ML
CYNABOLIN   80.5MG/ML
PSYCHBOLAN   80.5 MG/ML

LAURABOLIN
(NANDROLONE LAURATE)

Reported Characteristics
Active Life: 22-26 days
Drug Class: Anabolic/Androgenic Steroid (For injection)
Average Reported Dosage: Men 200-600mg weekly Women 50-100mg weekly
Acne: Rare
Water Retention: Low except in high dosage use
High Blood Pressure: Rare
Liver Toxic: None
Aromatization: Low except in high dosage use (norestrogen is aromatization product)
High Anabolic/Moderate Androgenic
Decreases HPTA function: Yes, moderately
DHT conversion: No, conversion is Nor DHT

Laurabolin is another nandrolone AAS and is quite comparable to Anadur in both effects and duration. This drug is intended for veterinary use, mostly with dogs. Like Anadur, Laurabolin is a very long lasting anabolic. In fact, a single injection remains active for over 3 weeks, and only a few days shorter than Anadur. Where as some women have reported good results from a single 4 ml injection for 3-4 weeks, the volume of a single injection required for an appreciable anabolic response for a male was considered too massive. (Gee, you think so? Picture 32-ml at one time!) Larabolin aromatizes lightly and only when an athlete utilized higher dosages of over 600 mg weekly. Water retention was low and there was no noted liver toxicity. Most male body builders obtained good but slow lean mass and strength gains with 200-400 mg weekly. Women users reported excellent results with a weekly dosage of 50-100mg with few virilization side effects. In both cases the resulting muscle mass gains seemed to be well retained after use was discontinued. As with all nandrolones, a protein intake of 1-2-gm per pound of body weight was almost unanimously considered a must due to nandrolones high nitrogen retention and high protein synthesis qualities.

Like all nandrolone esters it was common to stack so-called mass drugs such as testosterone, Anadrol-50, and/or Dianabol with the drug for mass type protocols. During calorie restricted or pre-contest prep periods many reported high quality lean mass tissue resulted when stanozolol, trenbolone, and thyroid hormones were co-administered.

The most common reported negative aspect of this drug was the low dosage per ml available. This was due to the volumous injections often utilized to establish the desired effects.

TRADE NAMES

FORTABOL   20-MG/ML-10/50-ML   LAURABOLIN   50-MG/ML 5/10/50 ML
FORTADEX   50-MG/ML 10/50ML   FORTADEX   25-MG/ML-5-ML
LAURABOLIN   25MG/ML 5/10/50 ML   LAURABOLIN   50MG/ML

TRENBOLONES AND DERIVATIVES

Trenbolone is a derivative of 19-Nortestosterone (Nandrolone) and one of the most powerful and considered effective AAS in existence today. It is a fact that milligram for milligram, Trenbolone was more effective for aiding muscle mass and strength augmentation than any testosterone. Some once dispute this by claiming 3 ML (Milliliters) of testosterone cypionate weekly would produce greater mass and strength gains than 3 ML of Finabolan weekly. And they were correct in a weird bodybuilding sort of way. First off, 3 ML of most brands of testosterone cypionate would provide 600 mg of that drug, whereas Finabolan or a Fina Kit would provide only 225 MG of Trenbolone per 3 ML. Second; there is the issue of water retention/weight. Trenbolone does not aromatize and testosterone does. So a significant portion of weight gained during testosterone use is water weight, which of course did have its place and benefits during personal specific protocols. However, 1MG per pound of body weight weekly of Testosterone Cypionate (600 MG for 200 LBS) administration did result in Trenbolone as the victor for lean mass gains. And gains were more permanent! Trenbolone is a very high androgen drug.

NOTED POSITIVE EFFECTS OF TRENBOLONE

*Amazing anabolic qualities.
*Rapid high quality lean tissue gains. (Dose dependent)
*Maximum post-cycle lean mass retention.
*Low-none water retention.
*Increased Erythropoies (Red blood cell production)
*Does not aromatize to estrogens.
*Superior strength and mass gain. (Lean)
*Extreme hardening of musculature and vascularity.
*Excellent protein sparing/anti-catabolic qualities.
*Reduction in fat stores and favorable distribution.
*Increased metabolic rate.
*Low-moderate HPTA function inhibition.
*Significant increase in muscle glycogen synthesis.
*Increase creatine phosphate (CP) synthesis.
*Improved muscle insulin receptor activity.
*Remains anabolic during calorie restricted periods. (High protein intake remains necessary)

POSSIBLE NEGATIVE EFFECTS TRENBOLONE

*Liver and Kidney toxicity.
*Growth of prostate tissue. (PSA test is wise)
*Male pattern baldness. (Accelerated genetic predisposition)
*Mild hallucinations. (High dosage -prolonged use)
*High blood pressure.

* A potential quality of Trenbolone was its ability to alter cortisol receptors during and after use. The result was cortisol inhibition to some degree on a "semi-permanent" basis and subsequent favorable alteration in the anabolic /catabolic ratio.

FINA JET
(TRENBOLONE ACETATE)

Reported Characteristics

Active-Life: 2-3 days
Drug Class: Anabolic/Androgenic steroid (for injection)
Average Reported Dosage: Men 30-60 mg every other day
Acne: Common
Water Retention: None
High Blood Pressure: Common
Liver Toxic: Though disputed, yes
Kidney Toxic: Yes
Noted Comments: High Anabolic/Very high Androgenic
Aromatization: None
Decreases HPTA Function: Moderately
DHT conversion: None

This was/is a very nasty but effective steroid that was removed from the market about 1987 or so. Not all that long ago it began showing up on the black market from Australia. Upon testing the 50-ml vials, it was discovered that it actually contained 31-mg/ml of Trenbolone acetate. Most Fina Jet now found is bogus. It contains either a testosterone ester, ground Finaplix pellets, or just oil. But the original has been discontinued. (There are several new brands of the drug trenbolone acetate)

Trenbolone acetate is a strong androgenic/anabolic steroid that caused a fast increase in strength and increased fat burning if the athlete's diet was right. Unless stacked with other steroids, this drug did not cause much in actual weight gain (dose dependent). Its main use was to harden the physique's appearance once body fat levels were low enough before competition. For the most part, bodybuilders have replaced Finajet/ Finaject with Parabolan or one of the many black market trenbolone products. Since Finajet did not cause gyno or water retention, one may assume it was fairly clean. Wrong! Even at dosages of 30-60-mg injected daily, side effects such as kidney toxicity, nose bleeds, headaches, high blood pressure, acne, and serious attitude problems were common.

Some creative and brave athletes have used the Finaplix 20 mg pellets which are intended for animal use. The pellets are shot into animal tissue for a slow release of Trenbolone. However some athletes (and black market crazies) have ground the pellets into a powder, mixed it with oil or water, and injected the *very un-sterile*
solution with 18 gauge needles. I can not stress enough how dangerous this is. The product is often labeled Finabolan. ("Finabolin" gives us a chance to discuss trenbolone in greater depth in a moment)

Another reported method of using the Finaplix pellets was to ground them into powder, mix the powder with a 50/50 solution of DMSO (DIMETHYL SULFOXIDE) and water. Then apply it to skin. The DMSO acts as a transporter that allows 14-18-MG of a 20MG pellet to be absorbed into the blood stream while the skin acts as a filter of sorts. Unfortunately this also allowed many toxins on the skin to enter as well.

Some individuals have claimed real hard-core status by using an animal pellet implant gun and taking one in the glute. Do not try this at home. The pain would be major and compared to being shot with a .177 pellet. The interesting side of this is that the lads who did this had been told that the Finaplex pellets were readily absorbed "rectally".

*Geez! And some bodybuilders wonder why we have the stigma of dull wittedness?

FINAPLIX /FINABOLAN
(TRENBOLONE ACETATE)

Reported Characteristics
Active-Life: About 2 days
Drug Class: High Androgenic/Anabolic Steroid (for injection)
Dosage: 1-3 ML (30-90mg) every one -to- 2 days
Acne: Yes
Aromatization: None
Water Retention: Low-None
High Blood Pressure: Rare
DHT Conversion: None
HPTA Suppression: Low-Moderate
Liver Toxic: Very

Finaplix and Finabolan are both non-legitimate pharmaceutical products. They are manufactured in underground labs of questionable means by crushing up 20 MG pellets of the cattle implant steroid Finaplix-H and dissolving them in a solution before suspension in oil. Each of the Finaplix-H pellets contains 20 MG of Trenbolone Acetate and is implanted into cattle using an implant pistol. (Do not try this at home. OUCH!) . However, the black market products I encountered did contain 30 or 75MG/ML of Trenbolone Acetate and were sold in 30 ML vials… usually.

Trenbolone Acetate has an active-life of about 2 days. Since it is short acting, most male bodybuilder injected 1-3 ML every one -to- 2 days. Though some did use as much as 120 mg daily. Administration seldom exceeded 6 weeks.

Most considered Finaplix to be as effective as Parabolan. The drug was often used pre-contest for its hardening effects and questionable fat metabolizing qualities. The drug is highly androgenic, does not aromatize, and it remains anabolic even in a low calorie/high protein environment. The strength gains and post-training recovery realized during administration was "remarkable". Quality lean mass gains were considered to be excellent and superior to those experienced from Masterone or Deca.

Trenbolone Acetate is highly liver and kidney toxic. For this reason, athletes reportedly consumed at least one gallon of water daily during use and used milk thistle during and after cycles. Gyno was not a problem with Trenbolone since the drug can not readily convert to estrogen. Prolonged or high dosage was said to lead to dark urine, and in some cases, blood in urine.

Trenbolones have a very high affinity for androgen receptor-sites. For this reason, the drug will inhibit other AAS from binding to muscle cell receptors adequately. It also means balding is quite possible if an athlete was genetically predisposed to a receding hair-line problem. Due to Trenbolone possessing very high androgen receptor-site affinity qualities, most athletes realized best results when stacked with drugs that are not dependant upon the same mode of cellular activation. Dianabol, Winstrol orals, and Anadrol-50 were common choices. Some athletes reported excellent results with few side effects when they had opted to stack Trenbolone with high receptor-site affinity drugs such as Nandrolones. Another preferred option was multiple stage type Max Androgen Phases. (See "Building The Perfect Beast", book two of this series)

An interesting aspect of all Trenbolone products is their apparent unique ability to permanently shut down existing cortisol receptor-sites. This explains, in part, the exceptional post-cycle lean mass retention realized after protocols utilizing Trenbolones were discontinued. Since Trenbolones are a derivative of Nortestosterone (the active drug in Deca), it should not have been a surprise to realize such exceptional results.

*There were individuals whom had incorporated the use of dissolving the crushed pellets in oil through a simple solvent and cold filtering process. The end product was said to create a reasonably sterile solution. ***Reasonably sterile? That is like asking if someone is a little pregnant!***

METRIBOLONE
(METHYLTRIENOLONE)

Reported Characteristics
Active-Life: About 24 hours
Drug Class: Androgenic/Anabolic Steroid (For injection)
Acne: Yes
Liver Toxic: Very
Water Retention: Low-None
High Blood Pressure: Rarely
Aromatization: None

Metribolone is the trade name for the drug Methyltrienolone, which is the most potent AAS produced. It is actually an orally active form of Trenbolone chemically altered into a 17-alkylated compound. Obviously, this means serious liver toxicity. In fact, even at microgram dosages, (1milligram = 1,000 micrograms) it is 15-20 times more toxic than Anadrol-50. That is toxic! Though orally active this AAS is provided in vials and meant for injection use only. But in truth, Metribolone is about 40-50 times more androgenic than Methyltestosterone, so a little goes a long way. The drug is fairly resistant to DHT conversion but does bind easily to scalp and prostate androgen receptor sites.

In clinical research, Metribolone is used to determine receptor-site affinity / displacement. Let me explain that. Metribolone is a very powerful androgen receptor-site stimulator and antagonist. I doubt there is any AAS more powerful. Since it binds so strongly to the receptor-site, researchers use the drug to see if other drugs can dislocate it, or for comparison. Not even Deca can kick it out of receptor-sites!

Metribolone is highly resistant to binding proteins such as SHBG. This means it remains highly active in the blood. If you recall, about 97-99% of our testosterone is in a "bound" state and only the remaining 1-3% is active or free. Only free or active androgens can fit into receptor-sites and trigger the anabolic mechanism. Some AAS are more resistant to these binding proteins than others. And Metribolone is the most resistant of all. Like I said, a little goes a long way. As example consider this for a moment. If all other factors of potency were equal, 1mg of unbound/free Metribolone would have the same activity as 97-100mg of testosterone due to the effects of binding proteins.

*Metribolone is like "Super Parabolan". The few individuals I know who have tried it reported the stuff was nothing short of amazing. This is an injectable form of course. Since Metribolone has a brief active-life, daily injections were reported as necessary. With mega-dosage use liver damage is not just a high concern, it is a fact. Since this drug is like "Super Parabolan", all negative side effects, results, and uses of the two drugs are interchangeable for the most part, with the obvious exception of reported dosages. I have seen only a few vials of the SP Labs product available on the black market as of yet. However, there is an injectable around that claims to be made by Denkall. It is an underground lab product actually and the mcg/ml is suspect as is sterile factors. Personally, I did/would not use the drug. It just amazes me that it exists.

PARABOLAN
(TRENBOLONE HEXAHYDROBENCYL CARBONATE)

Reported Characteristics

Active-Life: About 5-7 days

Drug Class: Androgenic/Anabolic Steroid (For injection)

Average Dosage: Men: 76-228-mg weekly; Women: 76-mg weekly (but should not use)

Acne: Rare

Water Retention: Rare, usually none

High Blood Pressure: Rare

Liver Toxic: Yes, highly toxic to kidneys also

Aromatization: None

DHT Conversion: None

Decreases HPTA function: Moderately

Parabolan was reported to be the most effective injectable anabolic/androgenic steroid available today. Real Parabolan provided users with a rapid build-up in strength and high quality muscle mass, while increasing fat burning (even when not dieting). The drug does not aromatize to estrogen or reduce to DHT. For this reason there was no noted water retention or feminizing effects. Parabolan sped up the metabolism as well. Due to the high androgenic quality, a hard, ripped, and vascular look with a dramatic increase in quality muscle mass resulted for all that reported use. This profile is what made Parabolan appear to be another all-purpose steroid.

So what's the problem? It was rare to find real Parabolan. Though the real product has a distinct odor, at least 95% seen was bogus. The real product is quite toxic to kidneys, so users mostly kept usage to 4-8 weeks and drank at least an additional gallon of water daily. Due to the high degree of potential toxicity dark urine and even blood in urine can result from high, prolonged use (as can prostate enlargement due to the drug's structural similarity to DHT).

Parabolan was commonly stacked with growth hormone, thyroid, and/or Clenbuterol during diet periods for the synergistic effects. A simple stack of 20-30-mg Oxandrolone daily and 152-228-mg Parabolan weekly consistently brought excellent high quality strength and muscle mass gains while decreasing body fat.

Women should not use Parabolan due to a very high virilizing effect. But many competitive female athletes still did. Some stacked 76-mg of Parabolan every 5-8 days with 80-120 mcg of Clenbuterol and either 15-20-mg of Winstrol tabs or 10-15-mg of Oxandrolone tabs daily.

I know of one female who is suffering from most of the possible side effects: missed periods, hair loss on the scalp, serious sex-drive (you should see her on an exercise bike) and clitoral hypertrophy. Facial hair growth can also result also.

Males usually obtained excellent results with 76-mg every 2-3 days.(Though some doubled this amount unnecessarily)

TRADE NAME

PARABOLAN   76-MG/1.5-ML

*Denkell is manufacturing a similar Trenbolone product for veterinary use.

ESTROGEN CONTROL AND HPTA REGENERATION DRUGS

The HPTA is the key to endogenous (natural: produced inside and by the body) androgen synthesis. It also regulates many other hormones and growth factors paramount to the anabolic/anti-catabolic process. The maintenance of normal or above function of the HPTA is therefore paramount as well. Estrogens play a major role in this equation. Elevated circulatory estrogen levels inhibit HPTA function significantly and low levels increase function. (Increase endogenous testosterone production results) Certain other types of estrogenic compounds increase HPTA function also. Confused? Good! Then take the time to read this section too.

ARIMIDEX
(ANASTOZOLE)

Reported Characteristics
Active-Life: 4-6 hours
Drug Class: Anti-estrogen /competitive inhibitor (Oral)
Average Reported Dosage: 0.5-3.0 mg daily
Acne: No
Water Retention: None
Liver Toxic: Yes dosage dependent
Decreases HPTA function: No, the drug has been accredited with HPTA up-regulating effects.

Arimidex is an anti-estrogen type drug. It is usually provided in 0.5 MG tabs. The drug works in a non-steroid form by inhibiting the aromatase enzyme which converts testosterone and other androgens into estrogen. This means that there is less estrogen to cause female pattern fat deposits, gyno, and water retention. In medicine, Arimidex is utilized to treat prostate cancer. In sports chemistry, the drug has been employed as a means of preventing excessive estrogenic side effects during AAS use and to aid in creating a harder appearing musculature for competitive bodybuilders. Unlike Nolvadex, which simply block estrogen receptor-sites, this drug prevents or reduces estrogen production. Though some estrogen presence is noted as necessary for AAS to reach full effectiveness, too much can cause a layer of fat, water retention, and breast tissue growth potentially with tumors called gynecomastia or bitch tits. Arimidex has a 75-85% aromatization inhibition rate.

Males who experienced excessive aromatization of AAS or who were extremely estrogen sensitive usually utilized a dosage of 0.5-3.0 mg daily. In fact, most realized excellent estrogen control with only 0.5mg/d (mg daily). Women usually showed excellent lean appearances (even in their legs) with 0.5-1.0 mg daily. Arimidex has a very short active-life so 0.5 mg dosages were often taken 2-6 times daily at equal intervals. Stacking 10-30 mg of Nolvadex with 1.0 mg of Arimidex has resulted in a near "0" estrogen activity situation regardless of the AAS protocol utilized. Directly following an AAS cycle, estrogen control has also become a problem (during periods intended for re-establishing HPTA function). In this case, the dosage was reduced from a higher starting dosage to a low dosage that was continued for 7-14 days after AAS discontinuance. This protocol was considered necessary to assure clearing of AAS induced estrogen build-up.

CLOMID
(CLOMIPHENE CITRATE) 25mg & 50mg TABS

Reported Characteristics

Active Life: about 8-12 hours
Drug Class: Synthetic estrogen/HPTA stimulator (Oral)
Average Reported Dosage: Men 50-100 mg daily
Water Retention: No
High Blood Pressure: Rare
Aromatization: None
Liver Toxic: Low, seldom reported.
Strong gonadotropin stimulator/mild anti-estrogen

Clomiphene is a synthetic estrogen clinically administered to help women ovulate. Bodybuilders, (male) following AAS cycles, seeking to jump start natural testosterone production (or those that were simply seeking a natural testosterone spike) have used this drug with great success. Clomiphene increases activity in the hypothalamus-pituitary-gonadol axis by stimulating the release of more gondotropin from the pituitary gland. Therefore, a higher/faster level of LH (luteinizing hormone) and FSH (follicle stimulating hormone) results. This creates a signal to the leydig cells in the testes which in turn produce more testosterone and sperm. Normally with Clomiphene this took 5-15 days. Most started with 50-mg twice daily for about 5 days, then reduced intake to 50 mg once a day for 5-10 more days. Due to Clomiphene providing a fast response time, I felt it was often beneficial to use a dosage of 100 mg total daily for 5 days, mid-cycle during longer AAS protocols. This drug was seldom utilized for longer than 15 days continuously simply due to it being unnecessary. The goal was to normalize testosterone production post AAS cycle as quickly as possible so as to minimize post-cycle strength and mass loss. Not create dependency.

HCG was combined with Clomiphene (Clomid) sometimes, or Clomiphene was used after HCG administration. This is because Clomiphene acts by affecting the hypothalamus and pituitary (hypophysis) and regenerating the whole regulating system, while HCG only "imitates" LH, thus stimulating the leydig cells in the testes to produce natural testosterone. (*Also see HCG)

*Some may wonder about Clomiphene being a synthetic estrogen. Yes, it is, but it works as an anti-estrogen. This is due to the fact that Clomiphene has a very low estrogenic effect. This means stronger and more active estrogen, such as those formed during the aromatization of many androgenic steroids, are blocked out of the receptor-site and less estrogenic activity results; less gyno, less water retention. Clomiphene was by no means as effective as Novladex or Proviron for estrogen suppression, but post-cycle it helped greatly.

TRADE NAMES

ARDOMON 50 MG TABS	CLOMIFEN 50MG TABS
CLOMID 50 MG TABS	CLOMIFEN 25MG CAPS
CLOMIPHEN-MERCK 50MG TABS	OMNIFIN 50 MG TABS
CLOSTIBEGYT 50MG TABS	TOKORMON 50MG TABS

81

CYCLOFENIL
(SAME CHEMICAL NAME)

Reported Characteristics

Active Life: 8-12 hours
Drug Class: Synthetic estrogen/gonadotropin stimulator/anti-estrogen (Oral)
Average Reported Dosage: Men-400-600mg daily
Acne: Rare/light
Water Retention: Rare
High Blood Pressure: Rare
Strong gonadotropin stimulator/anti-estrogen
Aromatization: None
Liver Toxic: None noted

Cyclofenil administration is quite similar to using HCG and CLOMID together. It is an anti-estrogen and a gonadotropin/testosterone stimulator. It does so by occupying estrogen receptors (antagonist) with a much weaker estrogenic compound and by shutting down the negative feed-back within the hypothalamus-pituitary-testes-axis (HPTA). The male body actually can produce much more testosterone than it does. Simply said, it sees no reason to do so. When the hypothalamus senses adequate testosterone/estrogen levels, either naturally (endogenous) or unnaturally (exogenous) provided, it shuts off gonadotropin release from the pituitary/hypothalamus. Thus, leydig cells in the testes do not receive the signal to produce more testosterone. Cyclofenil interferes with this negative feed-back/shut down production signal. This means that the hypothalamus - pituitary-testes-axis runs wide open to some extent, and more testosterone is produced. After about 5-6 weeks the hypothalamus figures this out and really shuts down the goodies production.

Though some strength and mass resulted with Cyclofenil use, it was not noted as a great growth drug. Some "natural" (okay) bodybuilders have used it with some results as have older individuals. However, the chemically assisted lads have used it to kick start natural testosterone production and even as a "during cycle anti-estrogen" very successfully. Normally 200 mg was taken 2-3 times daily for 4-6 weeks, either starting the last 3 weeks prior to the end of an AAS cycle or directly following a cycle. The prior method being reported as more effective since about a week is necessary for Cyclofenil to become effective and provide results. Side effects commonly reported have been; light acne, elevated sex-drive (that is a side effect?), and hot flashes.

TRADE NAMES

FERTODUR   200MG TABS
FERTODUR   200MG TABS
NEOCLYN   200MG TABS
ONDOGYNE   400MG TABS
REHIBIN   100MG TABS
SEXOVID   100MG TABS

*A note of interest; I have known several so-called natural bodybuilders who have utilized cyclofenil with a prohormone protocols in the United States with surprising results. This was effective for many reasons. Lower estrogen activity means a harder appearance. Testosterone both endogenous and exogenous combine resulted in significant total testosterone levels as well as a higher free testosterone level due to prohormones ability to uncouple testosterone from SHGB to some extent. The usual cycle consisted of 6 weeks of prohormones with 4 weeks of cyclofenil beginning week #5 of the prohormone cycle. Doing so extended the cycle 2 weeks and assured no post-cycle HPTA suppression to deal with for most athletes. Some athletes reported week #6-8 produced good secondary growth. This may have been due to an up- regulation of LH, FSH, and the conversion enzymes responsible for prohormones becoming testosterone in blood as well as decreased activity of estrogen. My concern would be the rush of estrogen post-cycle since cyclofenil only blocks estrogen receptors instead of suppressing estrogen production. In that example, for me personally, Arimidex would have been a wiser choice beginning week #5 also.

HCG
(HUMAN CHORIONIC GONADOTROPIN)

Reported Characteristics

Active-Life: 64 hours

Drug Class: leutenizing Hormone (LH) - Gonadotropin

Average Reported Dosage: Men 2000-5000 i.u. injected every 5th day

Acne: Yes

Water Retention: Yes, HCG is a female hormone.

Liver Toxic: None

Aromatization: None, however due to HCG use testosterone levels increased and aromatize was a potential side effect

HCG is used medically to positively influence ovulation in women, and to help produce estrogen. It is also utilized in fertility medicine to aid in ovulation.

Male bodybuilders used HCG for another important reason. HCG is almost exactly the same amino acid sequence as Luteinizing Hormone (LH). LH is normally produced in the pituitary gland which is then circulated to the testes where it contacts the Leydig cells. The Leydig cells then produce androgens such as testosterone. Obviously this means so-called natural bodybuilders reported use of HCG to increase endogenous (natural) testosterone levels. According to some clinical studies this works so well that an injection of 1500-2000 i.u. of HCG has increased plasma testosterone levels 200-300% over normal levels. For those males who utilized high aromatizing AAS, HCG was a "partial" cure for restarting natural testosterone production either mid or post-cycles.

When administering exogenous (occurring outside the body) androgens, such as AAS, the body's endocrine system shuts down (partially of completely) natural androgen production in an attempt to maintain homeostasis. This is simply because the hypothalamus senses the excess estrogens from AAS aromatization (and to a lesser degree elevated androgen levels) and signals the pituitary (hypophysis) to partially or completely stop producing LH and FSH (follicle stimulating hormone). Since the Leydig cells in the testes do not receive the signal from LH, they partially or completely shut down testosterone production. Sperm production is also reduced as a result of FSH down-regulation. Because the testes are not producing androgens and/or sperm at their normal level, the testes shrink. This often causes a drop in libido too. Many heavy AAS users reported sexual dysfunction for a brief (Brief?) period post-cycle.

So what did the men do about "the boy's"? HCG injections act as a replacement for the LH normally produced by the pituitary gland which normally stimulates androgen and sperm production by the testes. When 2000-5000 i.u. of HCG was injected every 5th day for 2-3 weeks, mid or post-cycle, the testes began to function again. Also an increase in total testosterone was realized and athletes often made some of their best gains at this point. It also helped to keep the "significant other" significantly happy! When HCG was administered beginning the last week of an AAS cycle and for an additional 1-2 weeks post-cycle, testes function normalized again and much of the common post- AAS cycle muscle mass and strength loss was avoided. However, our athletes were not out of the woods (with acceptable wood) quite yet. Earlier, I mentioned that HCG has been a utilized as a "partial cure" for the shut-down of the hypothalamus-pituitary-testes-axis (HPTA). HCG only "replaces" natural LH. The pituitary and hypothalamus part of the HPTA still sense no reason to produce gonadotropins and restore normal LH/FSH production. So ending HCG administration sometimes only brought on another crash. But staying on HCG for more than 3 weeks without at least a month off between HCG cycles could cause permanent gonadal dysfunction and/or a desensitizing of Leydig Cells. Male bodybuilders commonly used Clomid or Cyclofenil with HCG (*See Clomid for more info). Available literature shows that Clomid stimulates the pituitary to release more gonadotropin so a quicker and elevated level of LH and FSH are realized. By following an AAS cycle with 2000-5000 i.u. HCG every 5th day for 2-3 weeks and ingesting Clomid for the last 10-15 days of HCG administration many athletes noted that muscle mass and strength losses post AAS cycle were significantly avoided. Many athletes also used Clenbuterol at this point. (*See Clenbuterol for more info)

***It should be noted that administration of HCG will increase plasma testosterone levels 200-300% or more. Therefore all of the negative side effects of testosterone injections can apply to a lesser degree.**

TRADE NAMES

A.P.I.   5000I,U., 10,000 I,U, 20,000 I,U, AMPULE
BIOGONADYL   500I.U., 2000-I.U. AMPULE
CHORAGON   1500 I.U., 5000 I.U. AMPULE
CHOREX   5000-I.U., 10,000 I.U. AMPULE
CHORON 10   1000 I.U., 10,000 I.U. AMPULE
GESTYL 1000-I.U. AMPULE
GONADOTRPHON   5500-I.U., 0000 I.U., 5000-I.U.
GONADOTRAFON LH   125-I.U., 250-I.U. 1000-I.U.
GONADOTRAFON LH   2000-I.U., 5000-I.U. AMPULE
GONADOTRPYL   5000 I.U. AMPULE
HAVATROPIN   10,000 AMPULE
HCG   5000 I.U., 10,000 I.U. AMPULE
 PREGNYL 10,000 I.U. AMPULE
PREGNYL   1500 I.U., 5000 I.U. AMPULE
PROFASI   10,000 I.U. AMPULE,

There are several other HCG brands including veterinary. HCG always comes in two vials: one contains a packed powder and the other contains sterile water. Once the product is mixed (swirled not shaken) it must be refrigerated. HCG was often what bogus Growth Hormone (GH) vials contained. A simple test for real GH was to buy a pregnancy test kit and drop a few drops into the test. If your test read pregnant, you are also screwed. This is because most test kits test for elevated gonadotropins and HCG will test as such, but GH will not.

NOLVADEX
(TAMOXIFEN CITRATE)

Reported Characteristics

Active-Life: Less than 24 hours
Drug Class: Anti-estrogen/estrogen antagonist (Oral)
Average Reported Dosage: 10-30-mg daily
Acne: None
Water Retention: No
High Blood Pressure: Rare (not normally attributed to the drug itself)
Liver Toxic: Yes

Nolvadex is a drug commonly referred to as an anti-estrogen. This would suggest less or no estrogen is produced due to the drug's actions as in the case of Teslac. Actually, Nolvadex is an estrogen antagonist, meaning it competes with estrogen at estrogen receptor- sites. This prevents the active estrogen from entering its receptor and creating an estrogenic complex capable of activity. Since many AAS aromatize (covert to estrogen) to some degree, the control of feminizing side effects (males should pay attention here) is important. Males normally have a very low estrogen level. During AAS cycles, due to aromatization, estrogen levels rise considerably. This elevated estrogen level can cause feminizing side effects such as increased fat deposits, water retention, and gynecomastia (growth of breast gland tissue and painful tumors under the nipple). As a rule, it is more the ratio of androgens-to-estrogens than the simple increase in estrogen that actually initiates feminizing side effects.

It is important that the reader realizes that Nolvadex does not decrease estrogen production and that it simply blocks estrogen receptors. For this reason the sudden discontinuance of Nolvadex will allow the increased level of circulating estrogen to merge with the newly freed receptors and do feminine things to the body.

"Enter Proviron". At the end of a steroid cycle, the body's natural testosterone production can be impaired. Due to the aromatization of the AAS estrogen levels are significantly higher than normal and Nolvadex only helps by blocking the estrogen receptors. If an athlete abruptly ends an AAS protocol without regeneration of the HPTA under these conditions, much of the hard earned gains would disappear due to estrogen becoming the dominant hormone. So what did the boys (that didn't want to be a girl) do?

Proviron is an anti-estrogen (*See "Proviron" for more info) that helps to prevent estrogen production while elevating androgen levels. During the last week of an AAS cycle, some male bodybuilders began a HCG protocol (*See HCG) and administered 25-mg Proviron/10-20-mg Novladex 1-2 times daily. This was commonly noted to almost completely suppress post-cycle estrogen and its activity. Since Nolvadex increases the body's own testosterone production, as does HCG, much of the cycle gains were retained quite well. Nolvadex has a direct effect on the hypothalamus and therefore increases the release of Gonadotropic hormones to a minor degree. (The hormones that tell the Leydig cells in the testes to produce androgens such as testosterone are refereed to as Gonadotropics) Many added Clomid (*See Clomid) to their post-cycle stacks beginning 6-10 days after HCG and continued for the average reported two week duration. In most cases the result was athletes with normal (or above) sex drive and androgen production!

* High dosage use of Nolvadex can inhibit natural testosterone production. This is due to inhibition of enzymes needed for testosterone production by the testes.

Nolvadex was normally layered into any protocol utilizing high aromatizing steroids such as testosterone, Dianabol, or those that are progesterone receptor stimulators such as Anadrol-50. Those who were prone to high fat deposits, water retention, and gyno consistently reported inclusion of Nolvadex. Many are were to obtain excellent estrogenic activity suppression with only 10-mg daily while others noted the need for as much as 60-mg daily (20mg 3 times daily). The best results and guidelines were obtained by starting low and increasing dosages only when necessary.

It is important for the reader to realize that AAS must have some estrogen present in order to achieve their full positive potential effectiveness and provide the best commonly desired results. This is why many AAS lose their anabolic qualities when combined with anti-estrogens. It is also why Methandriol magnifies the effects of the same AAS. Those who used high anabolic/moderate-low androgenic steroids such as nandrolones, Primobolan, or Winstrol, and did not combine them with high aromatizing steroids (such as testosterone) often considered not using Nolvadex during cycles the best choice when increased mass was the primary intent.

Women who used Nolvadex usually did so because it aids in fat loss due to less estrogenic activity. I have yet to see a female compete whom was able to achieve truly cut legs with out it. Women athletes often combined 10-20mg of Nolvadex with 50-75mg Proviron daily for the last few weeks of dieting. Due to availability of Clenbuterol, Proviron dosages were reported lower as of late, at least in female fitness competitors. Women should be aware that birth control is an estrogen and Novladex will block its effectiveness. Women have note irregular menstrual cycles, weaker menstrual bleeding, and sometimes skip periods all together during Nolvadex use. I know several women who use Nolvadex for this reason and can not say I disagree with their choice. After all, the use of progestin type birth control as a means of regulating or even stopping menstruation is becoming accepted in the medical circles at last.

A few athletes have experienced a paradox when using high dosages of Nolvadex. Instead of lowering estrogenic activity, it increased it. What happened was that the Adrenal glands went into over drive producing a pro-hormone called DHEA. DHEA is actually an adrenal androgen normally secreted in lower levels. As circulating levels increased enzymic factors came into play. Research shows DHEA readily converts into androstenedione, and to some extent, estrogens in males. (That sucks!) The female endocrine system usually favors testosterone production from converted DHEA or androstenedione. The newly formed estrogen then overwhelmed the estrogen receptors blocking the intended qualities of Novladex. In this case, Proviron, and especially Teslac where notably better choices.

*Gyno that fails to react to these drugs normally must be removed by surgery. DHT derivatives can cause increases endogenous estrogen production also in some individuals. Cytadren was a commonly co-administered drug with Nolvadex.

TRADE NAMES

CRIOXIFELO   20-MG TABS
DEFAROL   10-MG TABS
JENOXIFEN   10,20,30-MG TABS
NOLVADEX   10-MG TABS
NOLVADEX   20,30,40-MG TABS
NOLVADEX D   20-MG TABS
NOLVADEX FORTE   40-MG TABS
TAMEXIN   10,20,30,40-MG TABS
TAMIFEN   40-MG TABS
TAMOXIFEN TABLETS 10-MG TABS
TAXUS   20-MG TABS
TECNOFEN   10,20MG TABS

*THERE ARE SEVERAL OTHER MANUFACTURERS NOT LISTED

PROVIRON
(MESTERONE)

Reported Characteristics

Active-Life: 8-12 hours (effects last about 24 hours)
Drug Class: Androgenic Steroid/Anti-Aromatization (Oral)
Average Reported Dosage: Men 25-200mg daily Women 25-50mg daily
Acne: Rare
Water Retention: No
High Blood Pressure: Rare
Liver Toxic: Low
Aromatization: None
Decreases HPTA Function: None

Proviron is a purely androgenic steroid with no anabolic qualities. The drug was used both as an anti-estrogen that "prevents" estrogen from being produced through the aromatization of sex steroids, and for its hardening effect upon musculature. Unlike Nolvadex (which only keeps estrogen from bonding with its receptors by blocking them), Proviron actually prevents the formation of estrogen. Due to lower estrogen levels, athletes retained less water and prevented (for the most part) the formation of gyno and female pattern fat deposits.

*If it worked perfectly, we would not see all the obvious gyno at bodybuilding shows.

Proviron was popular as a post-cycle anti-estrogen. (To keep estrogen from becoming the dominant hormone and to kick up sex drive lost due to low androgen levels) In fact, it is used in medicine as a drug to increase sperm production and eliminate sexual dysfunction in males. In some cases Proviron is prescribed to decrease flow or stop menstruation in females. For males this only replaces the androgens levels, not cures the problems of low testosterone production. Though the reader should note that the decrease in circulatory estrogen in itself promotes increased HPTA activity. At one time Proviron was commonly used year round by many appearance oriented athletes to maintain hardness. Now, according to recent polls, more athletes are using ephedrine and Clenbuterol to replaced Proviron for this purpose. By the way, frequent and sometimes painful erections are side effects of Proviron use. (So?) Actually, an erection that lasts days can cause permanent damage and erectile problems.

*I commonly extorted another physiological response provided from the use of this drug. Proviron possesses the ability to bind SHBG at a high rate. By doing so other co-administered AAS (or endogenous testosterone) remained in an unbound/free state. This resulted in greater anabolic and androgenic activity realization with lower dosage requirements.

As to dosages, males "usually" administered 25-200mg daily and often combined it with Nolvadex (*See Nolvadex). Women athletes commonly reported virilizing side effects when employing Proviron. It should be noted that most women who reported this side effect also co-administered other androgens. At a dosage of 25-50-mg daily

89

combined with Nolvadex most reported good results and few side effects. Teslac was believed to be a superior anti-aromatase drug (which shuts down estrogen production) but few considered it cost effective. 50mg Proviron and 250-1000mg Teslac, or 150mg Proviron and 20mg Nolvadex daily, was said to almost totally suppress estrogens. (Both during steroid cycles and after these dosages were quite effective)

TRADE NAMES

MESTORANUM   25-MG TABS
PROVIRON   10-MG TABS
PROVRON   20-MG TABS
PROVIRON   25-MG TABS
PROVIRON   50-MG TABS
VISTEMON   25-MG TABS

TESLAC
(TESTOLACTONE)

Reported Characteristics
Active-Life: 12-24 hours oral
Drug Class: Anti-estrogen/Aromatase enzyme inhibitor
Average Reported Dosage: Oral: 200-300mg daily; Injectable 100mg/1ml daily
Acne: Rare
Water Retention: None
High Blood Pressure: Rare
Liver Toxic: Not listed but unlikely
DHT Conversion: None
Decreases HPTA Function: No. (Actually increased HPTA activity)
Aromatization: None

Teslac is used as an anti-estrogen. Instead of acting as an estrogen antagonist (competing for estrogen receptor-sites), Teslac prevents the aromatization of androgens into estrogens by inhibiting the aromatase enzyme. Obviously this prevents or minimizes the negative effects of estrogen such as gyno, water retention, and female pattern fat deposits. Teslac is unique in that it is reputed to cause permanent irreversible suppression of estrogen production in males.

Technically speaking, Teslac is an oral androgenic steroid related to testosterone. However, it has only very low androgenic and no anabolic effect. Medical use of Teslac is for treatment of breast carcinoma in women. For male athletes, it is probably the best anti-estrogen available, and it causes an increase in natural (endogenous) testosterone production. Teslac elevates natural testosterone production by influencing the HYPOTHALAMUS to stimulate the PITUITARY to release more gonadotropin. This in turn simulates the testes Leydig cells to produce more testosterone at a significantly increased level (Comparable to HCG). Unlike HCG, Teslac takes several days to cause this effect. So administration over a prolonged period (several days) clinically considered necessary (under a doctors care). For this reason Teslac does "create" an improved anabolic/androgenic environment. Even so-called natural (like lifting tons of weight and drinking protein powders is natural) bodybuilders have employed benefits form this drug.

*Plasma calcium elevation has been during administration of Teslac.

Manufacturer inserts suggest a dosage of 250-1000mg daily. However, this is not reported as necessary for estrogen suppression. Normally 200-300mg daily divided into 2-3 doses was reported as quite effective. Some reported 100-mg of the injection form version was even more effective. Due to the high price of Teslac, many have stacked it with PROVIRON: Teslac-100-mg daily and Proviron 50-mg daily. Women users reported excellent hardening effects with few, if any, side effects such as virilization.

Side effects are very rare but could include nausea, vomiting, tongue infection, swelling and pain in arms and legs, prickling sensation and high blood pressure, as well as loss of appetite. As mentioned earlier, side effects were rare but women often skipped menstruation during use.

This is probably rated as the most effective overall anti-estrogen available whether during or post cycle as well as for pre-contest overall hardening effects.

TRADE NAMES

TESLAC   50-MG TABS,
FLUDESTRIN   50 or 100-MG/ML (For injection)

CYTADREN
(AMINOGLUTETHIMIDE)

Reported Characteristics
Active-Life: 8-12 hours
Drug Class: Steroid Biosynthesis Inhibitor (oral)
Average Reported Dosage: 500mg-2000mg Daily
Acne: None
Water Retention: None
High Blood Pressure: Unknown
Noted Comments: Powerful endogenous hormone inhibitor
Aromatization: None
Liver Toxic: High potential

Aminoglutethimide is normally prescribed for patients with breast cancer or Cushings Syndrome. In both cases patients suffer from catastrophic physiological decline. To a profound degree this is notably due to severe over production of endogenous glucocorticoids. The one glucocorticoid most readers would be familiar with is cortisol.

Bodybuilders and strength athletes have often utilized this drug as a means of inhibiting the P-450 and aromatase enzymes. This obviously refers to inhibition of the two potential pathways in which susceptible AAS are converted into estrogens. The result of administration of aminoglutethimide is partial or complete inhibition of endogenous hormone biosynthesis. When this drug is introduced into the body it blocks the conversion of cholesterol into pregnenolone. Since this is the first step in all hormone biosynthesis: By blocking the conversion of C-19 androgens into C-15 estrogens it functions as an anti-estrogen. This is one of the obvious intents reported users had in mind. But by inhibiting the conversion of cholesterol into pregnenolone it also proportionately inhibits the endogenous biosynthesis of all hormones including androgens, estrogens, aldosterone, and cortisol. This brings the discussion to the second reason this drug use was commonly reported. Cortisol is a catabolic hormone that just loves to eat muscle tissue. In fact it is a significant part of the equation that induces genetic limitations to muscular augmentation. Many authorities and athletes alike have realized on a few facts: (1) Less cortisol = less muscle catabolism (destruction) (2) Less estrogen = less fat accumulation and less gyno resulting in a leaner physique (3) Less aldosterone = less water retention and a harder appearance. But less conversion of cholesterol into pregnenolone = less endogenous testosterone. Most noted these effects were highly desirable since the absence of natural testosterone production was abundantly replace through AAS use. And it was generally acknowledged that the absence of competing hormones had a profound synergistic effect upon those the self-administered.

According to the available returns the average reported dosages were 500-750mg daily to inhibit excessive estrogen formation from AAS aromatization and 1000-2000mg daily for the purpose of cortisol inhibition. Most reported a scaled weekly dosage

93

increase was most effective: Week #1 250mg 2xd, week #2 250mg 3xd, week #3 & 4 500mg 2xd.

*My personal experience with this drug was that a 2 day on – 2 day off protocol worked best with fewer negative side effects.

Of the many side effects is that the drug inhibits the body's ability to react to inflammatory responses. This means it can prevent the body from inhibiting hemorrhaging (I do hope that no one cut themselves shaving!) and fight disease among other things. It can also make a bodybuilder a victim of CUSSING SYNDROME. Other side effects include: Sore joints from a reduction in glucocorticoids, reduced white/red blood cell counts, reduced platelet counts, and liver disease.

The package insert states 2-7   250-mg tabs daily for treatment of CUSHINGS SYNDROME. CUSHINGS victims have a "much" higher cortisol/cortisone production than even the most over trained athlete. For this reason 500 mg-1000 mg daily total was considered more than enough for a chemically enhanced bodybuilder for cortisol/cortisone suppression, and 250 mg -500 mg sufficient for use as an anti-estrogen and aldosterone control drug during cycles. It was also noted that Aminoglutethmide was not be utilized for more than 4-6 weeks. At that point, the body responded by increasing production of ACTH and a whole new series of catabolic effects resulted.

TRADE NAMES

AMINOGLUTETHIMIDE 250-MG TABS
CYTADREN   250MG TABS
ORIMETEN   250MG TABS
ORIMETENE   250MG TABS
RODAZOL   250MG TABS

DIURETICS

The use of diuretics in competitive bodybuilding is nothing new. Since Rich Gaspari showed striated glutes in the mid-1980's, diuretics have become a common phase in contest prep. Even after Mohammad Benaziza passed out and later died in 1992 due to complications from severe dehydration, athletes still utilize these drugs to rid their bodies of excess water. The idea is to suck as much water as possible from under the skin to create the "dry" look and further enhance the visual effects of very low body fat levels. Though effective, the practice of using diuretics is also very dangerous. Diuretic misuse can result in electrolyte imbalances and excessive dehydration triggering congestive heart failure. It only takes one mistake and results are final: DEATH! (No re-do's on this one)

We will discuss some common diuretic drugs used individually as this section progresses. However, a basic break-down of these drugs can be listed in three groups or classifications:

1. Potassium Sparing Diuretics

Potassium sparing diuretic drugs are often said to be the safest. Though I do not necessarily agree. Drugs such as Aldactone and Aldactazide are examples of this group and they act as Aldosterone antagonist. Aldosterone is the hormone the body uses to regulate water retention endogenously. In short, for now, Aldosterone elevation equals water retention/elevation. Since potassium-sparing diuretics work by inhibiting the activity of Aldosterone, the result is greater sodium and water excretion, and increased potassium retention. Problems arise when athletes ingest additional potassium without the guidance of a doctor daring use of these drugs. Some users assume muscle cramps are due to imbalances of other electrolytes in all but the rarest cases. Supplementation with over the counter potassium products during use can result in heart attack. Personally I disliked the anti-androgen effect of these drugs. Some athletes experience gyno during use and assume it is due to estrogenic activity. They often increase diuretic dosages assuming "with estrogen comes water". Since potassium sparing diuretics require 7-14 days to provide maximum results, dosages can again be easily misjudged. I believe they are not all that safe.

2. Thiazide Diuretics

Thiazide diuretics act upon the kidneys to stimulate urine production. This can also result in excessive loss of sodium chloride, bicarbonate, and potassium ions. It is common practice to increase supplemental potassium intake during Thiazide use. Normal reference ranges for potassium are:

Serum=3.5-5.1 m Eq/L   Plasma (heparin) =3.5-4.5 mEq/L

--For those under medical care. Maxide, Hydrodiuril are common brands of Thiazide diuretics and hydrachlorothiazide is a generic chemical name for popular Thiazide.

3. Loop Diuretics

Loop diuretics such as furosemide and ethacrynic acid are actually double trouble. They have a two level approach to ridding the body of endogenous water. First they act upon the kidneys like Thiazide diuretics to stimulate urine production. Obviously, this can result in excessive loss of sodium chloride, bicarbonate, and potassium as well. Second, loop diuretics negatively affect an area of the kidneys called the "Loop of Henle". This double action places a severe strain on kidneys already dealing with high dosages of certain anabolic/androgenic steroids and below normal water insertion as in a pre-contest period. These are probably the most dangerous diuretic drugs. But use was restricted to 1-3 days in most cases. Common brands of loop diuretics are Lasix and Bumex.

Diuretics and Blood Pressure

Diuretics are commonly prescribed for individuals with high blood pressure. Whereas 120 over 80 is considered normal for average individuals 160 over 100 is not unusual for a large athlete. Simply said, bigger people have greater circulatory needs and a larger more powerful heart to supply this. The heart is a muscle of course. This is not to say that this is an optimum or even healthy BP of course. Just that it is not all that uncommon.

When athletes utilize anabolic/androgenic steroids that aromatize to estrogens, the production of the water balance hormone Aldosterone is affected as well. When Aldosterone is elevated, the body excretes more potassium but spares sodium and water. The result is a greater full body water content. Including within the vascular system. More water in the vascular system results in increased total volume and pressure. (Which is the balloon faced look explanation) This in turn places severe strain on the heart. Individuals with high blood pressure resulting from anabolic/androgenic steroid use must control the problem. For this reason, it is not unusual for AAS users to also include low dose diuretic use during cycles as a means of controlling blood pressure. It is absolutely paramount that athletes replace the water excreted by drinking an increased level of fluids. During mass cycles, Gatorade-like sports electrolyte drinks are excellent for this purpose due to the 6% glucose / electrolyte solution.

GLYCEROL

Glycerol is similar in structure to alcohol and is found in fat stores in the body. In fact a triglyceride is a 3 fatty acid chain attached to a glycerol molecule and makes up about 95% of body fat stores. Get the idea that the body deals well with Glycerol? A much smaller amount of Glycerol is present in body fluids. This means it is present throughout the body's tissues. Supplemental Glycerol-loading increases fluid concentration in blood and muscle in a sort of hyperhydration that lasts for hours. The result is that the water will not be removed until the excess Glycerol is broken down.

If Glycerol-loading is applied to the salt/Aldosterone /water strategy for pre-contest preparation, the result is an increase in muscle fullness and vascularity due to increased fluid volume. Since Glycerol has no effect upon Aldosterone secretion, this can be a real plus because it therefore aids in pulling excess water from subcutaneous areas and into the blood. For some individuals, this works very well. The usual protocol calls for 10-20 ML of Glycerol 3 times daily on the last day of water/salt intake pre-contest. The alternative approach calls for 10 ML of Glycerine in 8 oz. of water with 50 grams dextrose and 5 grams of creatine 4 times in a 6 hour period ending 24 hours before show time.

Personally, I drink 15-30 ML of Glycerol first off in the morning with 16 oz. of water and again an hour before bed on training days during the summer. It creates a slightly leaner appearance and provides a noticeable training endurance increase in hot weather. It works for me and most of our clients. Great pumps, too!

SALT: THE PRE-CONTEST NUTRIENT

Since we are discussing diuretics and water retention it only seems logical to dispel another pre-contest myth as well. Salt is a bodybuilders friend, not enemy, pre-contest. Many bodybuilders eliminate sodium like an ex-spouse at a honeymoon assuming the result will be the coveted "dry look" on contest day.

When salt intake is reduced, a series of "dry look" nemesis arise. Salt contains sodium, and to a lesser degree potassium in the form of potassium iodide. When salt/sodium is reduced or eliminated from the diet the result is increased Aldosterone release. This makes the body excrete more potassium and hold more sodium/water. The resulting water retention gives the athlete a puffy wet look. This is due to electrolyte imbalances.

Reduced salt intake also negatively effects the all important sodium-potassium pump. This is the mechanism the body uses to shuttle many nutrients into cells like those that all muscle fibers are composed of. (Gee, ya think?) This would therefore inhibit creatine and some amino acid structures from adequately transporting, as well as inhibit glycogen synthesis.

If the salt content is reduced in muscles so is the water content. This means catabolism, flat muscles come show time, and a lack of vascularity. (It would inhibit erectile function also, but that is another issue all together.)

The body has three major areas it stores water and there is an actual hierarchy. The order of importance is:

THE BODY'S WATER HIERARCHY

*The most important water store is in blood and the vascular system. Without adequate water in the vascular system blood volume is compromised, and if severe enough, the result is death. So this rates a big number one in the water store hierarchy.

*The second on the big three list is muscle tissue. Water is required within all muscle tissues, both smooth and fibrous, to support life sustaining metabolic processes.

*The last area of importance for water storage is subcutaneous (under the skin) areas. For those who have not been paying attention, this is the area that a bodybuilder wants to eliminate as much water from as possible the day of a show. The results are a "make-it or break-it" issue. So how do we do it? Piece of cake! (But not during contest dieting!)

The key to subcutaneous water control depends upon control of the hormone Aldosterone. Obviously estrogen control is part of this hormone cascade action/reaction factor. But, our main focus is salt and water control, so Aldosterone is the key.

Beginning 15 days out from a show, an athlete should increase salt intake 20-30%. This of course means salt intake was never reduced to begin with. The amount must remain reasonably high and steady each day. This creates an environment in which the body does not have to release Aldosterone. This causes salt to stay in muscle tissue and the subsequent attraction of water stores there. Also, the all important maintaining of the sodium-potassium pump is accommodated as well. (During diet phases, this also reduces catabolism.)

During the 15 day period, water intake must absolutely remain high. 1.5-2.0 gallons daily is a base line in fact. This helps your body excrete any extra sodium, which of course it will, because Aldosterone secretion in the body has been controlled by elevated salt intake/water intake. The body will continue to dump all excess water and sodium as long as this is followed.

On the Friday night before a Sunday show, the athlete stops water intake. The body thinks it will still get the 1.5-2.0 gallons of water daily and continues to excrete water at its normal rate. This causes a decrease in blood volume and of course muscle water volume. Remember the body's water hierarchy? Well, as a survival response or reaction, the body gives up water from the area of least importance as a means of compensation. Yup, you got it. Subcutaneous water is pumped into blood and muscles. The result is vascularity, full muscle bellies, and paper thin skin.

*It's always a matter of working with, not against the body's action/reaction factors to accomplish the greatest progress and /or results.

*This works well with Creatine/Dextrose carb-loading also.

ALDACTAZIDE
(SPIRONOLACTONE/HYDROCHOLRTHIAZIDE)

Reported Characteristics
Active-Life: 10-12 hours
Drug Class: Diuretic (Oral)
Average Reported Dosage: 50-200mg (total) daily

Spironothiazid is a diureteic and an ALDOSTERONE antagonist. This means that it suppresses the water retaining actions of the hormone ALDOSTERONE while lowering water retention by lowering electrolytes (potassium, sodium, and calcium). The advantage of the combination is that the potassium absorption effect by the spironolactone can be mediated by the hydrochlorthiazide. Because of this, some of the potassium loss side effects can be avoided. This is probably a safer choice than LASIX though any diuretic use should be medically monitored. Thiazides also lead to a lower loss of calcium.

Side effects are commonly due to imbalances in electrolytes and fluids. They can include irregular pulse rate, cramps, and light headiness. Since the drug has ANTI-ANDROGENIC quality (spironolactone), men can experience possible gyno, and impotence due to higher dosage and/or prolonged use. These were noted to not occur due to the brief administration period normally employed. According to available literature, it is best to avoid higher potassium intake during use. Dosages were usually 50-150mg a day for no more than 3 days. Dosages were divided into 2-3 daily dosages.

TRADE NAMES

Aldactazide   25/15-MG TABS
Aldactazide   25/50-MG TABS
Spironothiazid   25/25-MG TABS

*THERE ARE SEVERAL OTHER MANUFACTURERS NOT LISTED

99

LASIX
(FUROSEMIDE)

Reported Characteristics
Active-Life: About 6-8 hours (Diuretic effects)
Drug Class: Loop Diuretic (Oral)
Average Reported Dosage: 40-100mg total in a 12 hour period
Acne: None
Water Retention: You must be joking!
High Blood Pressure: None
Liver Toxic: Unknown
Aromatization: Does not apply

Lasix is probably one of the most dangerous drugs some pre-contest bodybuilders used. Even the IFBB tests for diuretics, and that is saying something

Lasix was used to excrete excess water during the last day or two before a show. This was said to be especially effective with subcutaneous water (under the skin) so a *"ripped to the bone, dry, and hard"* look was achieved. Lasix was also used by some to lose weight for weight class oriented sports.

Loop diuretics work by increasing the excretion of electrolytes (sodium, chloride, potassium) which the body normally uses to maintain intra cellular and extracellular water. Monitoring of the re-absorption of potassium, sodium, and chloride ions during use should have been a must, but few did so. Lasix can and has caused death.

As to dosages, it depended upon the effect achieved. Normally 20-40-mg was taken and (over a periods of 2-4 hours) the bodybuilder evaluates the results. This was followed once or twice more at 4 hour intervals if more water loss was necessary. Too much water loss makes the body appear flat with no vascularity and makes it impossible to pump-up before walking out onto the stage. The effects of Lasix begin within about an hour of administration and continue for 6-8 hours. Once "the look" was achieved, it was unnecessary to ingest more to maintain "the look".

Lasix is very strong and was reported to cause diarrhea, dehydration, dizziness, muscle cramps, circulatory disorders, vomiting, circulatory collapse, fainting, and cardiac arrest. It was considered far more safe to start with 20-mg and repeat every 4 hours than to use higher dosages for a shorter period of tome. Over 40-mg per dosage increased side effects dramatically!

Most serious noted comment:
NEVER USE A 250 or 500MG TAB!!!!

TRADE NAMES

DIUNRAL   5,10,20,40,250,500-MG TABS
DIURAPID 40/500 40,500-MG TABS
DURAFURID   40-MG TAB
FURANTHRIL 40,500-MG TAB
FUROMEX   40-MG TAB
FUROMIN   40-MG TAB
FURON   40-MG TAB
FURONET   40-MG TAB
FUROSEMIDE 20,40,80-MG TAB
FUROSIFAR   40-MG TAB
LASIX   20-MG TAB
LASIX   25MG TAB
SEMID   40-MG TAB
VESIX   40-MG TAB

"INJECTABLE SOLUTION"-LASIX 20 or 40 MG/2ML or 4ML
SEMID   20MG/2ML
TROFURIT   20-MG/2-ML
VESIX   10-MG/1-ML

*THERE ARE SEVERAL MORE FUROSEMIDE PRODUCTS NOT LISTED

TARAXACUM OFFICINALE

Reported Characteristics

Drug Class: Diuretic (Oral)

Average Reported Dosage: 500-1000mg 3 times daily for 3 days.

I realize some may consider Taraxacum Officinale an unlikely effective diuretic simply because it is naturally occurring as dandelion root. But testosterone is naturally occurring also and nobody laughs at its effectiveness. Taraxacum is actually a very potent diuretic with the unusual advantage of possessing a natural built-in source of potassium. Since water shedding increases potassium excretion, this is potentially a health benefit that adds to the over all effectiveness. The active extract is water soluble, and oral ingestion is highly absorbed for this reason.

As discussed prior, diuretics were often utilized by many of the competing athletes polled during AAS use as a means of controlling blood pressure elevation. Taraxacum was probably the safest product used for this purpose. Fortunately, it is a commonly found ingredient in many OTC weight loss supplements.

THYROID HORMONES

Thyroid hormones were most likely one of the most misunderstood and underrated drug groups in the bodybuilder's so-called arsenal. Based upon personal experiences, they certainly increased the rate and efficiency of fat loss during diet periods. And they acted synergistically to increase the rate of lean tissue growth during mass gaining periods....if used correctly.

The noted positive physiological effects of reasonable dosages of thyroid hormones included:

*Increased protein synthesis rate.
*Increased rate of fat oxidation.
*Increased sensitivity of receptors for androgens, Insulin, GH, IGF-1, PGE-1, PGF-2, Clenbuterol, Ephedrine, Creatine, and others.
*Increased metabolization of proteins, carbohydrates, fats and micronutrients.
*Increased metabolic rate and calories expenditure.
*Enhanced oxygen consumption by most body tissues
*Improved recovery time.

The noted negative physiological effects of excessive dosages of thyroid hormones included:

*Loss of lean mass tissue.
*Increased heart rate and palpitations.
*Insomnia.
*Diarrhea.
*Vomiting.

Thyroid hormones govern the body's metabolic rate. This means that the metabolism of nutrients and subsequent cellular utilization or storage rate is dependent upon blood circulatory thyroid hormone levels. Higher levels result in elevated over all metabolic rate providing that other metabolic factors are accommodated also.

THYROID HORMONES AND CALORIE EXPENDITURE

Those who are familiar with, or have read the section on DNP are aware of the term "oxidative phosphorylation". This is a process by which cells/mitochondria convert ADP (Adenosine Diphosphate) into ATP (Adenosine Triphosphate). Basically this means adding another phosphate molecule to ADP so that it can be converted back into the body's energy /ATP. But the term keeps kids flunking biology anyway. DNP makes cells waste calories and burn fat by "uncoupling" the oxidative phosphorylation process and making it less efficient, even when at rest.

Thyroid hormones are powerful uncouplers of oxidative phosphorylation. However this is a different method of action than that induced by DNP. Thyroid hormones increase cell/mitochondrial substrate oxidation by effecting both cytochrome-C reducers and cytochrome-C oxidizers. This increases metabolic rate and substrate (nutrient/food) use as fuel for either ATP or heat production. Heat production by a cell is referred to as thermalgenesis, in this case the conversion of fat into heat. Though other substrates such as glucose /glycogen can be used for heat production also under adverse conditions.

THYROID HORMONES AND FAT OXIDATION

Fat oxidation or thermalgenesis involves the conversion of fat calories into heat. In the case of thermalgenesis caused by thyroid hormones it is due to "special uncoupling proteins" found in fat, muscle, and organs called UCP-3. Two things before we continue here. First UCP-3 stands for uncoupling protein -3 (big deal) and "special" refers to "specific", not "special" like the weirdo we all dated once and tried to explain later. When UCP-3 is increased, the calorie expenditure through thermalgenesis increases. But decreases will result in an increase in fat stores. As example, supraphysiological T-3 levels increase UCP-3 600 % and below normal levels results in a 300 % decrease. This is why calorie restricted diets significantly decrease in results after 2-4 weeks. The body down-regulates thyroid hormone production to save calories and reduce calorie expenditure as heat. The result is less UCP-3 and slower metabolism.

Thermalgenesis and oxidative phosphorylation uncoupling is the reason athletes used synthetic thyroid hormones during calorie restricted or diet phases. The individuals were able to ingest more calories than normal while still burning fat. It should be noted that a minimum of 2 grams of protein per pound of body weight was ingested daily during exogenous thyroid hormone use to prevent excessive muscle catabolism or loss. Athletes commonly stacked adrenalgenic beta-agonist drugs like Clenbuterol, Ephedrine/Norephedrine, or Fenoterol to increase UCP-3 levels and act synergistically with thyroid hormones to favor fat oxidation and reduce muscle loss. DNP was another option commonly used as well. Obviously, anabolic/androgenic steroids, Insulin, GH, and other growth enhancement drugs were commonly stacked with thyroid hormones too.

THYROID HORMONES ARE ANABOLIC

Many athletes were not aware of the fact that thyroid hormones are a true form of absolute anabolic. The usual method of employment for thyroid hormones was during pre-contest periods. Obviously, this is because increased thyroid hormone levels means elevated metabolic rate and resulting increased calorie expenditure or use. This explanation itself suggests the noted anabolic potential.

Thyroid hormones govern or regulate our metabolic-rate or metabolism. Metabolic rate is the speed or rate at which all chemical and physical processes occur. This is true of every living cell in our bodies. This means that the rate of nutrient metabolism, absorption, and utilization is vastly dependent upon thyroid hormones. In fact the levels of thyroid hormones in our body determines if the food we eat is stored as adipose (fat) tissue, utilized for regeneration and building, or burned as heat /energy. How often have you heard some whale claim "it's glandular" as they stuff another box of donuts in their mouth? In some cases it is actually the truth. So fix it!! Low thyroid hormone levels slow the healing / growth process while increasing fat stores. Overly high thyroid hormone level results in tissue catabolism or wasting. But thyroid hormone levels matched to nutrient supply and demand were commonly considered to be seriously anabolic. Remember, training and chemical muscle enhancement protocols created a massive nutrient demand. If thyroid hormone levels are too low, no amount of calories will be an adequate supply simply because they are not metabolized at the necessary rate. This is why athletes often got needlessly big-time fat. They ate to keep up with major muscle chemistry, but failed to provide a metabolic rate to match.

*The administration of thyroid hormones should be under a doctors care only.

WHY ARE THYROID HORMONES ANABOLIC?

Thyroid hormones trigger the release of fat stores so other cells can convert the long chain triglycerides (fat) into heat, energy, ATP. By increasing ATP, muscle cells are better able to regenerate, and do so at an increased rate. Thyroid hormones increase creatine transport and increase androgen/GH/IGF-1/IGF-2 receptor-site sensitivity. Thyroid hormones increase the rate of nutrient metabolism, absorption, and utilization. Gee, sounds like the perfect growth environment to me when considering the fact that growing children do this naturally so well. It also meant major chemical muscle enhancement synergy for those whom reported use.

Many would be surprised to realize how many top bodybuilders remained "on cycle" with thyroid hormones all year long. This allowed maximum growth and recovery rates while preventing excessive fat accumulation even in the very brief "off season". The difference in diet and mass phases was dosage, though some altered the term dosage to mean "available". Why did they include thyroid hormones in their mass stacks?

Thyroid hormones can have a re-partitioning effect upon body composition or muscle-to-fat ratio. As example were the many athletes whose weight was 250 LBS but only 10% bodyfat when total daily circulating thyroid hormone levels were elevated 10-50%. This would be due to thyroid hormone activity inducing improved nutrient metabolization and cellular efficiency combined with other hormone synergy. Of course, this is what "Absolute Anabolic Phases" were all about. But those who read about" Frank N. Steroid" already know about this effect and how it was created.

NATURAL THYROID HORMONE PRODUCTION IN HUMANS

The thyroid is a part of the endocrine system. The endocrine system monitors and manufactures or synthesizes many hormones and hormone-like substances. For this reason, the endocrine system and its sub-systems have many built in "checks and balances" to assure proper substance ratio or synergy. It is no surprise that thyroid functions are no exception.

*Endogenous thyroid hormone production begins when neuro-input tells the hypothalamus to synthesize an release Thyroptropin -Releasing -Hormone. (TRH)

*TRH stimulates the anterior pituitary gland to release or secrete Thyroid-Stimulating-Hormone (TSH) (also referred to as Thyrotropin on some lab chem. Panels)

*When TSH contacts its receptor-sites located throughout the thyroid gland a series of enzymic reactions occur using tyrosine and iodine as substrates or raw materials to produce and/or release L-Thyroxine (T-4). This is then released into the vascular system so it can circulate. It should be noted that T-4 is an active form of thyroid hormone.

*The active T-4 circulating in the vascular system merges with receptors and triggers metabolic activity; but when it reaches the liver it is changed into the more active thyroid hormone L-Triiodothyronine (T-3) by an enzyme called 5-deiodinase. T-3 is about 5 times more active than T-4. The newly formed T-3 is released into the vascular system where it may contact and merge with cellular receptors which initiates all the metabolic activity discussed earlier.

FEED-BACK MECHANISMS and FEED-BACK LOOPS

Of course the thyroid does not simply produce T-4 continuously. This is due to the "checks and balances" nature included called "feedback-mechanisms". In the care of thyroid function the feedback-mechanism or loop involves the hypothalamus (secretes TRH), pituitary gland (secretes TSH), thyroid gland (secretes T-4), and the liver (converts T-4 into T-3). A feedback-mechanism or loop can trigger the release of another hormone (positive feed-back), or inhibit its release (negative feed-back) thus maintaining that balance. This means high levels of T-4 or T-3 initiate a negative feed-back loop that tells the hypothalamus to produce less TRH, and low levels of T-4 or T-3 initiate a positive feed-back loop that tells the hypothalamus to produce more TRH.

*Individuals reported the utilization of doctor prescribed blood tests for their personal average thyroid hormone levels before, during, and after thyroid drug administration as a means of base line dosage requirements and assessment.

*Thyroid gland function also regulates calcitonin which combats elevated levels of calcium.

*The normal thyroid gland (human) contains about 200 MCG of T-4, and 15 MCG of T-3 per gram)

*About 80% of circulatory T-3 comes from Monodeiodination (T-4 to T-3 liver conversion) of T-4.

*It should be noted that only "free" or unbound thyroid hormones are active and the bound form is not. When reviewing blood test results and reference ranges this is an important factor to assess. The human body normally produces about 76 MCG/daily of T-4 and 26 MCG/daily of T-3. A mid range test result/reference would express these approximate averages. Over 99% circulating hormones are bound. Thyroid Binding Globulin (TBg) Thyroid binding pre albumin (TBPA) and albumin (TBA) .

HEALTHY THYROID HORMONE REFERENCE RANGES

TSH (Thyroid Stimulating Hormone Serum/Plasma 2-10 M U/L
T-4 (L-Thyroxine) Total serum 65-155 NMOL/L
T-4 (L-Thyroxine) Free Serum 0.8-2.4 NG/DL (or) 10-31 PMOL/L
TBG (Thyroxine Binding Globulin) Serum 15.0-34.0 MG/L
T-3 (L-Triiodothyronine) Serum 100-200 NG/DL (or) 1.54-3.08 MMOL/L
T-3 (L-Triiodothyronine) Serum 260-480 PG/DL (or) 4.0-7.4 PMOL/4L

NOTES OF INTERESTS

*According to researchers, calorie restricted periods that provide less than 2 grams of complete protein per pound of bodyweight daily during thyroid drug administration usually resulted in weight loss consisting of 75% fat and 25 % muscle in most cases.

*The 5-deiodinase enzyme activity necessary for liver conversion of T-4 into T-3 requires adequate levels of zinc and selenium. During calorie restricted periods lasting more than 2-3 weeks T-4 conversion to the more active T-3 decreases dramatically greatly reducing fat loss. Adequate zinc intake and absorption prevents the decline in 5-deiodinase that causes this negative by about 67% and adequate selenium levels prevents the decline by about 47%. Obviously both in sufficient amounts are best.

*Thyroid hormones were commonly cycled with Insulin, AAS, GH, IGF-1, PGF-2, Ephedrine, Clenbuterol, and other drugs by athletes.

....

ARMOUR THYROID
(Desiccated Thyroid Gland)

Reported Characteristics
Drug Class: Natural Thyroid Hormone complex (Prescription Only) Oral
Average Reported Dosage: 1.0-4.0 grains daily
Noted Comments: Significant suppression of thyroid function during use.

Armour thyroid is a brand of desiccated porcine thyroid gland. The product provides the following active thyroid hormones:

T-4 (L-Thyroxine) 19 MCG
T-3 (L-Triiodothyronine) 4.3 MCG
*Trace levels of T-2 (L-diiodothyronine) and Triacana (Triiodothyroacetic Acid)

Most readers would assume that the low percentage of T-4 and T-3 provided by Armour was ineffective. In fact, the combination was often considered more effective than either drug alone and is at the correct human ratio. The trace levels of T-2 and Triacana create a complete synergystic and effective thyroid hormone drug. Most athletes realized an increased metabolic rate with only 1.5-2.0 grains daily.

CYTOMEL
(T-3/Triiodothyronine/Liothyronine Sodium)

Reported Characteristics
Drug Class: Synthetic thyroid hormone.
Average Reported Dosage: 25-150 MCG daily.
Noted Comments: Significant suppression of Thyroid function during use.

Cytomel is the synthetic form of T-3/L-triiodothyronine and was a commonly known trade or brand name among athletes. T-3/L-triiodothyronine is used as a form of thyroid hormone therapy mostly in Europe. Most bodybuilders favored this drug over synthetic forms of T-4/L-thyroxine due to its vastly superior activity level.

An advantage of T-3/L-triiodothyronine administration over T-4/L-thyroxine was the lack of dependence upon the liver enzyme responsible for T-4/T-3 conversion. During diet restricted periods the liver naturally decreases the liver enzyme levels as a control measure to prevent metabolic rate induced starvation. Just as the liver increases production of this enzyme in response to elevated calorie intake it also reduces levels in response to decreased calorie intake. Remember that T-4 /L-thyroxine is only 20% as active as T-3/L-triiodothyronine.

The abuse of synthetic T-3/L-triiodothyronine will result in severe suppression of natural (endogenous) thyroid function. This is especially true of this drug because it actually circumvents the normal thyroid hormone manufacturing process the body utilizes to produce endogenous forms as required. Simplified this is because T-3/L-triiodothyronine is the most potent thyroid hormone so the body shuts down each level required for production to try to reduce circulatory T-3/L-triiodothyronine levels. Of course this does not reduce the level if the hormone is being administered exogenously (from outside the body).

Since long term use of T-3 /L-triiodothyronine will lead to thyroid function suppression the issue of rebound should be briefly discussed. It is commonly stated that synthetic thyroid hormone abuse will lead to permanent thyroid gland dysfunction. Though it is definitely a physiological possibility, I have not yet found a case study to support this statement. However, there is a common occurrence of thyroid gland/function *rebound* in natural endogenous thyroid hormone production. It seems that it was common for individuals to realize an "increase" in endogenous thyroid hormone production of 120-130 % within 3-15 days after drug discontinuance. This means an individual would commonly see an increase in their thyroid hormone production of 20-30% above their normal pre-drug administration levels, in many cases.

COLEUS FORSKOHLII
(FORSKOLIN)

Drug Class: Herbal thyroid stimulator. (Oral)
Average Reported Dosage: (Standardized for 10% forskolin) 165-250 MG 3-4 times daily.
*Significant stimulation of thyroid gland and adenylate cyclase production.

Why is an herbal supplement in a book intended to report upon the things hardcore athletes have done? It should be recalled that most AAS synthesis begins with a plant extract as does ephedrine, methamphetamine, and heroin. The point being that powerful things come from many places...sometimes.

Coleus Forskohlii increases cyclic AMP (cAMP) in cells and up-regulates thyroid gland function. Why is cellular cAMP so cool? The active substrate in Coleus Forskohlii is a diterpene derivative called forskolin. Well, forskolin stimulates the production of an enzyme called Adenylate-Cyclase (AC) which is sort of a master enzyme in the body that positively effects many other enzymes that regulate muscle growth and fat loss. In this case, AC increases cAMP which in turn activates Protein-Kinase (PK). This event allows a PK/phosphorylation reaction resulting in the active form of Hormone-Sensitive-Lipase (HSL). Finally ...HSL stimulates the release of fatty acids from adipose tissue (fat cells) so muscle cells can use them as an energy (ATP) and fuel for heat source. Remember, UCP-3's earlier in this section? Well, forskolin stimulates thyroid gland activity similarly to Thyroid-Stimulating-Hormone (TSH). TSH is also sometimes called thyrotropin. When the thyroid gland stimulated it begins the thyroid hormone cascade by releasing T-4 and so on. Since this results in an increase in circulatory thyroids hormone levels and an increase in (yup!) UCP-3's, more of that newly released fatty acids supply is burned off. The reason the basic biochemistry was explained here is simple. First, anything that affects any of the biochemicals we briefly discussed, also effects body composition. This includes all thermalgenics, AAS, insulin, GH, and most other anabolic chemistries. Second, the basic knowledge may prevent the reader from falling for supplement ad scams by knowing why something will or will not actually have value.

Most products containing Coleus Forskohlii should be (but rarely actually are) standardized for a 10% forskolin content. An effective dosage of the 10% standardized product has been 165-250 MG, 3-4 times daily. So far there is some existing research that supports the listed effects of Coleus Forskohlii. And anecdotal /personal evaluations are positive thus far. It seems finding an actual standardized source is the most difficult aspect of acquiring favorable results.

A note of interest.

The use of Coleus Forskohlii seems to have possible cardiovascular benefits by acting as a vasodilator (lowers blood pressure) , inhibition of platelet aggregation (reduced blood clotting), and positive inotropic activity in the heart (increased contractile force).

The use of Coleus Forskohlii does not seem to inhibit endogenous TSH production. There is a synergy between this product and beta-andrenergic drugs such as Clenbuterol, ephedrine, synephrine, and norephedrine.

GUGGULSTERONES

Reported Characteristics
Drug Class: Thyroid hormone stimulator. (Oral)
Average Reported Dosage: 20 MG (pure extract) 3-4 times daily.
*Significant stimulation of thyroid function during use.

Guggulsterone are an extract of the herb Commiphora Mukul, clinically proven to restore lagging metabolic rate caused by dietary calorie deficiency such as during diet phases. Ayurvedic medicine has utilized the unprocessed herb for centuries to treat energy deficiencies related ailments.

Guggulsterones Z and E seem to have the greatest effect upon stimulation of thyroid hormone, though other substrates of the herb commiphora mukul may effect different metabolic factors as well. Thus far, research suggests this is a result of guggulsterones Z & E stimulation of TSH (Thyroid-Stimulating-Hormone) production. This results in an increase in Thyroid gland T-4 production and subsequent liver conversion to the more active T-3 hormone.

Guggulsterones can be very beneficial to dieting athletes. When calorie intake is decreased, the body naturally decreases metabolic rate or calorie expenditure. This is why dieters often hit a fat loss wall after 2-4 weeks. Since TSH production begins the entire thyroid hormone cascade, guggulsterones can be very helpful at restoring "normal" metabolic rate at this point. It should be noted that guggulsterones do not inhibit normal thyroid activity or induce a negative feed-back loop. It is very unlikely that the use of this extract will lead to above normal accepted TSH, T-4, T-3 reference range production.

Other benefits of guggulsterone supplementation include reduced blood cholesterol and triglyceride levels, increased fat oxidation (fat burning), increased energy, and better post-training recovery during diet restriction phases. Reduced acne has been noted.

Please note that other diet defiencies can lead to reduced metabolic rate including phosphates, niacin, selenium, and magnesium among others, such as Zinc.

Some athletes used guggulsterones to regenerate thyroid function after discontinuance of synthetic T-3/T-4 protocols. Those who thought ahead, utilized guggulsterones " synthetic T-3/T-4 thyroid hormone use to prevent thyroid function suppression even temporarily. This usually was initiated 10-14 days prior to synthetic thyroid administration discontinuance. Coleus Forskohlii, the amino acid tyrosine, and iodine also had a noted great deal of value for this purpose.

SYNTHROID
(T-4/L-THYROXINE)

Reported Characteristics

Drug Class: Synthetic Thyroid Hormone. (Oral)
Average Reported Dosage: 100-400 MCG daily.
Noted Comments: Significant suppression of thyroid function during use.

Synthroid is a man-made synthetically manufactured version of T-4/L-thyroxine. The average person produces about 76 MCG/d of T-4/L-thyroxine which is then converted by the liver into the more active T-3/L-triiodothyronine. This is true of the oral T-4/L-thyroxine medications as well. The average conversion rate of T-4 to T-3 is about 30-33%/ MCG. Since the conversion of T-4 to T-3 is dependent upon adequate levels of since and selenium, athletes commonly increase daily intake of these minerals during synthetic T-4/L-thyroxine use.

As is the case with all thyroid hormone drug use, most athletes were noted as wiser to begin at a lower dosage of 100 MCG/d and slowly progress to their chosen dosage. Daily dosages of T-4/L-thyroxine that exceed 400 MCG will not increase metabolic rate beyond what is realized at 400 + MCG/d.

Dosages that were increased too rapidly or that were too high commonly resulted in diarrhea, excessive sweating, rapid heart beat, nausea, vomiting, insomnia and trembling.

T-4 drugs suppress endogenous thyroid hormone production significantly. After discontinuance, most athletes experienced a metabolic lag period of 3-15 days before thyroid function rebound occurred. Interesting fact is that most monitored athletes experienced a 120-130 % increase in endogenous thyroid hormones at that point. And some maintain that level permanently.

*See guggulsterones for other possibilities.

113

T-2
(L-diiodothyronine or 3, 5-diiodo-L-thyronine)

Drug Class: Thyroid Hormone. (Oral)
Average Reported Dosage: 150-600 MCG daily.
*Minor noted suppression of thyroid function during lower dosage short term (30-35 days) administration.

There are two well known synthetic thyroid hormones commonly administered by bodybuilders known as T-4 and T-3. (*See "Synthroid" and "Cytomel" for more info) However, some have not yet heard of another natural thyroid hormone called T-2 or L-diiodothyronine. The good new is that it is highly active and naturally occurring in some foods such as beef products. It is also non-prescription in many countries...so far. The bad news is that since it works quite well and offers individuals freedom of choice, it probably will not be legal for long.

So far, T-2 seems to be slightly more effective for fat oxidation (burning) than either T-4 or T-3 alone while offering an improved protein sparing-like result. This may be true. T-2 stimulates cellular mitochondria (cellular energy producers) more so than the cell nucleus. This means, unlike T-4 and T-3, T-2 is less likely to activate other cellular functions and more likely to focus upon increased metabolic rate or energy expenditure. Personal experience had shown an excellent synergistic effect between T-2, Norephedrine, and ephedrine plus caffeine. This is due to an interesting interplay between the substances.

DRUG SUMMARY

1. T-2 increases resting metabolic rate by stimulating mitochondria expenditure of energy from calories. T-2 also increases Adenylate Cyclase production. Adenylate Cyclase is like a master enzyme in our bodies that positively effects most other fat burning and muscle building enzymes and hormones. As example, adenylate Cyclase elevation results in an increased rate of production of cyclic AMP (cAMP) from ATP. This forces fat cells to give their stores to be used as fuel for energy production. The result is an increase in fatty acid (fat) oxidation and a protein sparing effect because fat becomes favored muscle cell food.

2. Norephedrine and ephedrine mimic and stimulate the release of the adrenal hormones norepinephrine and epinephrine. Norephinephrine raises heart rate and epinephrine stimulates carbohydrate metabolism resulting in an increased metabolic rate, fatty acids release from lipocytes (fat cells), and a protein sparing effect. Caffeine simply prolongs the effect.

T-3 is about 5 times more active than T-4, and some research suggests T-2 is more active than T-3. My experience to date has been that this just is not the truth. But, T-2 does offer a reasonably safe non-prescription alternative to the use of synthetic T-4 or

T-3 drugs in countries where it is still an OTC product. Of course some idiots somewhere will find a way to hurt themselves with it and show up on day time talk shows. Like the guy who discovered nail guns can inflict a law suit based injury if held to one head just so. (This really happened)

There is also the drug synergy that results from a T-4, T-3, T-2 stack to consider for overall effectiveness and reduced dosage requirements. Some athletes have reported an improved rate of fat loss and better lean tissue retention with this technique.

Most T-2 users reported an increase in metabolic rate and activity proportionate to dosages as listed. This supplement has been noted as exceptionally beneficial for individuals who have a slower metabolic rate naturally that results in above normal fat storage and poor post-training recovery at a dosage of 50 MG, 4 times daily. Others had found the higher listed dosages necessary for rapid fat loss at maximum rates. Most reported improved rate of recovery, improved lean mass to fat ratio, and often an increase in libido. (No Joke)

T-2 has a half-life of 4-6 hours. Due to this brief period of activity users reportedly divided dosages into 3-4 daily administrations to maintain constant circulating T-2 levels and the resulting metabolic rate increase.

T-2 use can create a negative feedback loop at higher dosages and due to prolonged use. The result was often metabolic lag usually for 3-7 days after discontinuance. (See guggulsterones and Coleus Forskohlii for common reported solutions)

Athletes also used T-2 post-AAS use as a means of avoiding post-cycle metabolic lag. (50 MG 4 times daily)

TRIACANA
(TIRATRICOL)

Reported Characteristics

Drug Class: Thyroid Hormone Metabolite. (Oral)
Average Reported Dosage: 1 MG per 50 LBS of bodyweight daily.
Noted Comments: Significant stimulator of thyroid activity / suppression of thyroid function during use.

Triacana is a trade or brand name for the thyroid drug Tiratricol. The body naturally (endogenously) produces T-4/L-thyroxine, T-3/L-triiodothyronine, and T-2 /L-diiodothyronine. Triacana is simply a synthetic form of these three thyroid hormones natural metabolite product, Triiodothyroacetic acid, or tiratricol for short. This means the body naturally produces Triacana as a metabolic by-product of other thyroid hormones.

Triacana is sold in Europe as a prescription synthetic thyroid drug intended to restore natural metabolic rate. And of course it did not take long before bodybuilders began importing the drug with anabolic/androgenic steroids into Canada and the United States. This lead to custom agents adding Triacana to drug alert list and confiscation. Interesting since the chemical itself is not a controlled substance in most of the U.S. at this time. Have no fear though, the FDA and DEA are actively pursuing reclassifying Triacana /Tiratricol/Triiodothyroacetic acid as a controlled substance there.

Triacana reaches maximum effects at a daily dosage of about 1 MG per 50 LBS of bodyweight. (Daily, meaning "total") Since the chemical possesses a 6 hour half-life, this "daily dosage" was reported to be divided into 4 equal dosages. So a 200 pound athlete required 1 MG 4 times daily. Beyond this dosage no subsequent increase in metabolic rate occurs. What many, including the FDA, fail to realize is that Triacana administration will not induce a true replacement metabolic rate like other thyroid hormones. This means any polled athlete was able to increase their metabolic rate only equivalent to the upper range considered normal and acceptable through administration. So an individual whom employed this chemical realized a metabolic rate about equal to a so-called ectomorph only. Which is, in truth, a very significant increase and considered highly effective by all but a few users. This would make Triacana one of the *safer* thyroid drugs.

*I have not found post administration thyroid function suppression from Triacana as of yet. But it is possible if use were prolonged. Obviously someone, somewhere, will somehow find a way to be the one exception who sues and does T.V. talk shows decrying the evils of this drug. No doubt while smoking cigarettes and drinking alcohol. (Another case of a day without the lifeguard monitoring the gene pool)

NON -AAS GROWTH FACTORS

AND RELATED SUBSTANCES

The human body is a constant miracle ever unfolding within. Some of the more amazing events are mediated or caused by other factors of metabolism very different yet synergistic to AAS. Many fail to realize that the body functions in a very synergistic way dependent upon these various factors. Sadly enough is the fact that research has only begun to accept many of the findings athletes have been aware of for years. So much more is possible when the body, or research, is seen in a synergistic format. Equally sad is the realization that many athletes have lost faith in the medical and research community in return.

HUMAN GROWTH HORMONE
(GH/SOMATROPIN/STH)

Reported Characteristics

Active-Life: Varies upon injection method
Drug Class: Growth Hormone/IGF-1 Precursor (For injection)
Average Reported Dosage: 2-16 i.u. total daily (1mg=2.7 i.u)
Acne: None
Water Retention: Very rare
High Blood Pressure: Very rare
Liver Toxic: None
Aromatization: None
High Anabolic/No Androgenic Effects

Human Growth Hormone (GH) has been a subject of debate since I was a kid. Natural (endogenous) GH is produced by the pituitary gland. Children produce 2 i.u. "spurts" 4-7 times per day for 4-5 non-consecutive days during a 2-3 week period (during growth spurts). That would equal 32-70 i.u. in only a 4-5 day span. A healthy adult's pituitary releases only 0.5-1.5 i.u. daily.

Until the mid 1980's, the only available form of exogenous (occurring outside the body) GH was manufactured by taking the pituitary glands of dead corpses (like there are a lot of "live" corpses running around?) and grinding them up. (I am not joking!). The GH was then extracted and purified through a series of expensive procedures, packed and sold by prescription only for use by children suffering from stunted growth. About 1987, this form of GH was linked to a fatal brain disease called CREUTZFELD-JAKOB DISEASE, and removed from the market.

Enter Genetech and synthetic GH. The first synthetic GH was produced by genetically altering transformed mouse cells /Ecoli. Natural GH has a 191 amino acid sequence where as the Protropin brand of GH produced by Genetech contains 192 amino acids in its sequence. This may have the affect of causing the body to produce GH antibodies which deactivate the GH. Most synthetics now contain the normal 191 amino acid sequence, of which there are over a dozen available today.

GH has 3 effects any athlete desires: GH helps the body burn more adipose (fat) tissue by promoting the release of fatty acids to be used as energy. Normally at rest, the body uses about an equal division of fat and carbohydrate calories. When the endocrine system senses a low circulatory level of glucose, the hypothalamus-pituitary-axis (HPA) reacts by releasing GH. The GH then triggers (through a series of enzymic/chemical reactions) the release of fatty acids from adipose stores so metabolic energy requirements can be met. This means exogenous GH administration has been well documented to do the same.

GH has a very potent anabolic (protein synthesis/tissue building) effect. In exerting anabolic effects, it can cause both hyperplasia (an increase in the number of muscle cells) and muscular hypertrophy (the enlargement of muscle cells). This change in cell number is permanent and therefore means more cells to make bigger. GH also has an anabolic effect on soft tissues such as tendons, cartilage, and other connective tissue. This means old injuries repair and strength increases due to stronger connective tissue… both at an accelerated rate. It is a well known fact that GH is a powerful anti-catabolic agent (protein sparing). This effect has allowed modern bodybuilders to retain or even add significant lean mass tissue during calorie restricted periods (cutting phases) and become the shredded monsters of the new era.

When using GH many athletes were less than satisfied with their results. Most likely this was because they bought bogus GH. It was common to find GH for a hard-core pro bodybuilder cost about $35,000 or more, yearly. To test GH, most simply bought a pregnancy test kit, mix a vial of (hopefully) GH and place a drop or two in the test area. If the test result was "pregnant"..they had been screwed. Most pregnancy test kits test for elevated gonadoltropins (which HCG is and GH is not). For those few, whose bodies manufactured GH anti-bodies (and GH failed to work for you) sorry about your luck. GH, used properly, has overwhelmingly been renowned as a genetic equalizer if used for that purpose.

Any polled athlete chose to use GH as a performance enhancing drug should have first understand at least the basics of its actions.

GH itself is not responsible for the majority of the effects seen from GH use. Actually GH is only a precursor to the so-called "good stuff". When GH passes through the liver, it is converted into INSULIN-LIKE GROWTH FACTORS (such as IGF-1). IGF-1 is a very active but unstable chemical, which is why the body waits until the last second to make it naturally. The liver has a limited capacity to convert excess GH into IGF-1 unless other chemical hormone levels are also elevated. Insulin, T-4/T-3 thyroid hormones, gonadotropins, androgens/anabolic hormones, and even estrogen and corticosteroids all play an important role in the positive effects of GH. So they too were often exogenously elevated in what was considered "the correct ratios" by the largest of the self administering athletes. For the liver to convert high levels of GH to IGF-1 several times a day and cause a high quality anabolic response, it was commonly noted that T-3 thyroid hormone and insulin also needed be increased to accomplish the desired effect. Triacana may be strong enough to increase thyroid activity, but Cytomel was considered to be a better choice. Though some seemed to disagree, most emphatically believed that a fast-acting insulin such as HUMULIN-R or Humalog was a better and safer choice of exogenous insulin since they allowed better timing and have a much shorter effective period. This allowed the athletes to time insulin activity with the active period of GH at the optimum absorption times such as upon waking and the first few hours after a work-out. The result was less chance of fat accumulation and a heightened anabolic response. Since GH suppresses natural T-3 thyroid hormone release, the exogenous administration of Triacana or Cytomel allowed for an elevated calorie intake that was utilized more for building muscle and soft tissue than for adipose tissue storage. Many pro bodybuilders used Clenbuterol and/or ephedrine stacks with GH while dieting. Since Clenbuterol and

Ephedrine both suppress natural insulin release, they usually stacked the GH and Clenbuterol /Ephedrine with a synthetic T-3 thyroid hormone and sometimes with insulin as well. The use of insulin was dependent upon whether it was a bulking or dieting phase and depending on how their body responded to exogenous insulin use.

*I can not stress enough how dangerous insulin use can be. Comas and death are quite possible if used wrong. If you wish to use it, please see a doctor for monitoring.

AAS and/or Clenbuterol further enhance the anabolic effects of GH. From all but a few polled it was reported that excellent muscle mass gains resulted with the use of GH when other chosen hormone levels were also met (*also see "cycles") and one could afford it. Also, beware of fake GH. It is more common than you may realize. It is an illegal drug and the black market is not always honest.

The question of dosage was a big one. For the purpose of stunted growth manufacturers of GH (due to pituitary hyophysially caused stunted growth) state 0.3 i.u. weekly per LB of body weight. So for a 235 LB bodybuilder that would equal 70.5 i.u. weekly, meaning a daily total of about 10-i.u. However, even 2-3i.u. daily did produce some nice results over a 6-8 week period when the other reported hormone requirements were met as well. Short high dosage burst cycles too were noted to create these results (which will be discussed later) by the more elite of those polled.

*GH is medically administered intramuscularly or subcutaneously (under the skin).
*When multiple injections were utilized, I personally noted better results with subcutaneous administration.
*1-mg=2.7 i.u. of GH and some products are listed as such.

With exception of those few whose insert states otherwise, the dry unmixed GH substance maybe stored at room temperature. Once the solution has been mixed with the dry GH powder, (SWIRLED, DO NOT SHAKEN) the mixture must be refrigerated and lasts for 24-hours before it begins to degrade. An interesting product has become available called DEPO-NUTROPIN that has an active-life of about a month. This would allow for fewer injections and a reduced price. Also, several patents run out this year so many overseas and less expensive GH preparation will soon be available in the U.S. by prescription only.

*Though no negative side effects were reported, the available literature does list several serious ones: Kidneys and heart enlargement, high blood pressure, diabetes, thyroid hormone deficiency, and acromegaly. For the most part, they are rare to say the least and usually would be from extreme dosages and lengths of cycles. But like most hormones, you just do not know until it is a fact for you. Kind of scary, huh?

When GH was utilized with an insulin protocol, it was considered important to space injection periods between GH and insulin about an hour. Also if GH was utilized only twice daily, it was reported best to avoid natural high points of GH release such as first thing in the a.m., post-work out, and right before bed. This was if GH was utilized without insulin.

TRADE NAMES

CORPORMON   4 I.U
GENOTONORM   4 I.U.
GENOTROPIN   2,3,4,12 I.U.
GENOTROPIN   16 I.U.
GRORM   2,4 I.U
HUMATROPE   4 I.U.
HUMATROPE   5MG
HUMATROPE   16 I.U.
NORDITROPIN   12 I.U.
NUTROPIN   10 MG
PROTROPIN 10 MG..
SAIZEN   10 I.U.
SOMATOHORM   4 I.U.
ZOMACTORS   4,12 I.U.

HUMULIN-R
(FAST ACTING INSULIN)

Reported Characteristics
Active-Life: Up to 8 hours
Drug Class: Injectable Insulin

Insulin is a storage hormone produced by the pancreas. Insulin shuttles nutrients, such as carbohydrates, fats and amino acids (derived from proteins) into cells. The main function of insulin is to maintain homeostasis of circulatory glucose, and intracellular glycogen storage. It also aids in fat storage.

Many top bodybuilders utilized insulin to increases intracellular amino acid and supplement storage. This means nutrients such as glucose, amino acids, and supplements such as creatine and glutamine were forced into cells at a much higher rate and volume. Since insulin is not site-specific, and both fat and muscle cells have insulin receptor-sites, nutrient storage is in both areas as well as in organs. The actual partitioning of nutrients is highly dependent upon receptor sensitivity. For this reason individuals who have developed insulin resistance (receptor insensitivity) gained significant fat tissue during insulin administration. Insulin is highly anabolic and anti-catabolic.

*Before I continue, it is paramount that the reader realizes just how dangerous exogenous insulin use is. Where as years of abuse of the most toxic steroid may destroy your liver, a single mistake when using insulin can cause coma, brain damage, or death. THIS IS A FACT! Use of exogenous insulin should only be considered under a qualified medical supervision.

Since insulin acts synergistically with other anabolic/androgenic chemicals, there are several methods, stacks, and protocols that were reported as effectively utilized by athletes. There are also basic safety (Insulin is safe? NO!) protocols wiser bodybuilders were said to have followed:

1. A maximum single dosage of 1-i.u. per 15 LBS of body weight was used and not more than twice daily. (200 LB bodybuilder used 13 i.u. 200 /15 = 13.3)
2. A cycle length of 15-28 days was a maximum use period with a 4-8 week off period. Longer periods lost effectiveness
3. A minimum of 10g of carbohydrates was ingested for each I.U. of insulin injected. (This was cutting it dangerously close) Some say this was too many calories. I disagree!
4. The two most effective times insulin was utilized was during the two highest insulin sensitivity periods (Which are also high cortisol level periods):
      1. First thing in the morning (Upon waking)
      2. Immediately after an intense workout.
5. Insulin activity is increased by anabolic/androgenic steroids. This means dosages were often reported as lower (less exogenous insulin) when stacking with AAS and other anabolic substances.

*Improper use of insulin can cause diabetes or hyperglycemia.

6. Never utilize insulin protocols where the half- life of the exogenous insulin over lap. This means that since HUMULIN-R has a 4 hour half- life, a minimum of 4 hours passed between injections.

7. Never use insulin without a qualified medical doctor's guidance and monitoring. Buy and learn how to use blood glucose test kits.

Negative side effects of insulin are: sudden sweating, heart racing, light headiness, mental confusion, weakness, hunger, blurry vision, impaired speech. If left untreated, coma, brains damage, and death can result. The earlier side effects are a warning that not enough carbohydrates were ingested or not often enough.

HUMULIN-R CYCLE EXAMPLES

WARNING

Before we begin to discuss the following protocols it is paramount that the reader realize that these are examples of cycles that were most commonly reported as "highly effective" by the polled athletes and from my own past personal experiences. There is a great deal of general agreed upon perceptions expressed and as such should not be taken as clinical proof. In no way are these examples meant as a guide or endorsement. The practice of self-administration of insulin is illegal and extremely dangerous without the proper medical supervision.

Dan's Approach

This dosing protocol was outlined by the late Dan Duchaine for mass weight gains: Dan claimed 30g of high glycemic carbs per international unit (iu) of insulin was the necessary amount his athletes consumed over a 4 hour period when utilizing fast acting HUMULIN-R. So a 200 LB athlete would have basically ingested 100g of fast acting carbs (dextrose, Gatorade, glucose polymers/matlodextrins) every hour for 4 consecutive hours; and that one "1" i.u. per 15 LBS of bodyweight was the maximum dosage of Insulin. So 200 LBS /15=13.3 I.U., 13.3 of Insulin. And 13 i.u. x 30g =390 grams of carbohydrates total and about 100 grams each hour for 4 consecutive hours.

HUMULIN-R / AAS CYCLE   EXAMPLE #1

HUMULIN-R day #1-7 was injected first thing upon waking then again 4-6 hours later, immediately after a work-out. 100g of high glycemic carbs was consumed each hour for 4-6 consecutive hours following injections. Each HUMULIN-R injection was 13 i.u. The two injections were not allowed to over lap (6-8 hours apart).

Testosterone suspension day #1-7 was injected twice daily, 50-mg per injection. This was done with HUMULIN -R injections. Since testosterone suspension is very fast acting (about 1 hour) and has a short half -life, the combination acted synergistically. Testosterone suspension is highly androgenic and anabolic. (An increase in IGF-1 was also realized during use) Testosterone propionate was utilized as a replacement by some. Testosterones helped to limit fat synthesis by blocking fat storage enzymes. This was an obvious plus when administering insulin without a GH layer.

Deca Durabolin administration began on day #1. Based upon prior sited characteristics, an injection site from Deca Durabolin only expels half of its dosage in 7-8 days. This means circulatory levels from the initial and following injections did not peak for about 14-16 days. Oxandrolone was added beginning day #7. The combination aided in post-cycle lean mass retention while solidifying gains made during testosterone /HUMULIN-R administration. The use of HCG/Clomid was commonly considered beneficial beginning day #30 (*See Clomid and HCG for more info) Clenbuterol was also an option.

(*Please see the next page for example chart)

HUMULIN-R /AAS CYCLE   EXAMPLE #1 (CHART)

Day #1	Hum-R 13iu 2xd	Test. Sus 50mg 2xd	Deca 200mg	
Day #2	Hum-R 13iu 2xd	Test. Sus 50mg 2xd		
Day #3	Hum-R 13iu 2xd	Test. Sus 50mg 2xd		
Day #4	Hum-R 13iu 2xd	Test. Sus 50mg 2xd	Deca 200 mg	
Day #5	Hum-R 13iu 2xd	Test. Sus 50mg 2xd		
Day #6	Hum-R 13iu 2xd	Test. Sus 50mg 2xd		
Day #7	Hum-R 13iu 2xd	Test. Sus 50mg 2xd	Deca 200 mg	Oxandrolone 15 mg
Day #8				Oxandrolone 15 mg
Day #9				Oxandrolone 15 mg
Day #10			Deca 200 mg	Oxandrolone 15 mg
Day #11				Oxandrolone 15 mg
Day #12				Oxandrolone 15 mg
Day #13			Deca 200 mg	Oxandrolone 15 mg
Day #14				Oxandrolone 15 mg
Day #15				Oxandrolone 15 mg
Day #16			Deca 200 mg	Oxandrolone 15 mg
Day #17				Oxandrolone 15 mg
Day #18				Oxandrolone 15 mg
Day #19			Deca 200 mg	Oxandrolone 15 mg
Day #20				Oxandrolone 15 mg
Day #21				Oxandrolone 15 mg
Day #22			Deca 200 mg	Oxandrolone 15 mg
Day #23				Oxandrolone 15 mg
Day #24				Oxandrolone 15 mg
Day #25				Oxandrolone 15 mg
Day #26				Oxandrolone 15 mg
Day #27				Oxandrolone 15 mg
Day #28				Oxandrolone 15 mg
Day #29				Oxandrolone 15 mg
Day #30				Oxandrolone 15 mg

*Most athletes made excellent progress using only 5 iu of fast acting insulin, 2 times daily. 13 iu was considered an intermediate or advanced level.

*Oxandrolone administration was divided into 3 equal daily dosages.

*HCG/Clomid administration was not reported necessary for most individuals.

Hum-R = Humulin type R insulin
Test. Sus. = Testosterone Suspension
Deca = Deca Durabolin

125

HUMULIN-R / GH /T-3 CYCLE   EXAMPLE #2

This cycle is quite similar to the Blitz Cycle example listed in Cycles. However, it was utilized without an Anabolic/Androgenic steroid (AAS) layer. This was usually considered a much more controllable method of Insulin use. There is a profound synergystic effect between Insulin, GH, and thyroid hormone T-3. In fact, it is a case of 1+1=3 when speaking of anabolic activity. Elevated T-3 levels increased protein synthesis as long as levels were not too high. 25-mcg daily would replace normal T-3 production if Cytomel was the drug utilized. However 25 mcg 2 times daily did cause a rapid turn-over in calories and accelerated protein synthesis. GH increases fat burning, is very anabolic and anti-catabolic. Insulin is quite anabolic but non-specific in its areas of calorie storage. This means fat deposits increased when insulin alone was administered. Since Cytomel burned excess calories and aided in GH conversion to IGF-1, fat storage was not an issue for those who reported this to be their most effective insulin protocol previously used. Additionally, intracellular nutrient stores were better focused upon muscle tissue. If HCG and Clomid were utilized, natural androgen production was elevated significantly again adding to the over all synergistic effect of this example. In this example 6 i.u. of HUMULIN-R, 2-I.U/ of Growth Hormone (GH), and 25-mcg of Cytomel were administered twice daily: Immediately following a work-out and upon waking in the morning. These are the two most insulin sensitive periods. However, it was obviously paramount that the two periods did not overlap. This means Insulin injections were administered at least 6 hours apart. A minimum of 10g of carbohydrates was commonly ingested per I.U. of HUMULIN-R injected within 1 hour of administration. So a 6 i.u. HUMULIN-R injection required a minimum of 60 g of carbohydrates to avoid negative and *dangerous* reactions. More carbs would probably have been better. A drink containing 50g of whey protein, 60g of maltodextrins or Dextrose, 5g of Creatine Monohydrate, and 4-20g of Glutamine was considered to be even better, AT LEAST TWICE within the 6 hour period with the first drink ingested within the first hour following injection of insulin.

*A note of interest: 200-mg of ALFA LIPOIC ACID or 50 mg of D-PINITOL will significantly increase insulin sensitivity. A vial of GLUCAGON (an Insulin antagonist) being handy and a blood glucose test kit was considered to be wise. Consider if any of the symptoms listed had arisen. Some athletes would have known that they screwed up. (Call 911! Better yet, do not try Insulin use without a doctor's guidance)

HUMULIN-R / GH / T-3 CYCLE   EXAMPLE #2 (CHART)

Day#	Humulin-R	GH	T-3	HCG/Clomid
1.	6 iu 2xd	2 iu 2xd	25 mcg 2xd	500iu/50mg 2xd
2.	6 iu 2xd	2 iu 2xd	25 mcg 2xd	500iu/50mg 2xd
3.	6 iu 2xd	2 iu 2xd	25 mcg 2xd	500iu/50mg 2xd
4.	6 iu 2xd	2 iu 2xd	25 mcg 2xd	500iu/50mg 2xd
5.	6 iu 2xd	2 iu 2xd	25 mcg 2xd	500iu/50mg 2xd
6.	6 iu 2xd	2 iu 2xd	25 mcg 2xd	500iu/50mg
7.	6 iu 2xd	2 iu 2xd	25 mcg 2xd	500iu/50mg
8.	6 iu 2xd	2 iu 2xd	25 mcg 2xd	500iu/50mg
9.	6 iu 2xd	2 iu 2xd	25 mcg 2xd	500iu/50mg
10.	6 iu 2xd	2 iu 2xd	25 mcg 2xd	500iu/50mg
11.				500iu/50mg
12.				500iu/50mg
13.				500iu/50mg
14.				500iu/50mg
15.				500iu/50mg

*Clomid/HCG use significantly elevated both 17-BHSD and 3-BHSD enzyme levels/production. These are the enzymes responsible for prohormone conversion to Testosterone and Nortestosterone. (And a light bulb should go on about now!) Obviously the use of Clomid/HCG was generally considered optional and dependent upon cycle intent or goal.

GLUCOPHAGE (Metformin HCL Tablets)
&
GLUCOPHAGE-XR (Metformin HCL Extended Release Tablets)

Reported Characteristics
Drug Class: Receptor Stimulator
Average Reported Dosage: 500-850 MG 1-2 times daily
Water Retention: Low-Moderate
High Blood Pressure: Rare

Glucophage is an antidiabetic drug prescribed to treat Type II diabetes. Type II diabetes is also called non-insulin-dependent diabetes mellitus. Individuals who have Type II diabetes are usually unable to produce enough insulin naturally (in response to the food they ingest) or suffer cell insulin receptor-site insensitivity. However, Glucophage can be prescribed by a doctor for Type I diabetics as a means of additional glucose (blood sugar) control in unison with insulin injections.

Clinical use of Glucophage for diabetics is fairly common. What the drug does is

(1) Increase cell insulin receptor-site number and sensitivity.
(2) Decreases the amount of glucose/sugar the intestines absorb.
(3) Decrease the amount of glucose/sugar the liver manufactures. (One source of liver glucose production is amino acids/protein).

These three effects explain why clinical administration of Glucophage seldom results in reports of added hypoglycemic effects during administration of the drug alone. However, when combined with insulin injections and/or sulfonylureas (Glipizide) a significant increase in carbohydrate requirements and weight gain is realized.

Polled bodybuilders utilized the effects of Glucophage differently for different phases;

1. During mass gain phases utilizing exogenous insulin, 500-850 MG 1-2 times daily of Glucophage increased the effective value of insulin. This was due to an elevation in receptor-site number and sensitivity. Glucophage also decreased the amount of insulin needed for maximum results.

2. During pancreatic regeneration or protocols that included Glipizide, Glyburide, or other pancreatic/insulin stimulation, Glucophage increased the effectiveness and amplified results. 500 MG 2 x daily was the common Glucophage dosage for this purpose.

3. During diet phases, bodybuilders have utilized Glucophage as a means of decreasing glucose production by the liver and glucose absorption by the intestines. This in itself decreases insulin secretion by the pancreas and increases the body's dependence upon fat stores for energy requirements. This was employed especially so during GH and PGF-2 use, and was synergistic with anabolic/androgenic steroids. SINCE cell insulin receptor-sites are more sensitive and since there is an existing cross-over stimulation between IGF-1 and Insulin (and their opposing receptor-sites) lean mass retention was notably increased. This effect helped decrease the negative effects dieting has upon IGF-1 production endogenously.

*Since less IGF-1 is produced during diet phases, less lean mass is normally retained. If cell receptor-sites are more plentiful and sensitive, less IGF-1 is required for stimulation. 500MG daily of Glucophage was usually considered effective for this.

Glucophage was taken with meals and never less than 6 hours before sleeping. Individuals with kidney problems did not take Glucophage and most athletes were aware of the fact that in some cases stacking with oral 17-alfa-alkylated drugs could induce even greater liver damage.

The drug insert gives some insight into the potential dangers of non-monitored use:

Combining Glucophage with Digoxin (Lanoxin), furosemide (Lasix), or any diuretic is dangerous for individuals with heart problems. Glucophage has also been known to encourage lactic acidosis. Lactic acidosis is a build-up of lactic acid in the blood stream. Prolonged excessive lactic acid build-up in blood can cause serious damage. Alcohol use increases the risk of lactic acidosis during periods of Glucophage use. A doctor should be consulted for monitoring prior to use.

~SIGNS OF LACTIC ACIDOSIS

**Dizzy or lightheaded.
**Feeling very tired, weak, or uncomfortable.
**Unusual muscular pains.

** Slow or irregular heart beat.
**Feeling cold.
**Unusual stomach discomfort

AVANDIA
(ROSIGLITAZONE MALEATE TABS)

Reported Characteristics

Drug Class: Thiazolidinedione (Oral)
Average Reported Dosage: 2-8 MG 1-2 times daily
Water Retention: Moderate (Similar to low dose insulin use in some individuals)
High Blood Pressure: Rare

Avandia is a prescription antidiabetic drug similar in action to Glucophage (Metformin HCl) and belongs to a fairly new class of drugs called thiazolidinediones (Thigh-a-zoe-lid-een-die-owns). Medical use for Avandia is confined to treating type II diabetes. What the drug actually does is increase cell insulin receptor-site number and sensitivity. This in turn allows the body to better utilize insulin and therefore feed cells nutrients they require for repair and growth. The need for drugs such as thiazolidinediones is due to the tendency of cell insulin receptor-site number and sensitivity down-regulation realized by long term diabetic treatments. This means diabetics become resistant to insulin and their cells begin to deteriorate. In fact, insulin resistance is an underlying cause of type II diabetes. Clinical treatment for diabetes has finally begun to address drug / hormone synergy.

The most elite bodybuilders polled realized that drug/hormone synergy/activity was the key to maximum growth rates. And in the case of drugs such as Avandia, the methodology for application was multifaceted.

Insulin is probably the most anabolic hormone there is. It was also noted to be highly synergistic with GH, IGF-1, PGF-2, Anabolic/Androgenic steroids, and several other growth inducing chemicals. However, maximum growth also required maximum receptor-site stimulation. (Which obviously is strongly dependant upon receptor-site number and sensitivity) There were several athletes who had hit growth plateaus due to insulin insensitivity. Sometimes this was due to over abuse of exogenous insulin during cycles and protocols. But it was more often due to either an athletes predisposition toward being a border-line diabetic or genetic limitations the endocrine system has placed upon growth. In either case, most of the elite group realized significant growth progress again by utilizing drugs like Avandia.

*5-10 pounds of additional mass gain were common during a normal seasons period.

Avandia is manufactured by Smith Kline Beech Pharmaceuticals and is provided as 2 MG, 4 MG, or 8 MG tablets. Athletes generally used Avandia in 12 week cycles with a progressive dosage:

Week 1-3 : 2 MG 2 times daily
Week 4-6 : 4 MG 2 times daily
Week 7-9 : 6 MG 2 times daily
Week 10-12 : 8 MG 2 times daily

According to available literature 12 weeks of continuous administration are required for Avandia to reach full effects in most individuals. A note of interest is that theoretically Avandia improved the results realized from IGF-1 use as well as insulin. This is due to the cross over stimulatory effect each of these hormones has upon the opposite receptor-sites. This may have had some positive effects upon GH use since GH converts to, and triggers IGF-1 release.

Noted Comments

*When athletes administered Avandia, hypoglycemia (Low blood sugar) occurred unless additional carbohydrates were ingested.

*The usual ratio of carbohydrates to insulin athletes used was 10 grams of carbohydrates for each I.U. of insulin administered. However, when athletes layered Avandia (or Glucophage) into a protocol that contained insulin or pancreatic stimulators (such as Glipizide) the ratio often increased to 12-15 grams of carbohydrates for every I.U. of insulin. (*See Insulin for more information)

*Failure to ingest adequate amounts of carbohydrates resulted in sweating, blurred vision, tremors, headaches, and confusion. Smarter athletes monitored their blood sugar (glucose) levels with test strips or metes.

*Liver enzyme values should be checked regularly before, during and after the use of Avandia (or Glucophage)

*It should be noted that additional negative side effects factually exist: Black outs, comas, and death to name a few. Insulin drugs were the most dangerous drugs utilized by athletes. FACT!

Since growth induced by Insulin and IGF-1/GH use was dependent upon the hormone's molecules merging with cell receptor-sites, it should seem apparent why Avandia was reported as quite effective for long term progress. Additionally, improved insulin sensitivity translates into an improved muscle to fat ratio body composition.

IGF-1
(INSULIN-LIKE GROWTH FACTOR-1)

Reported Characteristics
Drug Class: Growth Factor
Average Reported Dosage: 60-1000mcg daily
Water Retention: Diet dependent

IGF-1 is naturally produced in the liver as a result of GH (Growth Hormone) metabolism in the presence of insulin. Muscle tissue can also produce IGF-1 by way of an intracellular response. In fact, one of the benefits of training sets that result in an intense burn, or stretch position training, is the production of natural IGF-1. It is also a side effect of oral 17-ALFA ALKYLATED STEROIDS, which cause a higher release of IGF-1 from the liver. IGF-1 receptors exist throughout muscles and organs such as the heart, spleen, small intestines, and kidneys with a higher concentration of receptors exerting effects upon organs. IGF-1 is extremely anabolic, far more so than GH or Insulin.

Recombinant IGF-1 (genetically engineered) was reported to be effective when injected intramuscularly because it causes localized growth. This was the most popular method, and the agreed wisest for the most part. The drug has a half-life of about 10 minutes, and if it is or has been bound to IGF -BP-3, (INSULIN GROWTH FACTOR BINDING PROTEIN) the half- life is extended to about 12 hours. Pro's often stacked Insulin and/or GH with IGF-1 because IGF-1 shuts off natural GH production and GH causes Insulin resistance. IGF-1 is often referred to as Pro-insulin because it counteracts Insulin resistance and interacts with insulin. But this would actually be an untrue term for IGF-1.

IGF-1 can have all the side effect of GH or insulin use with an added negative: gastrointestinal (GI) growth. This is due to a higher number of IGF-1 receptors being located in the GI tract as compared to skeletal muscle. The latter has more GH receptors. This explains much of the bloat seen in pro bodybuilders of late.

IGF-1 is not stable in synthetic forms. A loud noise, shaking a vial, and sudden heat changes can render it nothing more than a bunch of expensive amino acids. Picture a piece of string folded up in a specific shape and held in that shape by a few fibers. This is what an amino acid sequence for GH or IGF-1 looks like, but the IGF-1 sequence has only 2 fibers keeping the active shape. The strand or string is a specific amino acid sequence. The shaping fibers holding the active shape are called disulfide bridges. Change the folding or break a bridge and the IGF-1 no longer fits into its receptor-site. Like a key must have a specific shape to actuate its lock, so must a drug have the right shape to actuate its receptor. Again, this explains the common noted necessity of careful preparation and site-specific injection (into the muscle group trained that day) when IGF-1 was administered.

Common stacks have been 0.25-0.50-mg of GH per KG of body weight stacked with 60-1000mcg of IGF-1 divided into 2-5 daily injections. Many had reported improved lean mass gains by combining both with insulin and high androgen AAS (Such as testosterone or orals such as DIANABOL and /or ANADROL-50) for 4-8 weeks. Many simply injected 40-mcg of IGF-1 directly into the muscle group trained that day after training. It is important to note that IGF-1 can cause hypoglycemia and blood sugar monitoring was considered paramount by most.

*The reader should note that IGF-1 has been used clinically on children at dosages of over 3-7mg daily. That is 3,000-7,000 mcg a day! No negative side effects were recorded, though none were expected... of course. The point being is that the 40-100 mcg of IGF-1 used by athletes is most likely insufficient, yet very expensive. However, the results some individuals have realized through IGF-1 use are amazing.

I have personally noted amazing new growth as a result of past IGF-1 administration. However it is important that readers realize that long term negative side effects have not been well studied. Anything that possesses genetic altering potential has equally negative potential as well.

DES (1-3) IGF-1
(NOT THE SAME AS IGF-1)

Most athletes have heard of IGF-1 (Insulin like growth factor-1) and the amazing anabolic effects it has been reported to have upon protein based tissue such as muscle. Des (1-3) IGF-1 is over 10 times (1000%) more anabolic than IGF-1. Now that is amazing!!

IGF-1 is actually produced from both Insulin and growth hormone in the liver and other tissues. IGF-1 is made up of 70 amino acids in a chain. Well, when a clever chemist removes the last 3 amino acids in the IGF-1 chain (the N-terminal tri-peptide) it becomes Des (1-3) IGF-1 and 1000% plus more anabolic. Why?

IGF-1 circulates through our blood stream and tissue 24 hours a day, 7 days a week. Unfortunately, most of the IGF-1 is inactive because it is bound by another protein called (get this) IGF-1 Binding Protein-3, or IGF-1-BP-3 for short. Since bound hormones can not fit into and trigger a receptor-site, the majority of circulating and muscle IGF-1 can not trigger an anabolic stimulus. Like tons of cellulite in a porno movie (who watches those?) there is little good stuff happening. However, when IGF-1 is altered and becomes Des (1-3) IGF-1 the binding protein IGF-1-BP-3 can not bind to it and it is totally active. Another reason Des (1-3) IGF-1 is so potent is its unique ability to fit into lactic acid altered IGF-1 receptor sites. (YUP) When we train we burn carbohydrates as a fuel to make cellular ATP. When cells switch to this ATP pathway, the by-product is Lactic Acid. This is of course the cause of most of the burn we feel during intense or higher rep sets. Well, the lactic acid build-up is called acidosis, and it destroys the shape of some receptor-sites for period of time. Therefore some anabolic/anti-catabolic hormones have difficulty merging with their respective receptor-site and triggering a response (such as even unbound IGF-1). Not so with Des (1-3) IGF-1, the super growth factor. It fits into the IGF-1 receptor-site even after acidosis. Des (1-3) IGF-1 is unbound, over 10 times more potent than IGF-1, and it picks receptor-site locks. Too bad it has only a few minute active-life.

Did you know that our body's make Des (1-3) IGF-1 naturally? Most un-informed individuals claim other wise, but it is true. When an athlete trains lactic acid builds up in muscle tissue. As we know, there is always IGF-1 / GH present in the blood stream and tissues (including muscle) from prior work-outs and other metabolic factors. That lactic acid burn triggers IGF-1/GH secretion from both prior and present work-outs. Unfortunately, lactic acid destroys some of the IGF-1 present in muscles being trained. But wait, this is good too!

Lactic acid also cuts (truncates) the last 3 amino acids off the 70 amino acid chain of "some" of the surviving IGF-1 and creates Des (I-3) IGF-1. So acidosis increases GH/IGF-1 production in the liver, "unbinds" IGF-1 locally in the muscle being trained (burned), destroys some of the IGF-1, and converts some IGF-1 into Des (I-3) IGF-1. Huh, good deal. And the synthetic form of this super anabolic stuff is beginning to show up on the black market more frequently.

INTERLEUKIN -15 (IL-15)

This is one of the newer drugs appearing on the bodybuilding scene that I would like to comment only briefly on. The human body produces several growth factors that are mediators and intermediates. In short this means they translate or decrease/increase the effect of hormones and other growth factors.

A study published in the Journal of Endocrinology in 1995 showed IL-15 doubled the rate of hypertrophy in skeletal muscle tissue. Interesting? Well the same study showed that stacking IL-15 with IGF-1 (insulin like growth factor-1; the stuff GH is converted into by the liver and other sites) increased muscular hypertrophy (excessive development/growth) by 500%. How is that for mediation? I have known only a few athletes whom have utilized this stack, and to be honest, I have always believed freaks can be created even from those with below average genetics anyway. Yes, the results were amazing. The down side of IL-15 use is that lack of research. Some have speculated that IL-15 can trigger cancer cell growth. However, available research has not shown a connection between IL-15 and organ growth as of yet. I will not, at this point, explain reported cycles or use. There is not enough research as of yet concerning possible negative side effects. However as more research becomes available, you can bet I will be happy to share the reported results.

*A note of serious interest. There is also an Interleukin-6 . DO NOT EVEN THINK ABOUT IT! It is used by AIDS patients as an immunocytochemical. This means it modulates an immune reaction to infection. It creates an inflammatory reaction and very high cortisol levels while suppressing IGF-1 and Androgen levels. So do not chase AIDS victims around asking for some. They have enough problems to deal with.

OXYTOCIN

Reported Characteristics
Drug Class: Vascular Contractile
Dosage: Unknown
Water Retention: None
High Blood Pressure: During Orgasms
HPTA Suppression: None

Oxytocin is a lessor known hormone produced in several areas of the body including the testes, pancreas, pineal gland, thymus, adrenal glands, and ovaries. So it would seem apparent that this is an important hormone. You don't know the half of it yet.

In women, the level of Oxytocin dictates orgasm level and number. In fact the higher the Oxytocin level, the greater the number of orgasms. This hormone is also responsible for some smooth muscle contractions in blood vessels and organs. This is why women's uterus spasm and contract during orgasms. Some individuals are not aware of this tell-tale sign of a woman's lower abs pulsating (meaning they are achieving an orgasm). Oxytocin levels can also affect sexual sensitivity positively.

In men, Oxytocin causes smooth muscle in the pelvic area and prostate to contract which aids in ejaculation. In fact, there would be no post- sexual debate over who sleeps on the wet spot without Oxytocin.

So why is this fun hormone listed in a book about chemical muscle enhancement? Well, beside the fact that it is fun to write about it, Oxytocin has had reported beneficial bodybuilding effects.

Oxytocin triggers production of GH, IGF-1, PGE-1, PGF-2, and testosterone. Obviously those who claim sex before athletic competition is a bad thing are not only frustrated, but wrong as well. Oxytocin also induces vascular contractions which translates into significant vascularity if an athlete is lean enough. Unfortunately, the effects only last 40-60 minutes. But long enough for pre-judging.

There are only two methods of inducing elevated Oxytocin levels. First would be a trip to the closet with ones lover just before stepping on stage. (Yes, it is actually done) The second, is an exogenous source. Oxytocin is utilized to induce labor in farm animals, and is available in a powder form at many feed stores. Since the hormone is orally active, the rest should seem obvious. (But is not suggested!)

Hopefully exogenous Oxytocin use is wisely not your thing, remember that a good sex romp burns an average of 250 calories and aids in anabolic hormone production. Who says aerobics can't be mutually beneficial?

WARNING: The misuse use of oxytocin can be dangerous resulting in severe cramping and projectile defecation. Only a qualified trained medical person should administer oxytocin.

PROSTAGLANDINS (PG's)

Prostaglandins (PG's) are naturally occurring intercellular messengers. In fact, many of the actions of anabolic substances fail to exert their protein synthesis actions without them. It is a clinical fact that there is a parallel between the rise of some levels of PG's and the degradation of catabolism. So they may in part be the relay between receptor-sites and translation to specific responses, or secondary messengers.

Research has shown a rapid and quite strong direct anabolic action from PG's in muscle cells. If PG's such as PGF-2 and PGE-2 are introduced into muscle cells, protein synthesis occurs at an incredible rate. If insulin is introduced into muscle cells with PGF-2 or PGE-2 there is a profound synergistic response. This places certain PG's among the most potent of anabolic activators. Perhaps far more so than anabolic steroids. This also suggests that the powerful anabolic actions of IGF-1, insulin, and amino acids are all mediated in one way or another by PG's.

Hang with me here. I need to explain your natural prostaglandin production process. Some prostaglandins called the PGE 2 series are made from a fatty acid found in the plasma membrane of your cells called Arachidonic acid. Under basal or non-training conditions, most of your arachidonic acid is in an esterified (bound) form inside the membrane phospholipids. Since only free (unbound) arachidonic acid can produce prostaglandins of the PGE 2 series, the basal synthesis of them is low. Pretty much like a balance of protein synthesis/degradation is normal (homeostasis). Due to the action of an enzyme called phospholipase A2, The esterified (bound) arachidonic acid is freed. The free arachidonic acid is converted into PGE 2s by another group of enzymes called Cyclooxygenase (COX). COX-1 and COX-2 are both found inside most cells and are responsible for the normal release of PG's. However, COX-2 is not normally present in the cells during basal states. When you train (creating a stress) COX-2 is quickly synthesized which in turn strongly stimulates prostaglandin release. Some PG's are mediators of inflammation, but our focus is upon PGF-2 which is an amazing anabolic stimulator. (COX-2 specific inhibitors such as Celebrex do partially block this activity)

*PG's are not stored like some hormones. They are quickly synthesized and then quickly destroyed. There are no PG reserves.

Cortisol, both natural and synthetic, are powerful PG inhibitors, though synthetic corticoids are even more powerful. Both reduce the activity of COX-1, COX-2, and phospholipase A-2.

A note of interest before I babble on. Intense muscular activity triggers specific muscle prostaglandins and the most intense of all stimuli is pure negative reps with very heavy loads. If you choose an exercise that contains a stretch position such as sissy-squats, incline curls, etc., more growth specific PG's are produced. The second most effective natural method of inducing elevated PG production is intense muscular burn. This is because Lactic acid build -up is a PG release stimulator.

Stretching is the third method. Stretching increases intermuscular IGF-1 and FGF (fiber blast growth factor) which triggers PG production.

Prostaglandins have shown up in a synthesized form on the black market since a few years ago. I have personally seen amazing transformations in those who had bravely injected PGF-2 site specifically 3-5 times per day. The injections were administered directly into the muscle group trained that day (usually with a fast-acting insulin such as Humulin R or Humalog). Due to extreme soreness, that body part could not be trained for a few days following injections. Since PGF-2 is site-specific, abdominal enlargement does not seem to occur as with IGF-1.

PGF-2 is the more active PG. Some of the elite group reported dramatic muscular hypertrophy (growth) at a dosage of 1-2 mg each 3-5 times per day. (3-10mg total per day) Side effects were serious soreness throughout the muscle injected. (Like a major cramp far worse than testosterone suspension). It was commonly known to avoid injections of PGF-2 anywhere near the intestines. (PGs of the 2 series will cause smooth muscles such as intestines and stomach to contract majorly. Some have experienced the worst bowel voiding of all times: the shits to end all shits) If injected, a small amount of the PGF-2 would reach the blood stream. This would explain the overall muscular growth reported. The reason, as I have stated prior, the injections were so frequent is due to PG's very short half- life.

Some interesting notes:

*Using androgens with PG'S were noted to be a bad idea for some individuals even if a legal method could be found. Users often reported that their muscles had difficulty functioning due to serious pumps. The upside was that androgen cycles after PGF-2 cycles became very effective again. According to some available literature, PGF-2 use seems to up- regulate androgen receptor counts at an amazing rate.

*PGF-2 prevented the fattening effects of insulin protocols by differentiation while increasing TGF (*See TGF). This was a benefit for those who were insulin resistant or during pre-contest periods.

*In women PGF-2 use would induce severe menstrual cramping.

*Arachidonic acid is found in red meat in fairly high levels. Unfortunately the activity of an enzyme called 5-Lipooxygenase (5-LO) upon arachidonic acid in the presence of estrogen has been linked to prostate cancer. An interesting finding is that inhibition of the 5-LO enzyme triggers massive apoptosis (programmed cell death) in human prostate cancer cells. Ginger seems to inhibit this enzyme and omega-3 fatty acids have a protective effect against prostate cancer.

As I wrote earlier, training and stretching trigger the release of prostaglandins by acting on the 2 enzymes that are responsible for their formation: Phospholipase A2 is increased which results in higher formation of free (unbound) Arachidonic Acid within muscle cells. Then muscular contractions increase COX-2, which transforms the freed arachidonic acid into PG's. The process can continue for days after a workout. At first, PGF-2 is the most elevated of PG production. FGF-2 synthesis is also elevated but in lower amounts at first. As the training induced muscle injury heals, the amount of PGF-2 production increases progressively. (Which is responsible for much of the anabolic reaction to training) It should be noted that there are several different PG's including PGE-1 which is used as an erectile function drug injected directly into the base of the penis. The result is a sort of inflammation: A woody.

The legal and far less effective but safer way to increase PG's is from the increased intake of essential fatty acids (EFA's). Specifically, Linoleic Acid, which is an OMEGA-6 fatty acid, and Alfa Linolenic Acid which is an Omega-3 fatty acid. Gamma Linoleic Acid (GLA) is another Omega-6 Fatty Acid essential for PGF-2 synthesizes. EFA'S are not just health and performance related. These EFA's are so necessary that without them, your body would simply deteriorate away and you die.

I have been amazed at how lacking many new clients diets are in EFA's. The best ratio seems to be 3:1, or about 6 grams of Omega-3 and 2 grams of Omega-6 fatty acids daily for most hard training bodybuilders. The best supplemental source for both is hemp seed oil. It contains the natural 3:1 ratio. Flax seed oil and evening primrose oil are both good sources, the latter, an excellent GLA provider. Yes, it is possible to test "dirty" for "weed" with enough hemp oil.

TGF
(TRANSFORMING GROWTH FACTOR)

Reported Characteristics
Drug Class: Adipocyte apoptosis stimulator
Water Retention: None
High Blood Pressure: Rare
DHT Conversion: None
HPTA Suppression: None

TGF is an endogenously produced hormone-like substance that plays a role in fat cell apoptosis (cell death). In times of starvation, such as long term carbohydrate depletion, adipose tissue produces TGF as a means of blocking fat cell anabolism, this means insulin in unable to trigger fat cell growth yet still possesses its powerful anabolic signal for muscle. This in turn facilitates the process of fatty acid mobilization (release from adipocytes/fat cells) and subsequent utilization as an energy source for the body. The result is fat cell starvation and eventual apoptosis. This is synergistic with natural PGF-2 elevation since localized increases in PGF-2 also result in an increase in TGF production. There also appears to be correlation between endogenous /exogenous GH levels and TGF. The higher the GH level, the more TGF produced in/by adipose tissue. This somewhat explains the extreme fat loss that occurs during GH administration even without a change in dietary habits.

Bodybuilders utilized exogenous forms of TGF as a means of fat cell eradication. Picture the number of fat cells in an athlete's body decreased by 20-50 %! During administration, fatty acids provide food for hard training muscle. Post administration, the athletes possessed a much lower potential for gaining fat tissue while creating a superior ability to utilize calories to build muscle. Simply stated, this means less mouths (cells) to feed = more calories for muscular repair and growth. Obviously there was a synergistic chemistry possibility utilized by athletes. TGF alone would be catabolic to lean mass tissue so an increase in the anabolic signal from GH, insulin, PGF-2, and/or IGF-1 was reported to be utilized by the few who had personally experimented with the drug. This was mostly done through TGF use to create an Absolute Anabolic Phase (See "Building The Perfect Beast" featuring "Frank N. Steroid" for more info on Absolute Anabolic Phases and Max Androgen Phases).There was a few report of pro bodybuilders who layered TGF into a Max Androgen Phase as a means of decreasing fat accumulation during mass weight gain protocols.

TNF
(TUMOR NECROSIS FACTOR)

Reported Characteristics
Drug Class: Adipocyte Necrosis Stimulator
HPTA Suppression: None

TNF should not be confused with TGF. Though similar in reaction, their action is through a different mechanism. Endogenous TNF production is normally a response to infections. Once released TNF kills fat cells through necrosis. Let me explain that. Every cell in genetic material contains specific DNA for cellular death. The exception is cancer cells. When the body has either the need for energy or factors contained within a cell the DNA is triggered through one or more chemical messengers to give up the factor. In the case of TNF, the message is "commit cellular suicide". When applied to fat cells (adipocyte) the result is a reduction in adipose tissue. It sounds cool, but the same signal can kill muscle cells as well.

OTHER SUBSTANCES

Athletes used a wide variety of substances in their quest for the ultimate physique or performance. Some truly health necessities...and some were insane alternatives to wiser choices. Many of these items can only be listed under ...*other substances*.

CATAPRES
(CLONIDINE HYDROCHLORIDE)

This is a drug used to treat high blood pressure (antihypertensive). Bodybuilders and other athletes using AAS often experience this problem due to increased water retention and elevated blood counts. The reason this drug is included here is simple: It raises serum levels of GROWTH HORMONE (GH) by stimulating production from the pituitary gland. Some athletes reported taking 0.3 mg -0.15 MG on an empty stomach both when going to bed and upon waking with a total of 0.18 mg per day, maximum. Personally I disliked the drug due to its many negative side effects such as potency problems, laziness, vertigo, and a few others. The use of antihypertensive drugs without a doctor's guidance is dangerous. Those prone to low blood pressure could die, those with high blood pressure could miss the safe dosage and do the same.

CLENBUTEROL
(CLENBUTEROL HYDROCHLORIDE) TABS .01-.02 MG

Reported Characteristics
Active-Life: Up to 68 hours
Drug Class: Beta-2-symphatonimetic, thermalgenic/anticatabolic (Oral)
Average Reported Dosage: Men 100-140 mcg per day Women 80-100 mcg per day
Acne: None
Water Retention: None
High Blood Pressure: Some reported high blood pressure
Aromatization: None
Liver Toxic: Unknown
Strong Anti-Catabolic/Thermalgenic

Clenbuterol is a quite strong anti-catabolic / thermalgenic drug that is not a steroid. During dieting periods, or post steroid cycles, this drug has reported dramatic effects on body composition. Since it suppresses the muscle wasting effects of cortisol/cortisone, a slight increase in total muscle protein synthesis was seen. When stacked with steroids the effect were synergistic and more profound. When used as a post-cycle drug, clenbuterol helped to maintain muscle gains after AAS were discontinued. In both cases the drug acted to reduce fat deposits by elevation of thermalgenesis. It was considered very important to all polled whom had utilized this drug to start with 1-2 tabs daily (2 on -2 off) and monitor body temperature. (Increased dosages can increase body temperature to dangerous levels) Most obtained excellent results in 4-8 weeks. Many also stacked clenbuterol with thyroid drugs and /or DNP to increase the rate of calorie expenditure.

Headaches, high blood pressure, and elevated body temperature were among noted side effects. Many reported side effects after 8-12 days. The body quickly adapts to clenbuterol so "on/off" periods were a must for successful results. By alternating between E/C (Ephedrine and caffeine) stacks and Clenbuterol, the effective period was extended and results increased. Rotations weekly such as clenbuterol, week #1, ephedrine/ caffeine week# 2, seem to have brought superior results.

The reason clenbuterol begins to lose effectiveness after only 2 weeks is that the beta-2-receptors it interacts with are quite sensitive. (These are adrenalgenic receptors) Once these receptors are over stimulated for a prolonged period of time they become insensitive. Oddly enough it appears that DNP and thyroid hormones help regenerate adrenalgenic receptor function.

TRADE NAMES

BRONODIL   0.02 MG TABS
BRONCOTEROL   0.02 MG TABS
CESBROW   0.02 MG TABS
CLENASMA   0.02 MG TABS
NOVEGAM   0.02 MG TABS
VENTIPULMIN   200MCG/ML (Liquid 355ml pump bottle)
SEVERAL MORE EXIST, BUT MOST COMMON ARE LISTED

Since Clenbuterol dilates blood vessels in skeletal muscle but relaxes smooth muscle blood vessels, the physical reactions are quite similar to the body's own epinephrine and can effect heart rate. It also reduces the level of the amino acid taurine in the heart which stabilizes cardiac rhythms, or the electrical activity in the heart. Increased intake for taurine during use was noted as wise.

Most bodybuilders don't realize that the anabolic effects of Clenbuterol are not due to increased anabolic activity. Clenbuterol is actually effective through a different mechanism. It decreases both protein synthesis and break down. The reason anti-catabolic effects result is simply because it hinders protein break down more which shifts the ratio in favor of anabolism. This means that clenbuterol had significant anti-catabolic effects when stacked with a cortisol inhibitor post or during AAS cycles. Cytadren was an often noted example. Again, since clenbuterol increases thermalgenesis, (calories released as heat) the common use of thyroid T-3 or T-4 in a stack with it caused a significant increase in body temperature. This was monitored closely by most.

Clenbuterol is utilized to treat asthma in several countries. The dosage for treatment is normally 20-30 mcg/d.

A note of interest, clenbuterol loses effectiveness quickly due to decreased beta-receptors. A drug called Zaditen (Ketotifen) helps maintain beta-receptors. The most reported down side of Ketotifen was that most users experienced drowsiness.

DNP
(2,4 DINITROPHENOL)

This was truly reported as chemical exercise. Normally the mitochondria process that converts ADP (adenosine diphosphate) into ATP (adenosine triphosphate) is about 60% efficient, which means there is a great deal of energy wasted. Those who have read the creatine section ahead of this are well aware of our good friend ATP. When we exercise, this process accelerates and raises our metabolic rate. (More calories are burned as a result) The process is called oxidative phosphorylation. Since ATP is the high-energy chemical our bodies utilize for intense training, anything that compromises this process will make cellular mitochondria work harder and expend more energy as heat. (Body temperature rises)

DNP is an oxidative phosphorylation uncoupler. It makes the process only about 40% efficient by uncoupling a high energy phosphate molecule from ATP and therefore turning ATP into ADP. To maintain an adequate supply of ATP, the body must step-up production. For this reason metabolism is significantly increased and an incredible amount of calories are burned. During this accelerated metabolic state, and due to the need for ATP production, most of the calories come from fatty acids (adipose/fat tissue). So little or no muscle is lost (With adequate protein intake).

Users experienced elevated body temperatures and perspiration even while sitting around. Simply stated, metabolic rates elevate 100-200% in only a few hours. *Sounds* great, but DNP can be deadly. Since increased energy is dissipated as body heat, too high of a dosage of DNP for to long of a period can actually COOK ORGANS!!!. No joke, I mean medium well done.

The issue of body temperature is of interest here and is a relevant point to discuss further. Clenbuterol and ephedrine are fairly easy to chart for effective results by checking body temperature. However, DNP is much different in this sense. When an athlete (Or anyone) used DNP, increased respiration, heart rate, and skin dilation occurred. Thus heat is quickly dissipated. This means that a person using DNP could feel warm but a thermometer can fail to show an increase in body temperature. According to available literature, in most cases a body temperature of near 100 degrees indicate a metabolic rate of about twice normal. It also means that the individual is in the very near the danger zone. This is wholly unnecessary, and it is the low cellular ATP level induced by high dosage DNP use that was most dangerous. The temperature or heat issue is secondary by comparison. Most reported users of DNP ingested a daily dosage of 6-8mg per kilogram of body weight. Realistically speaking, I can say from personal experience that this is not only an uncomfortable experience, but dangerous and unnecessary as well. My experience has been that 3-5mg/kg daily provided better results and did so even without a calorie decrease. Personally I feel a body temperature of 99.5-99.7 degreases was preferable also.

Before going on, I would like to say a few related points. Now we know that the mitochondrial process of converting ADP into ATP is called oxidative phosphorylation and that the process is normally 60% efficient. We know DNP is an oxidative phosphorylation uncoupler that will reduce the process efficiency to 40% and that this burns fat while raising metabolic rates 100-200% while increasing body temperature. (We also know misuse can cook our guts!). There are several products on the market, such as Usnic ACID using these terms and comparing their products to DNP.

Well, bull shit! Usnic acid even in pure form taken orally failed to raise metabolic rates significantly at the reported average dosage. Okay, second: DNP cannot be sold for supplemental use by law because idiots will think more is better and the media will again have a field day. (Funny how we see so many media interviewers in bars).

How did polled athletes utilize DNP? Well, pretty simple actually. 4-mg per kg of body weight divided into 4 equal dosages, take 4 hours apart was a common practice. So using a 220 LB bodybuilder, 220 lb = 2.2 = 100-kg. 100-kg x 4-mg = 400mg daily total, at 100mg taken every 4 hours. Using an oral thermometer, (rectal if preferred) the athletes temperature was taken upon waking before the first 100 mg DNP dosage and record. At one hour and again at hour 4 before the second dose the temperature was taken again and recorded. Any temperature above 100' was considered over kill on dosage, and therefore dosage was reduced or periods between dosages were increased due to half-life over lapping from previous dosages. Simple?

I did use DNP and followed a few obvious rules for *personal* use:

*I was always absolutely sure of the DNP quality and dosage I purchased. A mistake could have made me a cannibal's lunch.

*I never took DNP within 3 hours of bed time. If I made a mistake and I was awake, a cool bath tub of water could have saved my life.

*I drank atleast 1 gallon of pure water daily to aid in proper body cooling and to aid in removal of metabolic wastes.

*7mg per kg was the absolute maximum dosage of DNP and only for 5 days at this dosage. 7mg per kg was too high of a daily dosage and usually resulted in lean muscle mass loss, which sucked. 3-5mg/kg was wiser.

*I ate 2g of complete protein per pound at body weight daily, divided into 6-8 meals with at least 1g of carbs per pound of body weight daily.

*Never used DNP for more than 21 days consecutive. I lost about 11-18LBS of fat this way.

Note of interest: DNP also appeared to clean out androgenic receptor-sites and may have caused receptor-site up regulation!

Another factor of danger to consider is that after 48 hours of DNP use the liver experiences severe ATP depletion resulting in, among other things, almost all circulating T-4 thyroid hormone to be come unbound and excreted out of the body at a much higher rate. TSH, TRH, and thyroid gland secretion remain normal or above. But the body receives very little T-4 or T-3. This is why most DNP only users reported a decline in body temperature after two days of continuous use.

*It should be noted that DNP use causes an increase in free radical production. Those who used DNP supplemented their diet with additional anti-oxidants such as vitamins C & E, glutamine, and glutathione.

NUBAIN
(NALBUPHINE HCI)

Reported Characteristics
Drug Class: Narcotic/Analgesic (For injection)
Average Reported Dosage: 2.5-10.0 MG (0.25-1.0 ML) every 3 hours.
Noted Comments: HIGHLY ADDICTIVE

The first thing the reader should consider when reading this drug profile is "what is a narcotic drug doing in a book about bodybuilding chemistry?" And in no way, assume any good did or could come from its use.

Nubain is an injectable pain-killer similar to morphine in action and effect. In fact, the activity is about the same, as is its addictive potential, milligram for milligram. This is because Nubain is a synthetic opiate agonist/antagonist. The only positive aspect of Nubain is the fact that the drug is self-leveling (agonist/antagonist) which *mostly* prevents potential over-dosing.

Dan Duchaine (the original steroid guru) has been credited with introducing Nubain to the athletic world, though its use in sports pre-dates Dan's commentary. Dan speculated that Nubain maybe a viable anti-cortisol/anti-catabolic drug with Lipolytic (fat burning) qualities. Dan was a genius when it came to thinking outside the box. But he missed on this one. (And should not be totally blamed by those addicted to it)

Bodybuilders used Nubain (the crazy ones) as an intended thermogenic, anti-catabolic, and as a means of suppressing the pain of injuries from years of balls-out training. This may have some validity since the drug does reduce an individual's *perception* of stress, and is a powerful appetite suppressant. And like any opiate, the drug allowed some reported users to train well beyond the pain barrier threshold resulting in greater muscle fiber stimulation. So a lower perception of stress would slightly reduce total cortisol production. And an appetite fall-off would reduce total calorie intake while increased training intensity would increase calorie expenditure. But the fact is that the drug is no more thermogenic or anti-catabolic than any narcotic…just far more addictive.

Some have speculated that Nubain will be replaced by heroin. Don't laugh, Nubain is scheduled for manufacturer's discontinuance. If the reader has seen Nubain users during withdrawal, the facts speak unwell for the future.

Dan Duchaine was a very resourceful individual and, though an ass at times, supplied an answer to an urgent request for help to those he cared for. In this case, a client who suffered two prior attempts at kicking Nubain, and was ready for another try out of necessity. Dan's answer was a drug called Ultram, which is in the same drug class as Nubain but more like the clinical answer to heroin is Methadone. The client had a bit of an attitude but suffered no diarrhea no anxiety, no fever, or coughing, or sneezing. And he stated little or no Nubain craving resulted. He is Ultram/Nubain free still.

DAN'S KICK NUBAIN PROTOCOL

Week #1 Ultram 1 Tab 4 times daily.
Week #2 Ultram 1 Tab 3 times daily.
Week #3 Ultram 1 Tab 2 times daily.
Week #4 Ultram 1 Tab 1 time daily.

*Ultram is a prescription only drug in most countries (except Mexico) and should only be used under Dr.'s supervision.

I do have a few personal comments to add about Nubain. First that I have personally never tried it. Second that I feel this is an evil substance when utilized out side of the intended medical purpose. Last is that I have not seen a single individual who gained any actual benefit from it, but some that claimed they did while looking like shit.

PROSCAR
(FINASTERIDE)

Proscar is a DHT inhibitor. An inhibitor usually prevents something from being manufactured or converted, rather than simply blocking its receptor-sites. In the case of Proscar, the drug inhibits 5-alfa reductase enzyme which is the enzyme responsible for testosterone (nortestosterone converts to NOR-DHT) conversion to DHT (dihydrotestosterone). As you know by now, DHT is one of the hormones associated with accelerated balding and prostate enlargement. It is also responsible for many of the virilizing effects from androgenic steroids. (Like it also hardens musculature)

Proscar is a prescription drug utilized for preventing hair loss. About 83% of users reported a halt to hair loss. Unfortunately, some also report a reduced libido too. (Most sport wooded if the wind blew during AAS cycles). Since Proscar inhibits, or atleast reduces, the conversion of testosterones to DHT, theoretically there would be a greater anabolic effect possible during AAS cycles. But there was an obvious loss of hardness to the physique reported as well.

*Bodybuilders who were chemically assisted did not have to be concerned with the libido issue.

TRADE NAME

PROSCAR 1-5-MG TABS   MERCK U.S.

SYNTHOL/PUMP-N-POSE

This is not an anabolic steroid nor is it even an anabolic chemical except as a food. These were reported popular injectable products that contain a sterile (bacteria free and pure) medium chain triglyceride (MCT), an acid, and usually Procain or lidocaine (all of which have been made inert). The oil was injected deep into a muscle to add size. Usually this was done to smaller muscle groups such as biceps, triceps, delts, calves, and smaller round back muscles.

Most pro's who were using the stuff said that they had inject 2-3 cc's, 2-4 times per week directly into each target muscle for 2-4 weeks. They then followed this build-up with 3cc once a week for 15-25 weeks, which they had claimed made the gain in size permanent. On the noted plus side, this would stretch muscle fascia so that there is more room for muscle growth naturally. It had often been said that the results are a somewhat encapsulated oil pockets. But the size effects were admittedly dramatic. There were competing bodybuilders who admitted to over 100 weekly injection sites. Sad.

Fascia (the tissue that encases muscles) advantage aside, this could be a bad idea. The argument is that since MCT is a food product made from fatty acids and glycerol it could not hurt them. Well, many things good to eat could hurt you very bad if injected into the body! To be honest I have heard of no negative side effects as of yet except for the obvious loss of striations in delts and triceps, or when a vein was accidentally localized. I was of two minds on Synthol use until a year ago.

*Read "site injections " later.

REPORTED CYCLES
AND
EFFECTS

Before continuing I feel that it is again important to remind the reader that, like all that has been written and printed in this text, everything that follows is a report upon the crazy things that myself and other athletes have employed in our past quest for the ultimate beast physique. I do not endorse the use of drugs nor do I think anyone is wise to gamble upon their potential health and freedom by self administering any substance…especially those that are illegal.

I often find myself in a position were someone asks why I write about such things if I do not endorse the use of such substances. The answer is rather simplistic:

(1) I have a vast degree of research, personal and related experience to draw upon. Knowledge not shared, even for discussion purposes, is knowledge lost. I feel that, due largely to the medical hush placed on such research validation, there is a large number of individuals who will erroneously use the limited available knowledge resources to make very bad choices that will either result in health endangerment (or death) or a bad experience with the legal authorities.

(2) What I include in texts is simply the truth and opinions based upon these experiences and a disgustingly vast degree of viable research. In short, I am sadly qualified to do so.

(3) Chemistry is chemistry. It does not know political agendas nor have remorse for those whom erred with its existence. Having said that, please realize that many highly effective chemical muscle enhancing substances are not only health promoting but legal and readily available at health food stores. The hard part is separating the hype from the reality and facts. And that, dear reader, is why I write.

*In some instances athletes whom were surveyed were kind to provide validating blood work for their personal experiences. Personally it was common practice for my doctor to order a Chem. Panel, CBC, LH/FSH, and TSH tests. To a great degree my personal conclusions are additionally based upon these and much less on speculation.

REPORTED CYCLES and EFFECTS

As stated earlier, Anabolic / Androgenic steroids (AAS) come in injectable, oral, and sublingual forms. Each steroid has distinct effects that can be categorized as Anabolic and/or Androgenic. Due to alterations in chemical structure, scientists have created different ratios of Anabolic to Androgenic effects. As an example, testosterone is equally anabolic and androgenic whereas Deca Durabolin is highly anabolic and only moderately androgenic. These qualities manifest themselves in the following ways:

ANDROGENIC
Male personality characteristics like aggressiveness
Increased oil production by skin
Thicker, more dense facial and body hair
Growth of prostate tissue
Development of testes and sperm
Deeper voice
Increased sex drive
Increases adrenalgenic activity
Decreased catabolic activity
Faster recuperation
Reduced fat deposits

ANABOLIC
Increased muscle mass
Increases immune function
Male pattern fat deposits
Reduced body fat
Increased electrolyte retention
Increased hemoglobin and red blood cell count
Increased calcium deposits in bones
Increased nitrogen retention
Increased protein synthesis
Decreased catabolic ratio

*These lists are not a complete list of "negative side " effects: Only distinct characteristics, and the roll or function played by each.

REPORTED CYCLES and EFFECTS

Each steroid has distinct effects upon the body, both positive and negative, in different ratios. When multiple preparations of AAS were properly stacked together, a common noted synergystic effect resulted where the total dosage of 2 or more AAS was less, yet more effective, than a higher dosage of a single AAS.

AAS can be broken into 3 groups, rating negative side effects as High, Moderate, and Low. Be aware that all AAS can have some negative side effects, especially orals (different athletes reported higher or lower negative and positive effects). Based upon returns and interviews this depended greatly on sex, general health, age, receptor numbers/ distribution, diet, training stimuli, and regular tests for health monitoring among other factors and usually depended upon actual dosages that were administered. Those with the greatest training time (years, not hours per day) and experience achieved greater results as a rule.

*Read "Growth on the Cellular Level" and this will be explained better.

HIGH

Anadrol-50
Halotestin
Methyltestosterone
Dianabol
Metribolone

MODERATE

Trenbolones
Testosterones
Winstrol
Nilevar
Masteron

LOW

Deca Durabolin
Dynabolin
Equipoise
Oxandrolone
Androstanolone
Megagrisevit

M.D.
Andriol
Primobolan
Laurabolin
Anadur
Durabolin

CYCLES AND EFFECTS
~~AN OPINION~~

When it comes to dangerous side effects from AAS use liver toxicity is the *main* concern. I am not claiming steroids are safe for children per say, or that they can not negatively effect the body, but based upon research and personal experience it is my view that death threatening is pretty much a media hype for newspaper sales. In most cases the worst side effects AAS users faced were long prison terms and insane fines. Compare steroids to tobacco or alcohol and realize the two ends of the spectrum when one speaks of health risk. I do not endorse any illegal activity because that too is illegal. However, if an individual chooses to live in a society, then one also must live by its laws. I do not lecture or write as a means of endorsement of AAS use, nor to suggest a guide for users. Instead, my goal is to educate for discussion purposes only. Thus allowing readers to gain a degree of understanding only possible to achieve from those whom have been there and experienced the realities first hand.

I find it interesting that during the media hype concerning AAS over the past couple of decades, the media has focused solely on cases of one nature. Additionally, instead of distinguishing the toxic from the hormone induced side effects, they grouped them together so all steroids were equally bad. Which is not the truth at all. In fact, the cases the media made their money upon were exclusively "patients" who had under gone long term therapy of AAS and had already had extensive liver damage or other internal diseases before the use of medically prescribed steroids. Add this to the fact that in almost every case it was only one group of steroids (c17-alfa-alkylated oral androgenic) which were administered. (I wonder if the media is aware that birth control pills and injections are steroids and many are c17-alfa alkylated drugs) The two AAS most administered without discontinuance (for several years) were Methyltestosterone and Oxymetholone. Similar liver damage was only found in a couple of athletes who also had abused this group of oral AAS for years also. Compare that to any heavy alcohol drinker and AAS is relatively far less dangerous… even the 17-Alfa-alkylated orals. There simply is no evidence testosterone or its esters will "cause" liver cancer or disease. As a researcher, I find the controversy quite interesting. Since we are on this topic (and because I have a new crayon to write with), it seems quite the irony that the medical world has embraced the idea of prescribing testosterone, HCG, and GH for hormone replacement treatment, yet shuns nandrolones and other friendlier AAS.

REPORTED CYCLES AND EFFECTS

For the above mentioned reasons and concerns c17-alfa-alkylated oral steroids were used, if at all, for short periods. By stacking certain orals with injectable AAS a much lower dosage of orals notably create the same results with less negative side effects (due to toxicity). Personally, I find no use for Methyltestosterone nor could most justify the use of Oxymetholone for periods of more than 4 weeks.

OTHER SIDE EFFECTS OF AAS USE

As mentioned several times through out this book, AAS inhibit the normal function of the HPTA (HYPOTHALAMUS PITUITARY TESTES AXIS), reduce or stop natural androgen production, and decrease spermatogenesis. This results in shrunken testes (raisin-balls). This is further discusses under "HCG" and "CLOMID" to a greater degree. Loss of sex drive can develop in long term users.

Edema was common during the employment of aromatizing AAS due to imbalances in water and electrolytes. This was considered good to some degree because joints, connective tissue and muscle cells gained from it. Larger muscle cells containing more nutrients, stronger connective tissue, lubricated joints, and improved leverage, amounted to painfree workouts, better recovery, and increased strength. Different AAS effect edema differently and to varying degrees.

Oily skin causes acne, and higher androgenic AAS caused elevated secretion from sebaceous glands. This is because these gland receptor-sites have a higher affinity to DHT. Most AAS convert to DHT to some degree while others are DHT derivatives.

*Note: Many antibiotics prescribed for acne are anti-anabolic.

Feminizing effects due to AAS aromatization (to estrogens) such as gynecomastia (breast swelling and fat dposits), female pattern fat deposits, and extreme softness to muscle tissue is possible. Also after AAS cycles, due to decreased HPTA function, low androgen levels can cause estrogen to become the dominant sex hormone. (*Please see "HCG" for more info)

REPORTED CYCLES AND EFFECTS

Male pattern hair loss sometimes is another reported side effect. This *predominantly* effected individuals who were predisposed genetically to hair loss. Steroids that either convert to DHT at high rates (such as testosterones) and those which are DHT derivatives (such as Primobolan) can potentially cause premature balding. This is because DHT has a very high affinity for the receptor-sites in the scalp. This is not a reversible side effect and it can effect women too. An interesting note concerning Anadrol-50 is that has a progestin like effect upon progesterone receptors. Progestins can work with other estrogenic-like structures to stimulate hair loss also.

Psychological and sexual changes were common especially with high dosage utilization of highly androgenic AAS. Elevated libido initially occurred in most individuals especially women. High dosages can potentially increase aggressiveness, which is great, if this aspect were focused on training only. The sense of well-being and confidence did lead to *"roid rage"* for a few who were less in control of their adolescence (which is a common media term but in truth, I have found people who were assholes before AAS were even more so during AAS use).

157

Effects upon the cardiovascular system are possible. This is due to the fact that some AAS can elevate triglyceride and cholesterol levels. A decrease in HDL values and an increase in LDL levels are therefore possible. Normally HDL aids in protecting arteries by eliminating excess cholesterol that was not used for biosynthesis of endogenous hormones. LDL promotes the deposits of cholesterol on arterial walls. High blood pressure is another concern. These factors should be checked before considering the use of AAS and monitored by a health care professional. These factors were of special concern during bulk- up/ mass building phases for athletes who utilized poor dietary habits such as major simple sugars and heavy trans fats. Most values returned to normal (usually) after AAS use was terminated.

Elevated blood pressure was a concern for many AAS users. This was mostly due to an elevation in water and electrolyte retention caused by some AAS. This puts a strain on the cardiovascular system. Blood pressure should be monitored, and values higher than 140/90 should be treated by a doctor. This side effect usually normalized a few weeks after AAS are discontinued.

REPORTED CYCLES AND EFFECTS

Masculinization can be a negative side effect for women. The term virilization is used commonly concerning side effects of AAS use and women. But some aspects attributed are actually due to a significant decrease in body fat (a reduction in fatty breast tissue being the most notable). Males using AAS suffer HPTA function problems whereas women must be concerned with suppression of their natural hormonal balances in a different way. Simply stated, testosterone is what makes a man a man and it can make a woman one also. This is partially due to suppression of normal pituitary functions. This can manifest itself in many ways: Missed periods, acne, hirsutism which is increased facial and body hair, deeper voice or a distinct hoarseness to the voice, elevated libido (that's a bad thing?), aggressiveness, LH and FSH suppression, and clitoris enlargement/growth. Most of these side effects are permanent.

*Virilization is due to the androgenic effects of AAS, not anabolic.

Male prostate enlargement (growth) is possible but as of yet has not been statistically confirmed. However, it stands to reason that since some AAS convert to, or are derivatives of DHT and aromatize, that this is quite possible. It should be noted however that the connection between DHT and prostate tissue growth seems to require estrogen elevation above normal and testosterone level reduction to occur as well. Athletes over 40 years of age were wiser avoid high androgenic AAS that aromatize heavily, instead opting for nandrolones, Oxandrolone, Andriol, and Primobolan Depot (and enduring regular rectal exams). During AAS use, Finasteride (Proscar) was often considered.

Kidney damage is possible with some AAS. The discontinued Finajet actually caused athletes to urinate a dark colored or bloody secretion. Some authority somewhere will dispute this, but I for one have witnessed the event. Since the kidneys are filters for toxic by-products, it stands to reason c17-alfa-alkylated oral steroids could alter or damage the kidneys. Most AAS users drank at least one gallon of water daily.

REPORTED CYCLES AND EFFECTS
EXAMPLES

In a perfect bodybuilding world, anabolic/androgenic steroids (AAS) would have no negative side effects, would be free and legal without prescription, and athletes would use a great deal of intelligence while administrating them under medical supervision. (Also restaurants would feed us for free, but it's just a dream anyway) However, in the real world the dream is just a dream except in some of the more enlightened countries. I write the following examples for discussion purposes only and based on personal and reported experiences. These examples are not meant to be a guide or endorsement. They are not even a form of justification. They are simply facts experienced for better or worse by others. So no nasty letters, okay!?

Most reported first time AAS user were noted as wise to have at least 2-3 years of serious hard-core training experience before considering their first cycle. This point makes a great deal of sense and would be quite important when speaking of long term success and progress. First, untrained muscle does not respond very well to AAS. It takes time to acquire a good foundation in overall musculature, and an adequate series of neurological pathways between the brain and the individual muscle groups. It takes time to make this mind/muscle connection just as it takes time to learn to write and control your bladder. Okay, for those doubters…have you ever watched a first time squatter? Second, trained muscle contains more androgen, GH, and insulin (several others as well) receptors and more area to be potentially affected by AAS. Third, an untrained body has not developed the ability to deal with training induced waste by-products. How could it deal with AAS as well? Last, to use AAS before reaching training and growth plateaus was noted as a guaranteed method of limiting gains that could have been made physically and psychologically in the long run. In short, do not be a sissy, put your time in. Learn to train, eat, rest and diet first and foremost. Most athletes find that they are more than content with the progress they make without the inclusion of drugs. Fact, deal with it!

*I realize some experienced individuals will look at cycle examples and laugh at the lower dosages listed. This would likely be those who have joined the 2000mg weekly club and impaired their health and androgen receptors severely. (Due to prolonged "over-stimulation" not "down-regulation") For these individuals, Blitz Cycles and Max Androgen Phases were reported to be the best results producing AAS based cycles left. In truth, most steroids work bested, with the least side effects, when multiple AAS were stacked or, even better, rotated. This helped to avoid the adaptive response of the body (Action/Reaction Factors) while increasing effectiveness and decreasing negative side effects. After only a few weeks, many AAS became notably less effective anyway.

REPORTED CYCLES AND EFFECTS

As in most things in life there are many variations to common themes to which each individual prescribes. However, there are also many factors of commonality that the majority agrees upon which can not be denied due to experience. The following reported cycle explanations and examples were a result of the latter and are not meant as a guide in any way.

(*See "First Year Male Examples" chart also)

First Year Male Example Cycles week 1-4: First a series of urine and blood test were performed by a health care professional: HDL/LDL, BLOOD CELL COUNTS (CBC), LYMPHOCYTE, HEMOGLOBIN, and other health indicators including BLOOD PRESSURE were evaluated. Getting a copy of the results was always my goal for future comparisons. I would did this about 5 weeks after each cycle and again 2 months later if any results had altered negatively. Creating a training log containing: diet, training, cycles/effects good and bad was a must, of course.

The most common first cycle was brief (week #1-4). Deca Durabolin, 200-mg every 7th day. For those who were under 200-LBS, this short cycle provided good strength gains with lasting lean mass gains which were be mostly maintained after discontinuance of the AAS. Deca is a strong anabolic/moderately androgenic drug that promotes a high rate of protein synthesis. For this reason, a high protein intake of 1-2-g per LB of body weight daily was a must. Average total calorie intake was 18-20 calories per pound of body weight daily. Since the dosage was low and the cycle short, anti-estrogens were not utilized nor was there need for HPTA stimulating compounds post-cycle. According to available literature, Deca is very liver friendly (as is all Nandrolones) so toxicity was not an issue.

First year male examples weeks 9-12. The second cycle most commonly employed was a bit more aggressive than this but personally I used Primobolan Depot 100-mg twice weekly (Mon. & Thurs) stacked with Oxandrolone SPA. This cycle provided good strength gains and improved muscle mass with quality. However, my main goal was to harden the new mass acquired from my first cycle. Oxandrolone provided an increase in Phosphocreatine (CP) production and storage which translated into an increase in strength and improved nitrogen balance. The strong anabolic qualities of Primobolan Depot improved lean muscle mass to a respectable degree. I gained 6-8 LBS of lean mass during this brief cycle with improved body composition. Again, anti-estrogens were not necessary nor were HPTA stimulating compounds. This was due to Oxandrolone's lack of aromatization at any dosage. It also did not decrease HPTA function which was commonly confirmed by my own and other reported experiences. Primobolan Depot does not aromatize either and only slightly decreased HPTA function at higher dosages. I utilized a diet providing 1.5-2g of protein and 18-20 calories per pound of body weight daily. Post-cycle retention of new quality mass excellent.

REPORTED CYCLES AND EFFECTS

*Oxandrolone is a c17-Alfa-alkylated compound and liver toxic. However, in lower dosages for brief periods, toxicity is low-moderate. Primobolan Depot is only slightly liver toxic when administered in higher dosages.

<u>**First year male example weeks #17-34:**</u> Like most who opted to utilize AAS as part of a training regime my goal during and after my fist two AAS cycles was to gain as much quality muscle mass as possible. Since I was successful, repeating both cycles again before proceeding to stronger more androgenic combinations / stacks was prudent. Once I proceeded to higher dosages or stronger AAS, going backward had little augmentative value until I increased dosages.

The cycle example outlined in week #17-34 was a longer and stronger stack. Dosages were increased slowly to accommodate the body's adaptive ability, then tapered back down so as to avoid a sudden anabolic/androgenic crash (while HCG/Clomid kick-up endogenous androgen production). Though I did not necessarily agree with this protocols "tapered back down" aspect many reported this approach had lessor post-cycle psychological issues to deal with due to a gradual weening effect. Personally, I learned that this actually resulted in greater post-cycle lean mass tissue loss due to a prolonged negative feed-back loop within the HPTA.

The use of Novladex and Proviron to minimize estrogen, produced from aromatization of Dianabol, was reported as necessary by about half of those interviewed. However, the inclusion did result in reduced the effectiveness of this stack. Personally I introduced the anti-estrogens at the first sign of gyno or female pattern fat deposits only. Post cycle it was commonly necessary to utilize anti-estrogens as a means of avoiding an estrogen dominance while my HPTA function returns to normal. As with my prior cycle containing Deca, the gains made during this cycle were of a high quality muscle mass gain due to Deca's high protein synthesis inducing qualities. Most reported the same.

The use of the oral Dianabol greatly increased strength while creating water retention. Since Dianabol is a c17-alfa-alkylated oral AAS, liver toxicity was a concern. This stack usually resulted in a very rapid build-up of strength and weight with good regenerative qualities.

1.5-2-g of protein and 18-20 calories per pound of bodyweight daily were the normally agreed as "most productive". Since this was a mass phase type cycle, the higher calorie intake was necessary to realize optimal results. A reduction in calories to 17-18 calories per pound of body weight daily with out reducing protein intake was a necessary adjustment for those who already had excessive adipose (fat) tissue pre-cycle to avoid excess fat gain beginning week #33.

The use of HCG / Clomid was almost unanomously agreed to be necessary for those who reported this cycles use since higher dosages of Deca where utilized, and Dianabol does suppress /decrease HPTA function. Failing to do so often resulted in an anabolic/ androgenic lag period (which greatly reduced retention of mass gained during this AAS cycle). Continuing the cycle as outlined in weeks #27-34 usually depended upon negative side effects realized during the use of Dianabol during weeks #17-24. The use of HCG /Clomid during weeks #24-26 aided regeneration of the HPTA thus normalizing endogenous testosterone production and up-regulation of somewhat normal androgen receptor-site activity. This made the Winstrol Depot/Equipoise stack much more effective. The Winstrol Depot/Equipoise combination greatly reduced post-cycle muscle mass loss and had a hardening effect upon mass gained during the Deca Durabolin/Dianabol phase. This was obviously in comparison to protocols that did not employ this technique.

When I intended a competition date, it fell at the end of week #30 or 31. In that case, I begin the use of an anticatabolic/thermalgenic such as Ephedrine or Clenbuterol during week #27 and discontinued it at week #34-35. If I did not choose a competition date, I normally employed the use of Clenbuterol or Ephedrine for 4 weeks beginning week #32. This again reduced post-cycle losses. Winstrol Depot/Equipoise caused little water retention while creating a superior protein synthesis environment.

Most athletes who focused on long term results years later repeated this cycle after a 1-3 month "off period". The addition of other AAS was not considered by most until this cycle failed to provide effective results. I personally know of some NPC competitors who still used this first year cycle structure after several years with great success.

During week #17-24 the Dianabol was occationally replaced with Primobolan tabs to avoid liver toxicity issues: week #17-50MG/day, #18-75mg/day, #19-100mg/day, #20-125mg/day, #21-150mg/day, #22-150mg/day,#23-100mg/day, #24-50mg/day. The use of Nolvadex/Proviron for estrogen control was not reported to be necessary in this case. The use of Equipoise during weeks #27-32 was of little or no concern when liver toxicity was an issue since, according to available literature and based upon personal experience, it is not toxic at any dosage. Winstrol Depot was only somewhat liver toxic in the example dosage range and 6 week periods, in most cases. (And injections were less toxic than orals usually due to dosage differences)

First Year Male Examples Chart (Most common reported)

	Week #1	Week #2	Week #3	Week #4	Week #5	Week #6	Week #7	Week #8	Week #9	Week #10	Week #11	Week #12
Deca	200 mg/w	200 mg/w	200 mg/w	200 mg/w								
Prim. Dep.									200 mg/w	200 mg/w	200 mg/w	200 mg/w
Oxandrolone									25 mg/d	30 mg/d	35 mg/d	35 mg/d

	Week #13	Week #14	Week #15	Week #16	Week #17	Week #18	Week #19	Week #20	Week #21	Week #22	Week #23	Week #24
Deca				U/b/t	400 mg/w	400 mg/w	400 mg/w	400 mg/w	400 mg/w	400 mg/w	300 mg/w	200 mg/w
Diana-bol					20 mg/d	25 mg/d	30 mg/d	35 mg/d	35 mg/d	30 mg/d	25 mg/d	20 mg/d
Nol./Prov.									10/25 mg/d	10/25 mg/d	10/25 mg/d	10/25 mg/d
HCG												3000 iu 2xw

	Week #25	Week #26	Week #27	Week #28	Week #29	Week #30	Week #31	Week #32	Week #33	Week #34	Week #35	Week #36
Nov./Prov.	10/25 mg/g	10/25 mg/d										
HCG	3000 iu 2xw	3000 iu 2xw										
EQ			100 mg 3xw	100 mg 3xw	100 mg 3xw	100 mg 3xw	100 mg 3xw	100 mg 3xw				
Wins. Dep.			50 mg 3xw	50 mg 4xw	100 mg 3xw	50 mg 7xw	50 mg 7xw	100 mg 3xw				
HCG								3000 iu 2xw	3000 iu 2xw			
Clom.									50 mg 2xd	50 mg 1xd		

	Week #37	Week #38	Week #39	Week #40	Week #41	Week #42	Week #43	Week #44	Week #45	Week #46	Week #47	Week #48
	Off	Off	Off	Off	Off	Off						

REPORTED CYCLES AND EFFECTS

(See "Second Year Male Examples" chart also)

Second year male example cycles: This reported example was several interviewed athletes first cycle containing an injectable testosterone. Testosterone propionate was chosen due to a distinctly lower degree of water retention (due to active-life) and because it was only briefly active in the system. This allow myself and others to end administration of the testosterone quickly if unacceptable negative side effects resulted and circulatory levels reduced after 2-3 days. Kind of like avoiding a serious car wreck at the expense of a scratch.

This cycle provided a rapid build-up in mass and strength while exhibiting excellent regenerative qualities. During this mass phase utilizing a high calorie count of 19-21 calories per pound of bodyweight daily and our usual 1-2 g of protein per pound of body weight daily was considered the most effective approach. I have also used this cycle as a contest prep with a competition date during week #8 by beginning the use of Deca on week #4 and by continuing Testosterone Propionate an additional 2 weeks. Propionate was very effective at aiding intracellular muscle stores of glycogen so it was a real plus for me personally during carb-loading the last 2-3 days before competition. It also helped to protect against over training during diet restriction phases.

When employed as a contest prep protocol, Clenbuterol was added at the beginning of the cycle as well for both anti-catabolic and thermalgenic effects. However, I preferred this cycle to be utilized as a mass phase type cycle since Dianabol draws a great deal of water throughout the body causing a smooth appearance. This greatly reduced separation and definition of the musculature.

Use of Testosterone Propionate /Dianabol/Winstrol Depot caused a rapid increase in both strength and mass while adding additional quality to my musculature. By switching to Deca Durabolin at week #5 and adding Clenbuterol at week #9, I was able to further solidify the gains made during the mass phase and prevent excessive strength and mass loss post-cycle.

The use of HCG/Clomid was necessary due to the HPTA inhibiting effects of Testosterone Propionate and Dianabol. I was sensitive to highly androgenic AAS that aromatize so Nolvadex and Proviron used as an anti-estrogen needed to be continued as far as week #11 if I was not careful with my diet. The combination of Winstrol Depot and Dianabol caused some concern for liver toxicity. Primobolan tabs were reported as used in substitution for a better choice. However, the cycle lost some noted effectiveness as a result. The use of Deca Durabolin and Clenbuterol during weeks 4-10 was not indicated as highly liver toxic.

REPORTED CYCLES AND EFFECTS

(Second year male example reported cycles continued) This was be my personal first cycle intended for competition preparation. Since Dynabolan is milligram for milligram stronger than any other Nandrolone I was able use lower dosages. Stacked with first Dianabol then switching to Sustanon-250 will gave me a rapid and continuous build-up in muscle mass and strength. This was later solidified by the highly anabolic/androgenic (low aromatizing) combination of Equipoise, Winstrol Depot, and Masteron while I lost substantial water retention caused by the first period of this cycle. As my calorie intake slowly dropped during the period beginning at week #24, the addition of Clenbuterol and Cytomel increased metabolic rate and thermalgenesis (calorie burned as heat) while Clenbuterol acted as an anti-catabolic. The Nolvadex/Proviron anti-estrogen stack aided in preventing excess water retention while notably aiding in an overall hardening effect. Since I was sensitive to high androgenic AAS that aromatize, I begin the use of Nolvadex and Proviron as early as week #21 or 22. Most reported that this was not their response. I did not like limiting the potential growth of this phase, but accumulative side effects outweighed the value. (Yes, *some* estrogen was necessary for optimum results).

By tapering off all AAS and beginning HCG and most were able to retain much of my AAS gains. Clenbuterol was counted as quite important at this stage to protect against excessive muscle catabolism.

Personally I realized superior results due to a shorter protocol length from a lack of a so-called "tapering off" period.

As calories were reduced, the more elite athletes increased their protein intake to 2.5g per pound of bodyweight daily and begin trading some complex carb calories for MCT (medium chain triglyceride) oil calories (which is a fat that can not theoretically be stored as fat). *MCT oil contains 8.5-9 calories per gram.

Dynabolan was said to be slightly liver toxic, though this was not my experience. For this reason some replaced with Dynabolan with the more common Deca Durabolan or Anadur. Dianabol is an alkylated oral and is therefore quite liver toxic. Most agreed with this (which was further confirmed by the available hepatic test results provided). Again Primobolan tabs were utilized by some instead. Masteron and Equipoise were not noted as liver toxic while Winstrol Depot were moderately liver toxic at the listed example dosages.

Sustanon 250 is a mixture of Testosterones and therefore actually considered mild on the liver.

SECOND YEAR MALE EXAMPLES (Most common reported)

	WEEK #1	WEEK #2	WEEK #3	WEEK #4	WEEK #5	WEEK #6	WEEK #7	WEEK #8	WEEK #9	WEEK #10	WEEK #11	WEEK #12
DIAN A-BOL	35 mg/d	35 mg/d	35 mg/d	35 mg/d	30 mg/d	25 mg/d	20 mg/d	15 mg/d				
Win. Dep.					100 mg 2xw	100 mg 2xw	100 mg 2xw	100 mg 2xw				
Test. Prop.	150 mg 2xw	150 mg 2xw	150 mg 2xw	150 mg 2xw								
Deca					300 mg/w	300 mg/w	300 mg/w	300 mg/w	200 mg/w	100 mg/w		
Clen.									80 mcg/d	100 mcg/d	120 mcg/d	120 mcg/d
Nov./ Prov.					10/ 25 mg/d	10/ 50 mg/d	20/ 50 mg /d	20/ 50 mg/d	10/ 25 mg/d			
HCG									500iu /d	500iu /d	500iu /d	
Clom										50mg 2xd	50mg /d	

	Week #13	Week #14	Week #15	Week #16	Week #17	Week #18	Week #19	Week #20	Week #21	Week #22	Week #23	Week #24
Dyna								161 mg 2xw	161 mg 2xw	161 mg 2xw	161 mg 2xw	161 mg 2xw
Diana-bol							35mg/d	35mg/d	35mg/d	35mg/d	30mg/d	20mg/d
Sust											250 mg/w	250 mg 2xw
Nov./ Prov.												10/ 25 mg/d

REPORTED CYCLES AND EFFECTS

(See "Third Year Male Examples" chart also)

Third Year Male Examples: This cycle was quite long but was reported as very effective by all who had employed it. Due to the use of Masteron and Parabolan, it should be obvious the goal was to add quality and hardness to the muscle mass acquired over the years of AAS cycles. This cycle, combined with a high calorie diet providing 2-2.5 gm of protein per pound of body weight daily, resulted in a rapid and continuous increase in strength and quality mass. The resulting mass notably continued to become harder as the cycle progressed.

The brief use of Anadrol-50 during weeks #1-4 was long enough to obtain the best of its effects while mostly avoiding the negative potential of this drug. The following use of Dianabol during weeks #5-10 in a tapering structure as Equipoise and Winstrol Depot were added had a profound effect upon hardness and helped to maintain a highly anabolic state. Masteron was often replaced by Parabolan during week #5. This said to aid strength significantly and support Dianabol in the over bridge following the discontinuance of Anadrol-50. Since Parabolan is highly toxic, I kept use to about 2 weeks shorter than my own following contest prep cycle. The use of Equipoise and Winstrol Depot (or some replaced Winstrol with Deca) beginning week #7 allowed me to solidify gains made during the earlier mass phase. Excess water retention was lost during this phase and the results were more obvious.

The use of HCG/Clomid was quite prudent since Anadrol-50, Testosterone Enanthate, and Dianabol all decreased HPTA function. The use of Clenbuterol for atleast 4 weeks was just as prudent since catabolism is of concern during this post-cycle period. Anadrol-50, Parabolan, and Dianabol are all very liver toxic, while Winstrol Depot is moderately liver toxic in the listed reported dosage range.

*It was important to continue post-cycle blood test protocols and this cycle was no exception.

(Third year male example reported cycles continued) This was my earlier contest prep cycle. The stack provided good protection against over training during a calorie restricted period while maintaining or augmenting strength and lean muscle mass.

This combination of AAS did not aromatize to any significant extent. For this reason water retention was low and fat deposits increases were not a concern. Parabolan provided an elevated androgen level and improved overall hardness. Together with Masteron, Winstrol Depot, and Oxandrolone a highly anabolic (protein synthesis) and anti-catabolic (protein is spared) environment was maintained while improving muscle hardness. This is because Masteron is highly androgenic while Oxandrolone and Winstrol Depot are highly anabolic. The administration of Oxandrolone helped to maintain strength and improve hardness by elevating phosphocreatine synthesis and stores.

167

Clenbuterol accelerated fat loss through thermalgenesis (calories spent through heat production) while aiding as an anti-catabolic.

GH (growth hormone) is highly anabolic and quite anti-catabolic on one side (which means GH protects against muscle loss during calorie restricted diets while increasing muscle protein synthesis). On the other side, GH alters the ratio of fat/carbohydrates burned for energy in favor of fat. This means fat stores are burned up more easily. Cytomel, being a T-3 thyroid hormone, significantly increases whole body metabolism. (The amount of calories utilized in a given period.) This means I was able to maintain a higher calorie count "and" muscle fullness. The GH and Clenbuterol combination caused fat stores to be the main energy /calorie source during this elevated metabolic period of Cytomel use.

With the exception of the highly toxic Parabolan, this cycle example was mostly liver friendly. If Parabolan's toxic effects became a concern(significant SGOT/SGPT liver values), I used Masteron and Primobolan tabs through out the cycle instead of Parabolan. Oxandrolone was noted as moderately liver toxic at the listed dosages by a few interviewed, however unless blood tests following prior cycles containing Oxandrolone showed reason for concern, I made no other changes. The use of Nolvadex and Proviron was not "necessary", but the combination really improved over-all hardness and separation. HCG / Clomid were not noted to be necessary post cycle by most since this stack did not decrease HPTA function very much. However the HCG/Clomid induced endogenous testosterone elevation potentially would have aided in mass and strength retention post-cycle. This was a cycle I would have never used as an AAS novice and almost all agreed. (Estrogen suppression was utilized by some for an overall hardening effect, however)

THIRD YEAR MALE EXAMPLES CHART
(Most common reported)

	WK #1	WK #2	WK #3	WK #4	WK #5	WK #6	WK #7	WK #8	WK #9	WK #10	WK #11	WK #12
AD-50	50 mg/d	100 mg/d	150 mg/d	150 mg/d								
Test. Enan.	250mg 2xw	250mg 2xw	250mg 2xw	250mg 2xw	250mg 2xw	250 mg/w						
Mast.	300 mg/w	300 mg/w	300 mg/w	300 mg/w								
Diana-bol					40 mg/d	35 mg/d	30 mg/d	25 mg/d		15 mg/d		
Nol./Prov.			10-25mg/d	20-50mg/d	20-50mg/d	20-50mg/d	20-50mg/d	20-50mg/d	10-25mg/d	10-25mg/d		
HCG					500iu /d	500iu /d						
Para-bolan					76mg 2xw	76mg 2xw	76mg 2xw	76mg 2xw				
EQ							200 mg/w	300 mg/w	300 mg/w	300 mg/w	300 mg/w	200 mg/w
Wins. Dep.							50mg 2xw	50mg 2xw	50mg 3xw	50mg 3xw	50mg 2xw	50 mg/w

	WK #13	WK #14	WK #15	WK #16	WK #17	WK #18	WK #19	WK #20	WK #21	WK #22	WK #23	WK #24
HCG	3000iu 2xw	3000iu 2xw	3000iu 2xw									
Clom.			50mg 2xd	50mg /d								
Clen.	80 mcg/d	100 mcg/d	120 mcg/d	120 mcg/d								

	WK #25	WK #26	WK #27	WK #28	WK #29	WK #30	WK #31	WK #32	WK #33	WK #34	WK #35	WK #36
Wins. Dep.	50mg 3xw	50mg 3xw	50mg 3xw	50mg 3xw	50mg 3xw	50mg 3xw	50mg 3xw	50mg 3xw	50mg 3xw	50mg 3xw		
Oxan.	20mg/d	20 mg/d	20mg/d	25 mg/d	25 mg/d	25 mg/d	30 mg/d	30mg/d	30mg/d			
Mast.	100mg 3xw	100mg 3xw	100mg 3xw	100mg 3xw								
Para-bolan					76mg 2xw	76mg 2xw	76mg 2xw	76mg 3xw	76mg 3xw	76mg 3xw		
Clen.	80 mcg/d	100 mcg/d	120 mcg/d	120 mcg/d	120 mcg/d	120 mcg/d	120 mcg/d	120 mcg/d	120 mcg/d	120 mcg/d		
GH					2 iu 2xd	2 iu 2xd	2 iu 2xd	2 iu 2xd	2 iu 2xd	2 iu 2xd		
Cyto-mel					25 mcg/d	50 mcg/d	50 mcg/d	75 mcg/d	100 mcg/d	100 mcg/d		

AD-50 = Anadrol-50

Test. Enan. = Testosterone Enanthate

169

REPORTED CYCLES AND EFFECTS

(See: First Year Female Examples" chart also)

First Year Female Example Cycles: As we know, women are quite different than males (I am so thankful!!), and have reason to be concerned about virilization from AAS use. The first cycle most reported as "highly effective" began the day after an athlete's period had ended. It was considered absolutely paramount that this had to be a very low androgenic cycle.

*Oxandrolone has been utilized in medical fields to promote growth in children and treat or prevent osteoporosis in women. It provides improved strength and hardness by increasing phosphocreatine synthesis and storage. It is also mostly anabolic and quite low androgenically in its effects. Many steroid authors disagree claiming Oxandrolone is only good for promoting phosphocreatine synthesis. However, clinical studies on trained adults showed that 15 mg daily of Oxandrolone improved protein synthesis by over 40% in only 5 days. I would say that makes it clear Oxandrolone is very anabolic.

Though Deca Durabolin was often reported as utilized in this cycle, most had chosen Durabolin. This is due to Durabolin's relatively short half-life. This prevented androgen build-up thus avoiding virilization side effects unless someone was very androgen sensitive. Which relatively few women were. The highly anabolic qualities of Durabolin added strength, but noted more importantly transform the elevated strength from Oxandrolone into solid body mass. This combination was good for regeneration and recovery as well as reported liver friendly. Thanks to the very low androgenic qualities of this stack, no females reported the need for a mustache comb post-cycle. An elevated libido was a commonly noted experience during this cycle example and a sense of well being was said to result. Clenbuterol post-cycle was not necessary, but some reported good results and few negative side effects when they employed the drug. A high protein diet was a must during this cycle (1-2g per LB of bodyweight daily).

First year female weeks #13-18: This cycle was common and basically the same as the first. The goal was to improve muscle mass and quality while experiencing the effects of a stronger nandrolone, Deca Durabolin. As with the first cycle, a high protein intake was a must combined with a higher total calorie intake. 1-2g of protein with a total calorie count of 17-20 calories per pound of bodyweight daily was reported necessary to obtain the best results. Most did not continue on to the reported cycle example listed for weeks #25-34 until the two prior cycles repeated failed to provide adequate results. Total dosages of either Deca or Durabolin seldom went above 100 mg once weekly, with a close eye on virilization side effects. This cycle was noted as only slightly liver toxic due to the use of Oxandrolone.

*Based upon available literature, Deca is not liver toxic.

REPORTED CYCLES AND EFFECTS

(First year female example cycles continued) This cycle was not reported as "for novice female AAS users". If virilization side effects were not realized during prior cycles, I some women utilized Testosterone Propionate at this point for first time. Propionate is fast acting and out of the circulatory system quickly. This means use and effects can be discontinued quickly. Most who did experience Masculinization side effects did report discontinuance at the first sign of negative side effects. Durabolin was said to have been a better choice over Deca Durabolin for the same reason.

Oxandrolone provided good strength and anabolic qualities. The combination of Testosterone Propionate (due to androgenic qualities) and Oxandrolone increased strength rapidly while the mostly anabolic effects of the Oxandrolone /Deca (or Durabolin) combination will transformed the elevated strength into solid muscle mass. The tapering off period of Deca Durabolin and Oxandrolone after the discontinuance of Testosterone Propionate was said to be very effective at aiding in post cycle muscle mass/strength gains retention (in part due to psychological factors). The use of Clenbuterol beginning week #31 was often utilized to aid in post- cycle strength and muscle mass retention by acting as an anti-catabolic. The thermalgenic characteristics of Clenbuterol helped burn off any excess fat gained during the AAS phase of the cycle. (In most cases significant fat loss resulted when females utilize AAS)

The use of Nolvadex and/or Proviron was reported as not necessary in most cases since this was a mass phase cycle. Those who reported utilization of this cycle both with and without the co-administration of anti-estrogen drugs noted that blocking too much estrogen decreased overall effectiveness of the stack. This was a fairly liver friendly stack. According to available literature, Deca or Durabolin are not liver toxic. Testosterone Propionate was noted as very slightly liver toxic. Oxandrolone is moderately liver toxic but was not a major concern unless blood tests that followed prior Oxandrolone use showed negative results.

A high protein diet providing 1.5-2 g of protein and 17-20 calories per pound of bodyweight daily was commonly considered a must with this cycle example. Post cycle protein intake levels were continued while total calories are reduced to 15-17 calories per pound of bodyweight by those who retained the greatest lean mass tissue and the least adipose (fat) tissue. Since Testosterone converts to DHT fairly easily, hair loss of the scalp was monitored. If this became a concern, 1 mg of Finasteride (Proscar) was often co-administered and believed to be quite prudent (to block DHT conversion). It was almost unanimously said to be mandatory that Deca and Testosterone injections were alternated (Deca on Monday / Testosterone on Thursday) to avoid androgen build-up. By beginning Clenbuterol and Nolvadex/Proviron on week #25, this was noted to be an excellent contest prep cycle.

171

REPORTED CYCLES AND EFFECTS

(See "Second Year Female Examples" chart also)

Second year female example cycles: This was considered a hard-core cycle containing a mass phase and a contest prep phase. This was only considered necessary by seasoned athletes intending upper level competition who were willing to train very hard. There was a certain level of risk concerning virilization that most, but not all, strongly weigh against personal goals and values.

The weeks of #1-6 were very similar to weeks #25-31 of the prior years example cycle. So effects, results, diet and side effects were about the same. Week #7-10 contained Dianabol, a high androgenic/anabolic 17-alfa alkylated steroid that is liver toxic. Due to the short duration of use and low dosage (about the same as a male produces daily endogenously) side effects rare/low if any. The use of Dianabol at this point aided in strength and muscle mass retention from the period of weeks #1-6 while acting as an overbridge to begin the diet restriction phase of weeks that followed. Clenbuterol was commonly begun on week #6 and continued throughout the cycle to enhance thermalgenesis (fat burn) while acting as an anti-catabolic.

Winstrol Depot is androgenic and anabolic but does not aromatize to estrogens. For this reason estrogen and its effects were less of a concern. Primobolan tabs are an acetate ester. This means that it is an anabolic that was said to increase fat loss by some. Together Winstrol Depot and Primobolan tabs provided a distinct hardening to musculature while promoting protein synthesis. Therefore, muscle mass acquired during the mass phase was predominantly transformed into a high quality tissue. As the contest prep phase continued, the T-3 thyroid hormone Cytomel was added to increase metabolic rate and calorie burn. The Cytomel/AAS/Clenbuterol combination allowed for a higher calorie intake than would be normally possible for fat loss. This in turn promoted muscle growth and retention. Nolvadex and Proviron were utilized to reduce estrogen levels and effects for contest purposes.

Many women have reported difficulty acquiring hard legs during contest prep and the anti-estrogen stack of Nolvadex/Proviron solved this in most cases. Since Proviron is very androgenic (no anabolic qualities) a distinct hardness to musculature resulted. During carb loading 2-3 days prior to contest, 50 mg of Testosterone Propionate was often administered to promote glycogen storage intracellular in muscle tissue (which aids in muscle fullness and hardness). It also aided in vascularity to some extent. Those who felt that they were highly sensitive to water retention from Testosterone Propionate skipped that injection during carb-loading.

FIRST AND SECOND YEAR FEMALES EXAMPLES CHART
(Most commonly reported)

1st year female	Wk 1	Wk 2	Wk 3	Wk 4	Wk 5	Wk 6	Wk 7	Wk 8	Wk 9	Wk 10	Wk 11	Wk 12
Winstrol Tabs	10 mg/d	15 mg/d	15 mg/d	15 mg/d	15 mg/d	10 mg/d						
Dura Bolin	50 mg/w	50 mg/w	50 mg/w	50 mg/w	50 mg/w	25 mg/w						
	Wk 13	Wk 14	Wk 15	Wk 16	Wk 17	Wk 18	Wk 19	Wk 20	Wk 21	Wk 22	Wk 23	Wk 24
Deca Dura Bolin	50 mg/w	50 mg/w	50 mg/w	50 mg/w	50 mg/w	25 mg/w						
Oxan-droLone	10 mg/d	12.5 mg/d	15 mg/d	15 mg/d	10 mg/d							
	Wk 25	Wk 26	Wk 27	Wk 28	Wk 29	Wk 30	Wk 31	Wk 32	Wk 33	Wk 34	Wk 35	Wk 36
Deca Durabolin	50 mg/w	50 mg/w	50 mg/w	50 mg/w	50 mg/w	50 mg/w	25 mg/w					
Test Prop	25 mg/w	50 mg/w	50 mg/w	50 mg/w	50 mg/w	25 mg/w						
Oxan-droLone	10 mg/d	12.5 mg/d	15 mg/d	15 mg/d	12.5 mg/d	10 mg/d	7.5 mg/d					
Clen buterol							60 mcg/d	80 mcg/d	100 mcg/d	100 mcg/d		

2nd yr. Female	Wk 1	Wk 2	Wk 3	Wk 4	Wk 5	Wk 6	Wk 7	Wk 8	Wk 9	Wk 10	Wk 11	Wk 12
Deca Durabolin	50 mg/w	50 mg/w	50 mg/w	50 mg/w	50 mg/w	25 mg/w						
Test. Prop.	25 mg/w	50 mg/w	50 mg/w	50 mg/w	50 mg/w							
Oxan drolone	10 mg/d	12.5 mg/d	15 mg/d	15 mg/d	12.5 mg/d	7.5 mg/d						
Dianabol							10 mg/d	10 mg/d	10 mg/d	5 mg/d		
Winstrol Depot										25 mg/d	50 mg/d	50 mg/d
Primobolan tabs											50 mg/d	50 mg/d
Clen-buterol						80 mcg/d	80 mcg/d	80 mcg/d	80 mcg/d	80 mcg/d	80 mcg/d	80 mcg/d
	Wk 13	Wk 14	Wk 15	Wk 16	Wk 17	Wk 18	Wk 19	Wk 20	Wk 21	Wk 22	Wk 23	Wk 24
Winstrol Depot	50 mg/w	50 mg/w	50 mg/w	25 mg/w								
Primo-Bolan Tabs	75 mg/d	75 mg/d	50 mg/d	25 mg/d								
Clen-buterol	80 mcg/d	100 mcg/d	100 mcg/d	80 mcg/d	80 mcg/d	80 mcg/d	80 mcg/d					
Cytomel	25 mcg/d	50 mcg/d	50 mcg/d	50 mcg/d								
Nol./ Proviron	10/25 mcg/d	10/50 mg/d	2050 mg/d	2050 mg/d	10/50 mg/d	10/25 mg/d						

REPORTED CYCLES AND EFFECTS

Many female competitors used GH (Growth Hormone) also. Since it has no virilizing effects, aids in fat use for energy, is highly anabolic and anti-catabolic, this is no surprise. They worked very hard for their gains, too. The most beneficial period for GH use was reputed to be weeks #13-18. 2 I.U. once daily after training created impressive results. A second injection either upon waking or 12 after training was noted quite beneficial also. The second injection was also 2 I.U. in most cases, though some reported good progress from 1 I.U. 2xd. I have known many female athletes who used much higher dosages for greater periods of time. I just did not see the need when thinking about far sighted goals. By extending the use of GH to week #18, an increase in post-cycle muscle mass and strength retention was realized by those who employed this advanced principle. Women utilizing GH used very high protein diets. 2-3 g per pound of bodyweight daily improved results significantly.

There are several possible stacks females have reported superior benefit from:

1. Megagrisevit Mono-20 mg every second day/Durabolin (or Deca) 50-100 mg weekly/Testosterone Propionate-50 mg weekly provided strength/mass/hardness.
2. Orabolin 12-14 mg daily/Equipoise 50 mg weekly was noted as a very safe low toxic very low virilization concern stack for all around use.
3. Dynabolan 80.5 mg weekly / Primobolan tabs 50-100 mg daily was an effective low to moderate androgenic, highly anabolic stack with great versatility.
4. Deca Durabolin or Anadur 50-100 mg weekly/Winstrol tabs 10-16 mg daily was a moderately androgenic / highly anabolic stack that provided slightly better results than Oxandrolone /Deca Durabolin.
5. Equipoise 50 mg weekly/Winstrol tabs was a low toxic stack which provided slow and steady gains which were well retained post-cycle.

CYCLES AND EFFECTS
~~~BLITZ CYCLES~~~

Blitz Cycles are relatively new to so-called steroid authors but definitely not new to advanced "consultants" and elite competitors/steroid users. In practice the idea was mass saturation of androgen receptor-sites with very high dosages for brief periods of time. This protocol was no more effective than moderate dosages for beginning and intermediate AAS users due to muscle maturity. The reader must realize a few things. First, there are only so many androgen receptor-sites available to be activated. Second, those who utilized Blitz Cycles usually noted the need to do so because of the amazing amount of muscle mass/muscle cell androgen receptor-sites they possess and the lack of progress realized from any other protocol. At least brief Blitz Cycles were, in theory, safer and overall more effective than long term high dosage protocols. However, in some cases, Blitz Cycles utilizing GH and/ or insulin were far more effective for the purpose of muscle mass augmentation. But at what cost?

Let me say up front: Insulin can be deadly. Too high a dosage combined with too low an amount of carbohydrates can induce coma, brain damage, dizziness, cold sweats, blurred vision and other very bad negative side effects. Death is not reversible, nor is brain damage. This is not an endorsement of the protocols reported upon or even those I have previously experienced personally.

Things to Think About

When children experience growth spurts, their pituitary gland secretes about 2 I.U GH up to 7 times per day. But they only do so for a brief period of 4-5 days over (up to) a 3 week period.

The biggest problem with long term GH protocols was the expense to effect ratio. Furthermore, the longer the period of GH administration, the more Somastatin the endocrine system releases. What is Somatostatin? It is a natural/endogenous hormone your body uses to shut down GH and IGF-1 receptors to prevent a disturbance in homeostasis. The body hates change and Somatostatin blocks excessive change. Somatostatin can also be involved in GH production down-regulation. **BAD SOMATOSTATIN, BAD!** So considering the natural protocol growing children utilize for growth spurts (ever shop for a kid twice in one summer?) and the relative short periods, it seems intelligent to consider.

REPORTED CYCLES AND EFFECTS

There is a synergy between GH, Insulin, T-3 thyroid hormone, and high androgens. The combination was far superior for rapid growth than even the highest dosage of any one hormone alone. And in the case of insulin administration without a doctor's guidance, far more dangerous. (*Please see "Growth Hormone" for more info) Since it is the conversion of GH into IGF-1 (and other growth factors) we were most interested in, an androgen that also promotes IGF-1 production seemed an obvious choice in a Blitz Cycle. It also had to be very fast acting. Testosterone Propionate or Suspension were the best candidates, while Dianabol and Anadrol-50 were effective second choices. A fast acting short duration Insulin such as Humulin-R (which becomes active in about an hour and has a 4 hour half-life /8 hours of activity) was chosen since it was *somewhat* controllable. Cytomel (T-3) was the most effective thyroid hormone to utilize during GH administration. The liver converts GH into IGF-1 but has a limited capacity to do so. It seems that 2 I.U. of GH was acceptable in a span of about 2-3 hours and more closely followed the growing child protocol. So 2 I.U. 2-7 times per day was common. Now to put this info into a Blitz Cycle as it was employed.

~~BLITZ CYCLE EXAMPLE~~

	DAY #1	DAY #2	DAY #3	DAY #4	DAY #5	DAY #6	DAY #7
GH			2 I.U. 4 x D	2 I.U. 4 x D	2 I.U. 4 x D	2 I.U. 4 x D	2 I.U. 4 x D
Humulin-R			6 I.U. 2 x D	6 I.U. 2 x D	6 I.U. 2 x D	6 I.U. 2 x D	6 I.U. 2 x D
Cytomel			25 Mcg 2 x D	25 Mcg 2 x D	25 Mcg 2 x D	25 Mcg 2 x D	25 Mcg 2 x D
Test. Prop.	200 MG	200 MG	200 MG	200 MG	200 MG	200 MG	200 MG
Dianabol	50 MG	50 MG	50 MG	50 MG	50 MG	50 MG	50 MG

200 MG of fast acting Testosterone Propionate daily was begun on day #1 to allow circulatory saturation as was Dianabol 50 MG daily (divided into 3-5 dosages). This allowed circulatory androgen levels to be quite high before GH/ INSULIN/CYTOMEL administration began. 6 I.U. Humulin-R was injected twice daily 8-12 hours apart for best results. Humulin-R/Insulin injections were once, immediately after a work-out (with carbs/protein as stated earlier) and again 8-12 hours later. If an athlete trained at 5 p.m., the first injection of Insulin was administered upon waking at 5-7 a.m. and the second was after the work-out. Any signs of dizziness, hot flashes, cold sweats, and/or light headedness were immediately addressed with a protein shake containing 60 GMs. of Dextrose and 50 GMs. of whey protein. Both are very fast acting calorie sources. It was commonly said: "If symptoms did not totally disappear, call 911 and tell them you should never mess with Insulin if you are not a diabetic, and your address". A cycle of this nature promoted substantial long term growth when it was utilized 2-4 times throughout a year for all but a few who reported its employment.

REPORTED CYCLES AND EFFECTS

*Insulin use too often or too long can also make someone a permanent diabetic.

I utilized 3 such cycles some years back with remarkable results. I also ended up in an emergency room with someone else less fortunate.

This following section is a mixture of personal advanced AAS cycles and information gathered from both recent clinical data and some cutting edge lunatics I admired greatly, yet feared for their health. To say that some of these methods were controversial is an understatement at the least. What can I say except that they worked so darn well, and from reviewing blood tests, I feel most were *safer* than most long term protocols.

Results from these techniques truly were amazing, but I do not suggest or propose anyone utilize any of this information for illegal or unsafe purposes. There are laws against such free thinking in some closed minded countries. You know the logic of "What you do affecting only yourself is wrong if we disagree and we will put you in prison and fine you to protect you from yourself?" Sad, it is that mentality which caused so much misuse and possible negative side effects.

These protocols were quite advanced and predominantly utilized by elite competitive athletes only. The reason was simply a matter of physiological fact:: The effectiveness of the protocols were dependant upon an advanced neurological, vascular, muscle cell, training experience knowledge, and certain biological realities to utilize full possibilities and potential.

*There is uncontrolled growth within chaos for those who control the stimuli of the situation, and therefore controllable results.

These cycles employed short phase or staged protocols. Each of which involved the next logical step to achieve more permanent results in almost all cases. A great deal of synergy was employed by working "with", instead of "against" the body's natural responses to stimuli then utilizing each response to an advantage. These are the Action/Reaction Factors we discuss constantly. Traditional protocols failed to a great extent for this reason. Basic truth is that for every action there is a reaction. Try telling your wife you want to take her birthday and go to the game, but plan to invite her next year. Ya, hello Mr. Hand! That was an example a good idea with bad results...*Action/Reaction*. So let's look at some methods of actions that produced reactions of a mostly positive nature.

THIS IS ONLY THE TIP OF THE ICEBERG. MUCH MORE IS COMING IN: "BUILDING THE PERFECT BEAST"
The story of
"Frank N. Steroid"

REPORTED ADVANCED CYCLES AND EFFECTS

Personally I began 2 weeks before Stage 1/Phase1, I wanted to set the environment for serious growth. To do this, I needed to under eat and overtrain to cause an up-regulation of muscle receptor-sites for androgens, GH, IGF-1, and other goodies that focus or foster an emergency growth response. I wanted to force down-regulation enzymes that store fat or decrease nutrient absorption.

Think about it…

*Pre-contest bodybuilders under eat and overtrain for 8-12 weeks before a show. About 45 seconds after the show, they face slam about anything that does not eat them first. The rebound from this self induced catabolic state causes amazing weight gains _for a short period of time_, mostly lean muscle mass. Remember; it is not what we eat, it's what we absorb. A hint here is that AAS worked best in an initially catabolic environment. We have our ancestors to thank for this. Thousands of years ago they were hunters and scavengers who ate what they killed or found. Kind of like the IRS and banks. Anyway, days and weeks would pass with no food and their bodies would alter homeostasis for survival. Then something big, meaty, and hairy would fall off a cliff and they would gorge for days and grow due to a highly efficient storage system. This survival action/reaction factor is still with us.

Let me save you from another chemistry and biology lesson by saying this: If I increase training volume and intensity for 2 weeks while dropping 500-800 calories from my daily calorie count, my body will enter a controlled catabolic state. The body adapts in about 2 weeks to most hormone and enzyme affecting stimuli before altering for less desirable changes. This means I dropped some fat but not muscle during this period while setting peak conditions for major growth. If I return to my normal maintenance diet plus 25-35 % more calories (from increased protein intake) for 2 weeks, my body will "absorb" significantly more calories than normal and store most of it as lean tissue. When I utilized the right chemistry protocols for the ideal period, over compensation became super-over-compensation. I gained at least a pound of bodyweight per day during Stage 1/Phase1.

Theoretically speaking, (and I have seen the amazing results countless times) whether post-competition or after an intentionally induced controlled catabolic period, there was no other period more effective for growth when utilizing chemical muscle enhancement.

REPORTED ADVANCED CYCLES AND EFFECTS

So here is the basic outline I personally utilized. Beginning day #1 I stopped all supplements. (And was off cycle for at least 30 days)

LET'S DO CONTROLLED CATABOLISM

DAY #1
QUADS/HAMS/SHOULDERS
DAY #2
ARMS/CALVES/ABS
DAY #3
BACK/TRAPS
DAY #4
CHEST/ABS/CALVES

(1 g protein per LB of bodyweight daily/ 2 g complex carbs per pound of bodyweight daily. I Kept fat down to 20% of total calories.)

DAY #5
REST-Had fun -add 300-500 calories from junk food!!
Day #6
QUADS/HAMS/SHOULDERS
DAY #7
ARMS/CALVES/ABS
DAY #8
BACK/TRAPS
DAY #9
CHEST/ABS/CALVES

(1.5 gm protein per LB of bodyweight daily. 1.5 gm complex carbs per LB of bodyweight daily. Kept fat down to 20 % of total calories. 2 table spoons MCT oil/3 teaspoons flax seed oil daily.)

DAY #10
REST-Same as Day #5.
DAY #11
QUADS/HAMS/CALVES
DAY #12
CHEST/SHOULDERS/TRI's
DAY #13
BACK/TRAPS/BI's

(1 gm protein per LB of bodyweight daily. I gm complex carbs, per LB of bodyweight daily. (0.6 gm of protein) 3 table spoons MCT / 6 teaspoon flax seed oil/ fat down 20 % of total calories.)

DAY #14
REST-(0.6 gm of protein per LB of bodyweight daily)

I had now set the environment for amazing weight gains. During my 2 week catabolic periods I utilized a heavy negative-only set first, a drop-set second, and a high-rep-pump-set third on each exercise, using 6-9 sets total on legs, chest, back, traps, and 4-6 sets total on arms and delts with only high rep calve work of 3-6 sets. Why ? The heavy negatives first down-regulate androgen receptors then up-regulate them above normal about 10 days into this phase. The drop-set triggers an anabolic survival mechanism while adding to the glycogen depletion and prostaglandin production (which also triggers androgen receptor sensitivity) effects of the high rep set. Two full days of bed rest followed. At this point, my body was mass producing enzymes that clear androgen and other receptor-sites for major growth. But first I needed to get thyroid hormone activity back up quickly and stop the excessive cortisol production. I also introduced a high dosage of long acting androgen such as Testosterone Enanthate or a mixed Testosterone such as Sustanon-250.

I preferred the Enanthate because the Propionate in the Sustanon-250 kicked in too fast for this purpose unless my goal was a Max Androgen Phase. I also introduced some T-3 thyroid and a cortisol inhibitor. I preferred Cytadren, but Trilostane, which is a 3-beta hydroxysteroid dehydrogenase delta 5,4 isoerase inhibitor (60 mg 4x daily 2 days on and 2 days off for 18 days max) or metryapone which is an inhibitor of 11- beta hydroxylation in the adrenal cortex (250 mg-2x daily-2 days on and 2 days off for a max of 24 days) worked well also. I liked Cytadren because it mangled cortisol receptors for up to a year, which meant more mass retained post-cycle and a superior long term growth environment. And it suppressed estrogen production obviously. I would did use Trilostane when I planned site-injections with pro hormones later.

REPORTED ADVANCED CYCLES AND EFFECTS

Example 1 (Stage 1) Phase 1 *I wanted to super saturate androgen receptors

Day #1	500 mg Test. Enanthate	25 mcg Cytomel
Day #2	500 mg Test. Enanthate	25 mcg Cytomel
Day #3	500 mg Test. Enanthate	250mg Cytadren 3xd
Day #4	500 mg Test. Enanthate	250mg Cytadren 3xd
Day #5	400 mg Test. Enanthate	25 mcg Cytomel
Day #6	400 mg Test. Enanthate	25 mcg Cytomel
Day #7	400 mg Test. Enanthate	250 mg Cytadren 2xd
Day #8	400 mg Test. Enanthate	250 mg Cytadren 2xd
Day #9	300 mg Test. Enanthate	25 mcg Cytomel
Day #10	300 mg Test. Enanthate	25 mcg Cytomel
Day #11	300 mg Test. Enanthate	250 mg Cytadren 2xd
Day #12	300 mg Test. Enanthate	250 mg Cytadren 2xd
Day #13	200 mg Test. Enanthate	25 mcg Cytomel
Day #14	200 mg Test. Enanthate	25 mcg Cytomel

During (Stage 1) Phase 1: I ingested 2-2.5 g of protein per pound of body weight daily, 2.5-3 g of complex carbs (I drank a lot of D.E. 20 which is a maltodextrin powder from Hazardous Materials supplements), and added 6-9 teaspoons of flax seed oil and 3 table spoons of MCT oil while allowing other fats to fall where they may, to each days calorie total. The average normal person, (never met a "normal" bodybuilder) produces about 26 mcg of T-3 daily. During my controlled catabolic period my T-3 was suppressed but quickly returned to normal due to very high calorie intake. The Cytomel increased metabolic processes and nutrient absorption so that it was available for muscle cellular protein synthesis while it also increased cellular receptor clearing and kept fat deposits down. The Cytadren suppressed cortisol production (remember what would happen if I suppress catabolism 50% as stated at the beginning of this book?) and estrogen production therefore I was able to switch homeostasis in favor of anabolism. Since I had clean and fresh androgen receptors, I used a high dose protocol for Testosterone Enanthate to saturate the receptors before they could respond with a desensitized reaction. If any signs of excess estrogen did appear, I added either Arimidex (0.5 mg 2-4 times daily) or Nolvadex (10-20 mg AM and 10-20 mg PM) but this was rarely necessary, yet. I always had a very good appetite due to excess T-3 activity.

*Some athletes required 37.5 -50 MCG of Cytomel on listed days. The reason that 25mcg of T-3 was effective was due to the fact that the human body requires about 2 weeks to initiate the reactive process to most hormonal actions. So the 25 mcg acted in an additive manner since it was combined with my natural/endogenous T-3 production during the brief period.

REPORTED ADVANCED CYCLES AND EFFECTS

By day #14, my body was reaction ready and readjusting itself to begin shutting off storage mechanisms so it was time to switch to a highly anabolic environment. I commonly gained about one pound plus per day during Phase 1. During Phase 1, I returned to training each body part once a week on a 3 day on-one day off-2 day on-one day off schedule. Very heavy, few sets, total failure, and trained at a reasonable pace.

My first concern during Phase 2 was the circulatory cortisol my body was about to produce (which would have normally robbed me of much of my gains from Phase 1). So I wanted to either use chemistry that induced anabolism in spite of catabolism (such as Primobolan Depot or Parabolan)or use chemistry that acted as an anti-catabolic and anabolic (such as Insulin and GH) or both. Another choice that was sometimes taken will be exampled later.. My choice this time was GH/Insulin/T-3 so as to allow my receptors to clear again.

Example #1 (Stage 2) Phase 2 *I wanted to protect what I got and get more!
(Anabolic/Anti-catabolic)

Day #15	1. Humulin	10 I.U. 2xd/GH 2 I.U. 2xd/Cytomel 50mcg AM
Day #16	2. Humulin	10 I.U. 2xd/GH 2 I.U. 2xd/Cytomel 50mcg AM
Day #17	3. Humulin	10 I.U. 2xd/GH 2 I.U. 2xd
Day #18	4. Humulin	10 I.U. 2xd/GH 2 I.U. 2xd/Cytomel 50mcg AM
Day #19	5. Humulin	10 I.U. 2xd/GH 2 I.U. 2xd/Cytomel 50mcg AM
Day #20	6. Humulin	10 I.U. 2xd
Day #21	7. Humulin	10 I.U. 2xd
Day #22	8. Humulin	10 I.U. 2xd/Cytomel 50mcg AM
Day #23	9. Humulin	10 I.U. 2xd/Cytomel 50mcg AM
Day #24	10 .Humulin	10 I.U. 2xd
Day #25	11. Humulin	10 I.U. 2xd/GH 2 I.U. 4xd/Cytomel 50mcg AM
Day #26	12. Humulin	10 I.U. 2xd/GH 2 I.U. 2xd/Cytomel 50mcg AM
Day #27	13. Humulin	10 I.U. 2xd/GH 2 I.U. 2xd
Day #28	14. Humulin	10 I.U. 2xd/GH 2 I.U. 2xd/Cytomel 50mcg AM
Day #29	15. Humulin	10 I.U. 2xd/GH 2 I.U. 2xd/Cytomel 50mcg AM

*"Humulin" refers to Humulin-R

During Phase 2: I ate as I did during Phase 1 and added a few blender-solution-shakes. Training involved 1 heavy set, I pre-exhaust/compound set, and one high rep set per exercise as a means to increase glycogen /glucose turn over and hyperplasia. I also added 30 ml of glycerine in 16 oz of water with 2 grams of vitamin-C, first thing in the morning and before bed. I increased T-3 (Cytomel) while maintaining on-off-protocol to protect thyroid function, increase TSH (thyroid stimulating hormone) and ramp-up nutrient absorption and protein synthesis. This also helped clear androgen receptors. This was significantly effective when I opted to follow with another AAS protocol during Phase 3.

REPORTED ADVANCED CYCLES AND EFFECTS

Insulin was both anabolic and anti-catabolic in effect. Injections were before 2 large meals containing atleast 100 gms of carbs each. I avoided taking Insulin before training and at bed time for obvious reasons, and did not utilize Insulin and GH within one hour of each other. GH is very anabolic and anti-catabolic in some ways. It also, once altered by the liver, produces several growth factors including those that increase nerve and capillary structure into the new areas. This had a stabilizing effect upon the new tissue that I had added during Phase 1 or during previous site-injection protocols. The IGF-1 and IGF-2 produced during liver and cellular conversion was quite growth inducing as well. (DUH!) Since I ingested enough protein, carbs and fats, the Insulin act to assure cellular nutrient supply which was greatly influenced by the high nutrient absorption provided by Cytomel. I needed to eat, so that I could absorb, so that my body could transport enough nutrients. The result was enough raw materials around my muscle cells that when the nucleus said "grow", they did at a phenomenal rate. My self and other had also effectively utilized a variation to amplify IGF production by using 5 mg of Dianabol per 25 LBS of bodyweight on non-GH days. This had the addition effect of cortisol activity suppression. (Or I could used 300 mg of Testosterone Propionate to elevate androgen and IGF-1 levels on non-GH days for even more mass gain)

Example (Stage 3) Phase 3   *** I continued high androgen /high IGF-1**

DAY #

1. 300MG Test. Propionate/50MG Dianabol
2. 300MG Test. Propionate/50MG Dianabol
3. 300MG Test. Propionate/50MG Dianabol
4. 300MG Test. Propionate/50MG Dianabol
5. 300MG Test. Propionate/50MG Dianabol
6. 200MG Test. Propionate/40MG Dianabol/100MG Primobolan Depot
7. 200MG Test. Propionate/40MG Dianabol/100MG Primobolan Depot
8. 200MG Test. Propionate/40MG Dianabol/100MG Primobolan Depot
9. 200MG Test. Propionate/40MG Dianabol/100MG Primobolan Depot
10. 200MG Test. Propionate/40MG Dianabol/100MG Primobolan Depot
11. 100MG Test. Propionate/30MG Dianabol/100MG Primobolan Depot /50MG Winstrol Depot
12. 100MG Test. Propionate/30MG Dianabol/100MG Primobolan Depot/50MG Winstrol Depot
13. 100MG Test. Propionate/30MG Dianabol/100MG Primobolan Depot/50MG Winstrol Depot
14. 100MG Test. Propionate/30MG Dianabol/100MG Primabolan Depot/50MG Winstrol Depot

Testosterone Propionate and Dianabol orals really produced a great growth environment by causing a brief high production of IGF-1 and a very androgenic/anabolic environment that was perfect for previously cleared androgen receptor-sites (that were the reaction set-up from Phase 2). Dianabol orals also had a cortisol production suppression effect of 50-70%. By introducing Primobolan Depot, I prepared for an anti-catabolic/estrogen type suppression phase. Winstrol Depot is, like Primobolan, a DHT derivative. Though neither aromatize, it has been noted that the body will increase natural estrogen production to seek homeostasis (balance) to a minor extent during administration. The Primo/Winstrol combination made it easier to hold onto my mass gains during Phase 3 B. I sometimes chose to proceed to a site-injection protocol after Phase 2 or direct to an estrogen/cortisol suppression type protocol (with a site-injection maintenance phase) as exampled next. I had gained serious size at this point, next I had to adjust to it!

Example 1 (Stage 3) Phase 3 B.   **Cortisol/estrogen suppression.**

WEEK #

1. Cytadren 250 MG 2xd, 2 days on 2 days off/Arimidex 0.5 MG 4xd/ Nolvadex 20MG AM. & PM.
2. Cytadren 250 MG 3xd, 2 days on 2 days off/Arimidex 0.5 MG 4xd/Nolvadex 20MG AM & PM.
3. Cytadren 250 MG 3xd, 2 days on 2 days off/Arimidex 0.5 MG 3xd/Nolvadex 20MG AM & PM.
4. Cytadren 250 MG 2xd, 2 days on 2 days off/Arimidex 0.5 MG 2xd/Nolvadex 20MG AM. & PM.

Example 1 (Stage 3) Phase 3: My experience with this example has been that it suppressed cortisol and estrogen activity almost completely. When coming off AAS HPTA function was decreased so it is obvious cortisol and estrogens could have become the dominant hormones. Most athletes lost most of their gains and due to that fact, but it just was not necessary. By almost totally suppressing the two hormones responsible for losses (while the HPTA catches up) we can see why we experienced a shift from catabolism to anabolism. This is because even a small amount of endogenous testosterone was enough to become the dominant hormone when estrogen and cortisol activity was suppressed. A prime example of this is what happened when surveyed females reported taking just 250 MG daily of Cytadren with no other chemical protocol. They showed signs of masculization and lean muscle mass gains after only a few weeks. It was best to alternate Cytadren 2 days with Arimidex /Nolvadex for 2 days. This kept the protocol effective for up to 30 days before biological adaptive reactions initiated (such as run-away ATCH production in check) and minimized the rebound effect after termination. I have also utilized "Male Mix"/"Happy Sack" to aid HPTA function with about the same results as Clomid /HCG. I realized additional results when I had replace Nolvadex with Cyclofenil. This was due to an increase in endogenous testosterone.

REPORTED ADVANCED CYCLES AND EFFECTS

WEEK #   ALTERNATE (STAGE 1) PHASE 1   EXAMPLE #2

1. Anadrol-50 150mg/d-Test. Prop. 300mg/d-Deca Durabolin 100mg/d
2. Anadrol-50 100mg/d-Test. Prop. 200mg/d-Deca Durabolin 100mg/d-Primobolan Depot 50 mg/d
3. Anadrol-50 50mg/d-Test. Prop. 100mg/d-Primobolan Depot 100mg/d

This was an alternate to Phase 1 some had reported favorable utilization of. The Anadrol-50 was liver toxic but most only used it for 21 days total with this example. This caused a very rapid weight gain stacked with Testosterone Propionate. However most athletes androgen receptors were quite saturated by the end of week #2 or mid week #3, so it was notably wise that the more experienced individuals took their gains and ran (ended the protocol). This meant introducing a high anabolic/moderate androgenic. By beginning Deca Durabolin week #1, the anabolic effects began on day #6 of week #1 and slowly peaked until about a week after the end of week #3. This aided in turning the high weight and strength gains from Anadrol-50 and Testosterone Propionate into solid retainable mass. Primobolan Depot was introduced week #2 so as to be prepared for the high androgens loss and cortisol elevation. Remember that Primobolan Depot is an AAS that worked well in a high cortisol environment if there was enough protein available from diet.

During this protocol, an estrogen /cortisol suppression type protocol such as outlined in Phase 3 B example #1 or #2 was commonly used beginning mid to end week #1. This produced excellent muscle hardness as well as aided in over-all lean mass gains while suppressing cortisol/estrogen post AAS use. Where DHT conversion was a concern, much was avoided with 1 MG of Proscar daily and discontinued at the end of week #3. My personal calorie intake was atleast 20 calories per pound of body weight daily. The obvious following cycle was usually Phase 2 beginning at the end of an estrogen /cortisol suppression period. Most reportedly gained atleast one pound per day during this phase. However continuing with any AAS was counter productive beyond day #21.

*Remember; anti-estrogens and cortisol inhibitors are not AAS.

CONSIDER THIS....

I would like the reader to stop and ponder something for a few minutes. If, in theory, an athlete controlled proportionately all anabolic, androgenic, and catabolic hormones and enzymes with dominance upon protein based tissue growth, then supplied a correct ratio of amino acids, carbohydrates, and fats, the athlete would increase in protein based mass at a rate of body weight x 1.818 g daily. So a 250 pound bodybuilder in theory could add 454.5g daily in lean tissue. Though some or most would not agree, I

REPORTED ADVANCED CYCLES AND EFFECTS

have witnessed this in reality many times. There are also countable athletes who have successfully altered genetic shape of musculature. This would not be surprising to plastic surgeons of course, but to most in the athletic world this is pure fantasy. I assure it is not. There are many chemical enhancement protocols and techniques, as well as training specific methods joined with them, I have as of yet not written about. That is for future projects. So why have you, the reader (with a few very rare exceptions) been told other wise? If this is true, you should ask, then why doesn't anyone know this information? Simply said, you are reading it now, and as proof I suggest you review the current crop of top pro's and take another look, closely, at older pictures of them from only a few years ago. There will be some surprising competitors coming in the next few years. Genetic average athletes will be the super heroes in the near future. Picture 375-400 pound in shape pro bodybuilders. I assure you it can and will be done, and with fewer negative side effects. That should piss-off several experts. Again, this is only the first layer of many that have been done in the crazy and anything but pure health oriented world of chemically enhanced athletes.

I realize that this is a side track issue, but relevant all the same. Cycle protocols were an approach intended to facilitate optimal growth of muscle tissue. Remember there are two main muscle fiber types: Type I, which is endurance orientated, and Type II which is strength orientated. Type "IIa", "IIb", and Type "IIc" are responsible for most musculature size and have the greatest potential for growth. Testosterone increases the number of Type II fibers at the expense of the Type I transformation. Growth hormone, Insulin, IGF-1, and thyroid hormones effect growth and hyperplasia of both fiber types. This should be another key relating to protocols that were utilized and why.

What was that?

Synthol has become popular site-injection product both for chemically assisted and natural bodybuilders as of late. This is actually an illegal practice in many countries so the products are sold as topical "posing oils". The products contain an inert MCT oil which has been put through a series of processes to create a sterile product. Sometime back I was introduced to another but far more effective topical posing oil from a gray market supplement company called Hazardous Materials located in California.

This product had been re-labelled by some of the scummier black market steroid dealers as 50MG/ML Testosterone Propionate, Drive, and Nandrolone Decanoate 50MG/ML. I HATE THIEVES, but what would anyone expect to experience when dealing with people already committing a crime! What I found interesting was that the products brought "similar" results to the actual AAS and reports indicated that Protest was far superior to Synthol. Some reported utilizing one of the Protest products mixed with AAS to create a Max-Mix for site-injection protocols, while others have reported using the products "as is " between AAS cycles for the same purpose. Of course there are those who utilized the product for its intended purpose, which is as a topical/oral prohormone supplement.

REPORTED ADVANCED CYCLES AND EFFECTS

So is Protest sterile? The usual series of Agar plates with different nutritionate medium and warm autoclave, then a look under the microscope on days #1,3,6,9, and 12 revealed nothing. No growth of bad stuff. Three samples were analyzed for content. Protest contained 3 oils, a series of or single free prohormone and prosteroids, an interesting somewhat anti-catabolic product, and an estrogen receptor blocker. So yes, the vials tested were sterile.

As to effective, well blood tests revealed significant total testosterone increases of well over 400% and even better free testosterone levels. The creator obviously knew a thing or two. **Be aware, I am not suggesting anyone inject or miss use this product for any illegal purpose.** However, this does not mean that some have and with remarkable results such as over 2 inches increase in arm diameter, much wider delts, and an obvious improvement in overall body size and composition. Where such practices are legal this and other Hazardous Materials products may have been a natural bodybuilders dream come true and chemically assisted bodybuilders so-called best friend. I will briefly tell you about a few of their products. Personally, I have not received anything in return for this nor is this an endorsement. It was just rare to find effective products on the market that were legal in the United States.

PROTEST 1

"Topical androgen posing oil" sterile solution: 100MG free 4-androstene-3,17, diol, 50MG 17-hydroxy-androstane per ML. (And MCT oil with 2 other oils) This was reported to be a good androgenic/anticatabolic combination with estrogenic activity blocking effects. It also aided in clearing receptor-sites and displayed bound testosterone uncoupling qualities to some extent. This was the product re-labelled as Testosterone Propionate 50MG/ML by scum bags. Comparable to a testosterone/Primobolan stack.

PROTEST 2

"Topical androgen posing oil" sterile solution: 100MG free 1,4-androstane-3,17 diol,. This is the product re-labelled as both Drive, and as Boldenone 50MG/ML. I have to admit results did seem similar. Those utilizing 2-4ML daily had compared Protest II to 200-400MG of Equipoise per week.

MALE MIX (HAPPY SACK)

Male Mix: this is a sequenced amino acid product taken orally that I found quite interesting. In published clinical studies (in respectable medical publications) the product increased LH 629%, FSH 99%, and ACTH 106% (this is average) in trained athletes. I know the research well. Go re-read Clomid and HCG. The results are pretty much identical. In fact, the IOC had recommended banning the product for competitive use. I would not have used this product for more than 21-28 days. It could screw up the

REPORTED ADVANCED CYCLES AND EFFECTS

testosterone feed-back loop eventually. There were reports the product is as effective as Clomid/HCG. Personally I think Male Mix/Happy Sack was a good "off cycle" product after AAS or Prohormone use beginning the last week of the cycle.

D.E. 20: this was a maltodextrin that had a glycemic index (dextrose equivalent) rating of 20. Cheaper than food, easier to consume, excellent absorption, and goes well in protein shakes during any mass weight gain protocol.

The last time I spoke with them, they also had a good mixed protein with a great supply of glutamine in peptide form. SITE-INJECTION THEORY

SITE INJECTION

The idea behind site injection was pretty much a matter of introducing a substance between fascia and fibers. The substance forced itself between fascia and fibers which in turn made the muscle larger. This was similar to implants only in that the substance occupies space. The enlarged area slowly gained vascular tissue which promoted muscle tissue to expand into the greater area. For permanent size growth, it was noted as necessary to maintain a site-injection maintaining period of 5-8 months once the original size increasing site-injection protocol was discontinued. The oil, and anything else suspended in it, slowly migrated into the vascular system like any other metabolic compound. Then it entered the blood eventually making its way to the hepatic vein and into the liver. Once entering the liver, the oil was simply metabolized as food. The area where the injection protocol was applied then had more tissue area and greater mass. The first time this idea was brought to my attention was while reading a very old breast enlargement procedure which was silicon injections. I theorized incorrectly that the body would respond by creating a collagen capsule around the foreign compound. But why would it? The body does not encapsulate oil based steroids! I later read about a product containing a special MCT oil that had been put through a series of pressure, temperature, and other sterilizing processes. The product was being used for direct muscle injection. The light bulb went on! Several x-rays and MRI s were performed on users who had put inches on calves, arms, and delts about 3 months after discontinuance. Guess what? No oil pocket, just new tissue. I have seen 2 inches and more added to calves, arms, and delts in as little as 60 days and retained if the maintenance protocol was followed then discontinued after 5-8 months.

REPORTED ADVANCED CYCLES AND EFFECTS

INJECTION SITES (How was it done)

(ARMS)

Biceps: When I hit a double bi pose, the peak of the bicep was obvious. Marking each peak, I then relax the arm at the side. Trust me, the marks were much higher when relaxed. The injection site was directly into the mark about half way between bone and skin surface. So if the bicep was 2 inches thick, relaxed, the needle was inserted an inch into the muscle itself.

Tricep peak: Basic procedure was the same as biceps. Hit double bi pose, mark the peak, and inject at the mark with arm relaxed. Again, half way into the muscle was the focused site. (Tricep peak obviously)

Top of Tricep Horse Shoe: With my arm relaxed at side position and hanging straight down, I reached high and to the back of the Tricep with my other hand. Flexing in this position, I felt for the meatiest point of the upper horseshoe and marked it on both arms, then checked to be sure they were equal points on both arms. Again, same injection procedure was followed.

Delts: For round full lateral delts using my opposite hand, I followed my collar bone to the end with my finger. About one inch beyond and still in line with the collar, I put a mark on each lateral head. I inserted the needle 1-1.5 inches from the top as if it had fallen from above. The site was slightly behind the mid- muscle and pushed the whole area outward.

Any muscle could have been utilized for targeted site injection protocols. These were simply the most obvious since small muscles responded best to this technique. I preferred 1-3 ML per site and a 2 day on/2 day off protocol. This allowed me to train around each site so as to not disturb it too quickly. I once had seen biceps that had been site injected a few hours before an arm workout. Looked pretty bruised to say the least (Like snake bites). If I was hitting multiple sites, say delts, bi's and tri's, I simply trained chest/shoulders/tri's together and site injected/localized tri's and delts that and the next day. Back /traps/bi's followed on the next day after a rest day. Bi's with rear delts were injected. Simple huh? How about crazy? I always drew back on the syringe plunger to check for blood. If blood filled the rig, it was in a vein.

*Do not try this, Accidental localization of a vein can kill!

189

REPORTED ADVANCED CYCLES AND EFFECTS

COMMON INJECTION SITE MIXES

My favorite mixer became Protest by Hazardous Material. My perspective was why waste a shot on my ass? There are several AAS mixtures that brought excellent results. Usually it was fast acting AAS that work best:

Testosterone Propionate, Winstrol Depot, Durabolin, Deca Durabolan, even Parabolan if I could find it. I stacked one or more of these together with the rest of my cycle gear and added an AAS that worked well in a catabolic environment, preferably Primobolan Depot. 3 weeks with high AAS dosages was my max for site injection.

REPORTED EXAMPLE: MAX MIX 1 (in a 100ML vial)
*This was a favored all out weight /mass high androgenic.

    10 Sustanon-250
    15 Primobolan Depot 100 MG per ML
    30 ML Durabolan or Deca Durabolan 50 MG per ML
    10 ML Testosterone Propionate 50 MG per ML
    30 ML Protest (I or II) or Synthol

Note of interest: Some had also reportedly used site injections of Prostaglandin for 2 weeks before the beginning of AAS or prohormone site injection protocols. This created a dramatic up-regulation and sensitivity of androgen receptor sites. (*Go read Prostaglandins for more info) The localized growth from this procedure was crazy. This also worked quite well during the catabolic phase prior to Stage 1 (Phase 1).

REPORTED EXAMPLE MAX MIX 2 (in a 100 ML vial)
*This was a notably more conservative high anabolic protocol.

    20 ML Equipoise 50 MG per ML
    10 ML Primobolan Depot 100 MG per ML
    20 ML Testosterone Propionate 50 MG per ML
    50 ML Protest (I or II) or Synthol
    1 ML Benzyl Alcohol

*For maintenance periods, most alternated between Synthol and Protest, 2 weeks each. The maintenance period was usually 2.5 ML weekly in each prior localized muscle.

Winstrol Depot and Testosterone Propionate worked real well for site injections but pre-mixing water based with oil based AAS was a possible disaster. I pre-mixed Testosterone Propionate with Protest or other, then added Winstrol to the syringes prior to injection. Again this was about a 3 week cycle before utilizing a maintenance phase.

REPORTED ADVANCED CYCLES AND EFFECTS

REPORTED EXAMPLE MAX MIX 3 (in 100 ML vial)
*This was a common structure used for good specific site stimulation

21 ML Testosterone Propionate (50mg/ml)
58 ML Protest (I or II) or Synthol
1 ML Benzyl Alcohol

Personally I loaded 2 ML of Max Mix 3 into syringes then added ½ ML Winstrol Depot, set in hot water and (after cooling) utilized for site injection protocols. Some of the best pecs and tri's were built this way.

When trying to decide what is fast acting vs. slow acting esters, you could return to the drug description section. But from fastest to slowest they are:

Acetate
Undecanoate
Propionate
Isocaproate
Phenyl Propionate
Enanthate
Decanoate
Cypionate

A note of interest: In many cases bodybuilders reportedly injected non-sterile black market AAS. Sometimes abscessed or bacterial infections occurred. Usually Doxycyline-100 MG/d was prescribed for bacterial infections, and Augmentin for abscesses. For viral infections, Inosine Pranobex 4 tab/d for 10-20 days was said to be effective. However, a qualified medical professional was best consulted.

REPORTED ADVANCED CYCLES AND EFFECTS

DIRTIEST DIET AWARD

DAY #

1. DNP 6 MG/KG-CYTADREN 250 MG 2XD
2. DNP 6 MG/KG-CYTADREN 250 MG 2XD
3. DNP 6 MG/KG-NOLVADEX 20 MG AM/PM -ARIMIDEX 0.5 MG 3XD
4. DNP 6 MG/KG-NOLVADEX 20 MG AM/PM -ARIMIDEX 0.5 MG 3XD
5. DNP 6 MG/KG-CYTADREN 250 MG 2XD -PRIMOBOLAN DEPOT 100 MG -TEST. PROP. 300 MG
6. TEST. PROP.-300 MG-CYTADREN 250 MG 250 MG 2XD-PRIMO DEPOT 100 MG
7. TEST. PROP. 300 MG-NOLVADEX 20 MG AM/PM -ARIMIDEX 0.5 MG 4XD-PRIMO DEPOT 100 MG
8. TEST. PROP. 300MG-NOLVADEX 20 MG AM/PM-ARIMIDEX 0.5 MG 4 XD-PRIMO DEPOT 100 MG
9. TEST. PROP. 300 MG-CYTADREN 250 MG 3XD-PRIMO DEPOT
10. CYTADREN 250 MG 3XD
11. DNP 6 MG/KG-NOLVADEX 20 MG AM/30 MG PM-ARIMIDEX 0.5 MG 4XD
12. DNP 6 MG/KG-NOLVADEX 20 MG AM/30 MG PM-ARIMIDEX 0.5 MG 4 XD
13. DNP 6 MG/KG-CYTADREN 250 MG 3XD
14. DNP 6 MG/KG-CYTADREN 250 MG 3XD
15. DNP 6 MG/KG -NOLVADEX 20 MG AM / 30 MG PM-ARIMIDEX 0.5 MG 5XD-PARABOLAN 76 MG
16. GH 2 I.U. 3XD-NOLVADEX 20 MG AM/30 MG PM-ARIMIDEX 0.5 MG 5XD-PARABOLAN 76 MG -CYTOMEL 50 MCG AM
17. GH 2 I.U. 3XD-CYTADREN 250 MG 4XD-CYTOMEL 50 MCG AM-TEST. PROP. 200 MG-PARABOLAN 76 MG
18. GH 2 I.U. 3XD-CYTADREN 250 MG-4XD-TEST. PROP. 200 MG-PARABOLAN 76 MG
19. GH 2 I.U. 3XD-CYTOMEL 50 MCG AM-NOLVADEX 20 M.G. A.M./40 M.G. P.M. ARIMIDEX 0.5 M.G. 5XD-TEST. PROP. 200 M.G.-SPIRONOTHIAZID 25 M.G.
20. G.H. 2 I.U. 3XD-CYTOMEL 50 M.C.G. A.M.-NOLVADEX 30 M.G. A.M./30 M.G. P.M.-ARIMIDEX 0.5 M.G. 5XD-SPIRONOTHIAZID 50 M.G.
21. CYTADREN 250 M.G. 4XD-NOLVADEX 30 M.G. A.M./ 30 M.G. P.M. ARIMIDEX 0.5 M.G. 5XD-SPIRONOTHIAZID 50 M.G

What was that, huh? There was a bodybuilder who stated with tears, " I have 22 days before a show. If I don't compete, I lose my contract." He was 250 pounds at 9 % bodyfat which is 22.5 LBS of fat total. To reach 4 %, he needed to drop about 12.5 LBS of fat and a great deal of water. At least he was not 15% bodyfat. He followed this protocol and actually looked great, but he won the dirtiest diet award.

The strategy he utilized was a high estrogen suppression/high cortisol suppression protocol. He had an added problem of being one of those who encounter the paradox listed in "Nolvadex". His body reacted by over producing DHEA. The Cytadren eliminated that problem quite well.

REPORTED ADVANCED CYCLES AND EFFECTS

By utilizing brief high dosages of DNP and successfully timing Primobolan Depot and Parabolan, he was able to retain almost all of his lean mass. GH/Cytomel aided in kicking up metabolism and increased protein absorption. He ate 500 grams of protein daily and broccoli 6 times daily adding flax and olive oil. He also drank 30 ML of glycerine in 16 oz of water daily beginning day #1, then twice daily (AM & PM) beginning day 6. 20 grams of glutamine was ingested daily, divided into 5 separate dosages with 2 grams of vitamin c 3 times daily. On non-DNP days, he utilized 50 MG of ephedrine and 325 MG of caffeine twice daily. He carb-depleted on day #17 &18 and carb-loaded on day #19-21.

Since his body was not producing much Aldosterone (the hormone that causes most water retention) he was able to dump most of his remaining water using Spironothiazid for the last 3 days which of course also suppresses Aldosterone. He looked fairly dry and tight at 219 pounds on contest day with full muscle bellies due to Testosterone Propionate's reputed unique carb loading qualities and Parabolan's high androgenic profile. A few had utilized this protocol also but added Winstrol Depot on DNP days. The lad was a furnace the entire 3 weeks but swears he felt good on contest day. What can I say except sometime odd things worked.

There are several protocols which were very effective in a 28 day period. Utilized properly they were notably healthier than any 12 week AAS protocol and very effective. The only problem I had encountered was seriously bloated bodybuilders. 28 days is not enough time for skin to tighten up in some cases. The crying competitor is a good example of action/reaction and working with, instead of against, the body. He had spent months gaining quality mass and the body naturally fought back attempting homeostasis by way of weight loss. He simply helped it and switched priority toward weight loss from liposytes (fat cells) instead of protein based tissues. Since he also ingested Omega 3 and 6 fatty acids (flax and olive oils) his body did not fight him much, nor did he compromise his health as much as most do with crazy fat less diets. But I must add as the supreme skeptic that I wonder about some long term side effects he may experience. He was also smart enough to keep water intake high until day 18 through continuous sipping all day long. As we know by now, cortisol, estrogens, and aldosterone were the big enemies of cuts and separation.

REPORTED CYCLES AND EFFECTS

ANDROGENS AND LIBIDO

Part of the attraction of anabolic/androgenic steroid and pro hormone use was a distinct increase in sex drive and sexual pleasure. Those readers who have utilized androgens know the joy of being seriously horny and the elevated sensitivity of sexual arousal. The down side was post-cycle libido crash many experienced for 2-12 weeks following initial androgen discontinuance. How much was libido elevated during androgenic usage? Watch a woman who is employing androgen cycles ride an exercise bike sometime. In some cases it is a better voyeuristic experience than the strip-tease scene in True Lies.

Let's look at sexuality from a biological stand point first. (Sorry, pictures just do not seem appropriate). There are a multitude of receptors in the brain that constantly monitor internal biochemistry. In some cases, specific substances activate receptors that alter behavior and sensations. Androgens activate, or stimulate, receptors in the preoptic aspects of the hypothalamus. These aspects respond by increasing the sensitivity of the pudendal nerve that provides tactile data from the pubic area. These sensations make us more easily stimulated (horny). Heightened sensitivity is not the whole equation however. Though a strong wind was enough in high school to be cause for a large book held low. Cortical activity is another piece of the puzzle. Neurotransmitters are chemicals our neurons utilize to communicate with each other and with different areas of our bodies. Dopamine is a neurotransmitter which is released by neurons in the medial preoptic area of the hypothalamus in response to male sexual activity, such as sexual arousal. In turn, an erection results when dopamine activates D-1 receptor sites within the brain. This is due to moderate levels of dopamine. When dopamine levels increase above moderate levels, the D-2 receptor sites are activated which causes male ejaculation.

When exogenous forms of androgens are introduced into the body, various peptide amino acid levels increase. These amino acids can act as neuromodulators which inhibit or prolong the effects of neurotransmitters. Including the role of dopamine in sex. This means our cortical androgenic receptors (and obviously related sexual response mechanisms) send and receive signals, or impulses, to various sites which enhance sensory and behavioral processing activity that maintains our ability to have sex as well as sex drive. When supraphysiological levels of androgens are introduced from outside sources, there is an over abundance of receptor site stimulation in the hypothalamus and a subsequent increased production of neuromodulating peptides. This in
short, makes people very horny during the first 3-8 weeks of an androgenic cycle. After a period of time...
these receptors-sites and sexual response areas adjust to these heightened levels and libido returns to normal. Unfortunately post-cycle androgen levels are even lower than pre-cycle levels due to androgen induced suppression of the HPTA. This results in desensitized receptor-sites and sexual tissue. This is partially due to heightened stimulation thresholds in the pudendal nerve (which would decrease sexual sensitivity). Of course, the post-cycle decrease in dopamine release and uptake can limit our ability

and desire to have sex as well. All of this plus psychological factors can, in some cases, lead to a lack of sexual interests, and even erectile disjunction.

Though I have noted no permanent post-cycle dysfunction in any one, *as of yet*, it is possible. This is more due to psychological factors than with biological. In most cases, the use of HCG and/or Clomid quickly returned normal sexual interest, but I am sure some have sought psychological help as well.

Some interesting methods (which no doubt will be cause for nasty letters from OB GYNS) that may quickly solve the problem are simple. L-Dopa is a precursor for dopamine and is available in health food shops selling herbal remedies. Another play-time idea involved rubbing HPC cyclodextrin forms of 4-androstenediol into the clitoris, penis, and testes areas. Liposomal or topicals worked also, but some reported that they would have been wiser to watch out for those that include alcohol in their formulas. GH also aids in receptor regeneration but there is little need in most cases. Not a suggestion of course, just points of interest.

COMING OFF LONG AAS CYCLES

Many top competitors in bodybuilding and power lifting stayed on AAS cycles for years. This was due to many factors (none of which were health). For bodybuilders, it was a matter of being in top shape so as to make a living from guest appearances, and the almost year-long competition circuits now common. For all, the loss of performance and muscle mass created a real concern.

As explained in the beginning of this book, anabolic/androgenic steroids (AAS) have strong anti-catabolic effects as well. While an athlete was administering exogenous androgens at a much higher level than the HPTA naturally produces, the body had been trying to re-establish homeostasis (an equilibrium or balance between anabolism and catabolism) by over producing cortisol from the adrenal glands. As you
know, cortisol is a very catabolic (tissue wasting) hormone. This was okay during high androgen levels from exogenous sources (occurring outside the body) because the AAS molecules were blocking the cortisol receptors. Thus preventing the cortisol from entering and down-regulating muscle mass build- up. Once the exogenous androgen supply was gone (evil music please…) the high level of cortisol raped and pillaged that newly built muscle mass. Second: As you realize, all anabolic /androgenic steroids decrease HPTA function to some extent. This means natural testosterone production was either lower or non existent. So the body was not able to restore natural anabolism/catabolism homeostasis with much help from the Leydig's cells in the testes. Third; due to the aromatization of most steroids, estrogen levels were high and estrogen sometimes became the dominant hormone. You will bench like a sissy too!

Before males put on a dress and females refuse to come off steroids, please realize much of this was reported to be avoided. Note: I said "much", and not "all". The fall from high androgenics was worse than the milder high anabolic. This was mostly due to longer AAS use periods and aromatization issues.

REPORTED CYCLES AND EFFECTS

The following was theoretical information I once offered during an interview that was in reply to the question "What if someone could not handle the psychological issues relating to coming off steroids and the eminent shrinking?"

Start by setting a stop date. Set your mental state as "going into the next phase" not the end of an era. Do this right and you will keep much of your AAS aided mass gains while losing some bodyfat.

Psychological Fix

4 weeks prior to a stop date begin reducing all high androgen orals such as Oxymetholone, Dianabol, and Methyltestosterone. Reduce daily dosages evenly over a 14 day period; so two weeks before a stop date all high androgen orals are discontinued. This is effective for the more anabolic and milder orals such as Winstrol tabs, Oxandrolone, and Primobolan-S tabs. If you are using Sustanon-250, Testosterone, Parabolan or other high androgenic injectables, begin reducing dosages about 4 weeks out from your stop date. So as example, we are using Sustanon-250 at a 750 MG weekly level. Starting at week 4 and counting down, we would drop to 500 MG a week, 250 MG a week, 125 MG a week, 62.5 MG a week. Do the same with all other high androgens if you are using milder injectables do the same except where possible switch to Equipoise or Durabolin from Anadur. These have high anabolic qualities which are more easily maintained post-cycle. Some people are real psychological weenies! (The idea of tapering is unnecessary when more advanced protocols such as Max Androgen Phases are utilized to replace more traditional cycles)

First let's deal with the catabolism/cortisol problem. We need an anti-catabolic that will not inhibit natural HPTA function. Ephedrine is good, but Clenbuterol is better, and Growth Hormone is best. If you have access (legally of course) to Cytadren, take it (see Cytadren) for 20 days only beginning 10 days before your stop date. Since it stops cortisol production by stopping the biosynthesis of all hormones it would be a bad idea to take Cytadren only, during the period where you are trying to restart natural biosynthesis of testosterone by the HPTA. (DUH!). There are other chemicals that have anti-catabolic qualities that also do not negatively effect the HPTA. Methoxyisoflavone is an over the counter product that works pretty well at a daily dosage of 800-1200mg. An athlete would begin taking Clenbuterol on his or her stop date. (*See info contained in the Clenbuterol section) Clenbuterol blocks cortisol receptor activity fairly well and, if continued for a period of 6-8 weeks, will allow good retention of gains realized during a steroid cycle. A small amount of T-3 thyroid hormone is anabolic. So many athletes have added 3-4 MG daily of Triacana, or 25-50 MCG of Cytomel for the first 2-4 weeks after their stop date.

REPORTED CYCLES AND EFFECTS

Now for elevated estrogen level suppression. Those who have not been using anti-estrogens during their AAS cycle should consider beginning to do so about 10 days before their stop date 20-40 MG of Nolvadex and 25-50 MG of Proviron daily usually is plenty for most athletes at this point. Most are able to end anti-estrogen use after 20-30 days and due to Proviron's qualities, a rapid increase in estrogen production is unlikely. Proviron will also help AAS cycle effectiveness as well. Of course Teslac is an excellent replacement for the Nolvadex/Proviron combination.

Re-establishing HPTA function as quickly as possible is paramount to maintaining acquired muscle mass. HCG and Clomid do a pretty good job for males. (Women do not have testicles! Remember?). Since HCG also increases estrogen from the aromatization of elevated endogenous Testosterone levels, anti-estrogens are helpful here also. 9 days before a stop date an athlete should administer 3000-5000 I.U. of HCG once every 3rd day (4 shots) followed by 3000-5000 I.U. of HCG every 5th day for 3 more injections. 50 MG of Clomid is taken twice daily beginning on the athlete's stop date for 5 days followed by 5-10 days of 50 MG daily. Remember Clomid's actions are effective for up to 20 days after discontinuance. So the HCG gets "the boys" back to work and normal size, then the Clomid stabilizes Hypothalamus and Pituitary Gonadal functions. Some athletes experience a growth rebound effect during this last phase if their steroid dosages were not too high and if they tapered off properly. Personally I have found 5 GMS of Creatine and 2-5 GMS of Glutamine with 200 MG of Alfa Lipoic Acid 2-3 times daily, and 4 GMS of D-Ribose, after work-outs beginning 2-4 days before my stop date very helpful in maintaining the higher ATP and Phosphocreatine levels enjoyed during cycles.

As to diet: a high protein intake of 1.5-2.5 GMs per pound of bodyweight should have been adhered during steroid cycles. It should also be followed post-cycle. But total calorie count after mass phase steroid cycles should be decreased slowly by 20-30 %. Those using a little T-3 after stop dates maybe able to maintain a some what higher calorie count but should keep an eye on fat deposits.

Training: ya, it sucks if you have been using high dosages of androgens and post cycle weights are down. But by cutting training volume by 10-15%, (total amount moved during a single work-out) you will avoid adding more catabolism due to over training. It is important not to just give up because the numbers are not what they were. Psychologically… dig deep. You will find you retained much more than you thought. Usually sets in the 6-8 rep range are best for maintaining mass.

If you did everything right both during and after cycles you should maintain 50-90% of the steroid induced gains. So allow your body to normalize its functions before thinking about doing it all again and you will be way ahead of where you started.

REPORTED CYCLES AND EFFECTS

Many pro's used the Insulin/GH/Thyroid Stack listed in "Cycles " during off phases and gained muscle mass. Some hard-core ideas are not necessarily intelligent choices. However, when utilized properly and intelligently, these cycles increased mass, receptor-site activity, and prepared the body for following AAS protocols... or simply aided in long term mass retention. Also see "Reported Advanced Cycles And Effects" for other techniques and protocols that have been employed.

BLOOD SCREENS

Any athlete using AAS is foolish to not monitor blood and urine tests. There are possible long term negative side effects due to stress and/or damage to organs such as kidneys, liver and heart. These organs can be negatively affected due to toxicity especially from oral c17-alfa alkylated steroids such as Anadrol-50 and Methyltestosterone. If life is not important and only training and results matter (then you are the type that scares me) a regular blood testing protocol has been noted as a great aid in maximizing results.

Often blood tests are available through small clinics, college clinics, chiropractors, and nurse practitioners upon request and with privacy. Of course, I strongly believe a sports doctor is the only choice for dependable interpretation and advice, but much can be learned by athletes by simply learning a few basics. Personally I avoid most advice from ENT'S, GP'S, and dentists concerning athletic health. Simply put in my opinion, they do not have a clue when it applies to athletes. I do have to add to that in saying that I do know of some exceptions that turned out to be some of the brightest and most insightful of all. Of course many seem to feel "M.D." stands for "Major Deity" and bestow advice they themselves lack any extensive knowledge of, but hey, they are good in their fields! Why else would they charge so damn much? I fully apologize to any who have invested the years necessary to acquire applicable statistical knowledge based on facts. Gee, anyone wonder why I chose research over a medical practice? Back to blood screens...I asked for a copy. The results usually came back within a few days and cost $75.00-$150.00.

The most common type of blood tests that provided valuable information was a Chemistry Panel/CBC. Different labs may run different tests that are similar such as an SMA-22, SMA-25-HDL, SMA-24-HDL, or other. A CBC (complete blood count) was added to those that lack one.

REPORTED CYCLES AND EFFECTS

BLOOD SCREENING TEST APPLICATIONS:

LIVER: LDH, SGOT, SGPT, GGTP, BILIRUBIN, BLOOD UREA NITROGEN (BUN) ALKALINE PHOSPHATASE.,
KIDNEYS: BLOOD UREA NITROGEN, SODIUM, CHLORIDE, PHOSPHORUS, CALCIUM, POTASSIUM, URIC ACID, CO2, CREATININE/BUN RATIO
HEART: TRIGLYCERIDES, CHOLESTEROL, SGPT, SGOT, POTASSIUM.
BONES: CALCIUM, ALKALINE PHOSPHATASE.
IMMUNE SYSTEM: GLOBULIN.
DIABETES: GLUCOSE.
NERVOUS SYSTEM: POSTASSIUM, CHLORIDE, SODIUM.

It is important to remember that hard training athletes, especially high intensity bodybuilders, will have differences in their blood tests when compared to a couch potato. Changes in SGPT and SGOT would normally suggest liver stress in a couch potato. However, transient changes of this type in a bodybuilder usually mean there are metabolic events taking place such as muscle tissue being broken down from intense work-outs. If the SGOT was high accompanied by a high alkaline phosphatase and/or a high LDH reading during a AAS cycle it meant the steroid was negatively affecting the liver. I felt that a complete blood count (CBC) was also important to request as well as tests for T-3 and T-4 thyroid hormone uptake. Part of the CBC is white blood cell count. This is important to athletes due to indications of infections. An elevated red blood cell count beyond the normal range was noted as common for athletes, which was cool since it increases oxygen transport capabilities. Anadrol-50 usually elevated red blood cell counts significantly. This added to vascularity, but if it was allowed to elevate too much, circulatory problems resulted. Since T-3 and T-4 are indicators of metabolism and anabolism, a high T-3 reading (30-35) was preferred for athletes.

It was not uncommon for liver enzyme readings (SGPT, SGOT) to be elevated significantly during the first weeks of an AAS cycle. Often blood screens taken a few weeks later showed normal ranges. This change in values was usually considered merely an adaptive process. If these values remained high for prolonged periods, was taken seriously since this indicates excessive liver stress. For the most part, avoiding oral c17-alfa-alkylated AAS prevented this, or at least improved when most reduced their use to no more than 4-6 weeks with reasonable dosages.

When reviewing blood screens, the athlete will note a column of test values placed somewhere to the right of the tests requested/performed. This is the athletes results. There will also be a normal reference range for comparison in this area, and the measurement used such as units, NG/DL (nanograms per decaliter) and so on. An athlete can use this information to evaluate improvements and declines in over all health by maintaining a log containing each blood screen, training, and diet information, and AAS schedules utilized. If an athlete's HDL and triglyceride values failed to drop back to pre-steroid values within a 3-4 month off period, AAS schedules were commonly reported to be halted until they did, and measures to correct the problem were taken. I have found some AAS users thought they were super heroes during cycles. They over extended and over dosed oral c17-alfa alkylated steroids drank too much alcohol, ate too many high saturated fat meals as a base diet, slept too little, did not drink at least a gallon of water daily, and smoked. When reviewing blood screens, I have noted dramatic changes due to this abuse. I have even had clients lie about cycles and the previously mentioned bad practices.

Another test athletes benefited from was a serum testosterone / estrogen panel. Obviously, this was useful only after AAS had been discontinued for at least 2 months. The panel shows total and free testosterone/estrogen levels as well as a normal reference range. The use of HCG/Clomid, and Proviron usually corrected low testosterone levels and Proviron or Teslac usually normalized estrogen levels. These use of these measures have been known to throw test results off as well, if they were not discontinued for about a months before re-testing. By the way, Nolvadex did show up as estrogen if taken during testing periods. Like I had to explain that?

NUTRITION

When a new client comes to me, I ask them to create a log containing work-outs, weights, reps, sets, exercises, cycles of supplements and anything else they have or are putting into their body's (including any prescription medications especially birth control and antibiotics), and dietary intake in a nutrition/training journal. Of course, past and present medical history with any blood tests are included. I then explain nutrition is more important for health and athletic progress than any of the prior information. Many of you will say "DUH!!" at this point, but I am willing to bet you did not always know that. Read on, though simple, you may learn a thing or two to help dial it all in.

The human body is this amazing pharmacology lab that manifests itself in an ever changing living work of art. What else can stir primal instincts the way an attractive athletic body can? Strength, power, muscle mass, symmetry, and a hard physique simply are incredibly sexy. Okay, any of you day-time whine talk show types, (fat is not normally attractive to most healthy people) when was the last time you thought... "look at the rolls of fat on that sex god or goddess"(?) or "Gee I wonder if I could get Rosie and Roseanne to pose nude?" The truth is sexuality is based first on looks and second on personality traits. What does this have to do with nutrition? **Everything!** Eat Big Macs and super-size those fries too often and your body will revolt by becoming anything but what you train for. The body fat percentages reported by some so-called hard-core athletes simply dumbfounded me!

The body needs protein (complete) carbohydrates, and fats (yes fats) to repair, supply energy, and maintain good health. As a bodybuilder these basic macro-nutrients and micro-nutrient containing foods are the raw materials utilized to build and shape your living work of art. Buy and learn to use a nutritional almanac.

In order for any training or supplemental protocol to reap the greatest results, an adequate supply of calories are necessary... and in the right ratios. Not everybody is the same, but some basic guide-lines can be utilized concerning nutrition. *Please read on as there is applicable information that follows useful to natural athletes as well.*

First let's discuss calories. Both protein and carbohydrates supply 4 calories per gram while fats provide 9 calories per gram. The body has a basic metabolic rate (BMR) which is the amount of calories necessary to maintain homeostasis (neither gaining or losing weight) at rest. Though some may not agree, most hard-core bodybuilder's BMR is 15-17 calories per pound of bodyweight daily. So for a 200 LB bodybuilder, 3000-3400 calories must be ingested daily to maintain homeostasis. Normally, to gain weight, a calorie count of 16-21 calories per pound of bodyweight must be ingested daily. To lose weight, a calorie count of 10-14 calories per pound of bodyweight must be ingested daily.

Ratios of Macro-nutrients are also paramount to create an environment for the best athletic and /or aesthetic results. For most non-obese clients I advise a general Macro-nutrient calorie distribution/ratio of 30-40% protein, 40-50% carbohydrates, and 20% fats. Those who tend to more readily store fat are advised to utilize higher protein protocols. Using our 200 LB bodybuilder as an example (while in a mass weight gain phase) utilizing 20 calories per pound of bodyweight daily: 20 x 200 =4000 calories. 40% protein = 400 G, 40% carbohydrates =400 G, 20% fat= 88.8 G. So 1600 calories from protein (400G x 4C=1600 C), 1600 calories from carbohydrates (400 G x 4C =1600 C), and 800 calories from fats (88.8 G x 9C =799C). Another way to look at this example would be 2G of protein, 2G of carbohydrates, 0.45 of fats per pound of bodyweight daily. It is interesting to watch physical transitions for those who have not utilized higher protein intakes before. If they consume the same total calories per day as they had prior to switching to high protein intake, they will lose fat while increasing lean muscle mass. This is simple to explain. For every 100 calories of protein consumed, up to 25 calories will be burned through digestion and an increase in metabolism. But for every 100 calories of carbohydrates or fats consumed, only about 5 calories will be burned through digestion. This is also why most experience an increase in body temperature after eating a predominantly high protein meal, but get lazy after a mostly fat and/or complex carbohydrate meal. Protein not only increases metabolic rate (the rate at which calories are utilized for heat, building, and repair) it is also anabolic. And the body has more difficulty converting it to fat stores than it does carbohydrates and fats. Protein can also be quickly utilized as an energy source. Pretty cool, huh? However, carbohydrates and fats play very important roles in health and athletic success.

PROTEIN

Protein is the most under rated (and necessary) anabolic substance legally available anywhere. How important is it to bodybuilders and athletes? About 10% of your body's total protein is contained in skin while muscle contains about 50% of your body's total protein. The rest is contained in organs, enzymes, circulatory, etc.

Protein is made up of building blocks called amino acids. Amino acids are large molecules containing carbon, nitrogen, hydrogen and oxygen. Some amino acids include other organic chemicals in their compound such as phosphorus, copper, iodine, and sulfur. Basically speaking, this means that proteins are complex structures and each protein structure is an assembly of amino acids and other organic chemicals.

Amino acids are linked together by peptides, some of which are the body's vital nitrogenic compounds. For instance, Growth Hormone, Insulin, and Insulin-Like-Growth-Factor-1 are specific sequences of amino acids.

Proteins are either complete or incomplete. Complete protein simply means that it contains at least the minimal amounts of amino acids to sustain life. Which of course under lines the fact that a high protein "content" does not necessarily mean a high quality protein. It is the essential amino acid pattern and ratio that counts most. The essential amino acids are L-Leucine, L-Isoleucine, L-Valine, (These three are branch chain amino acids or BCAA'S) L-Lysine, L-Threonine, L-Methionine, L-Phenylalanine, and L-Tryptophan. The body can not make essential amino acids from others.

Non-essential amino acids are: L-Alanine, L-Arginine, Aspartic Acid, Glutamic Acid, L-Cystine, L-Glycine, L-Histidine, L-Proline, L-Serine, L-Tyrosine, and L-Glutamine. Non-essential amino acids can be made from other in the body's amino acid pool.

A note of interest: It is very difficult to get enough Glutamine and Arginine from normal diets. A hard training athlete should consume 20-100 G of Glutamine and 5G of a Arginine daily.

Protein digestion starts in the mouth and continues in your stomach and small intestines. This is due to pepsin, which is secreted in the saliva and obviously the gastric juice, followed by pancreatic enzymes, then absorbed by the mucosal cells in the small intestines. In short, the digestive system breaks down protein into its peptide amino acid structures so they can be absorbed in the small intestine via the
mucosal cells. When protein/amino acids enter the small intestines and transverse the mucosal membranes, they enter the circulatory system. From the there the amino acids enter the liver through the portal vein. Your liver decides amino acid intake, as well as the amount of assimilated amino acids your body can use to build- up muscle tissue. This is a major function of most anabolic chemistry. AAS increase the amount of amino acids passed into the blood stream to muscle tissue for growth and repair. Which of course means AAS are protein sparing in this respect as well. Duh!

Your liver is also a site for amino acid synthesis such as Serine, Glycine, Glutamic acid and Glutamine. This means that the liver will hang on to some amino acids for bio-synthesis while passing others onto the general circulation for transportation to other organs and tissue.

I had a client whom thought Anadrol-50 was candy. He had damaged his liver enzymic process to a point where synthesis of Glutamine was quite poor. Since Glutamine makes up 50-70% of total muscle amino acid pools, and is used to repair and replace the stomach lining every few days, growth stopped.

Your body has no long-term storage system for protein as it does for carbs and fats. The liver and circulatory system stores amino acids for a very short term, while muscle mass serves as the largest "temporary" store house of free amino acids. Maintaining these amino acid stores requires eating/drinking complete proteins every 2.5-3 hours. If not, then when your organs and muscle tissue can not get what they need from circulation, the muscle is catabolized. 2 steps forward and one step back makes for poor progress. Remember, the body can also convert branch chain amino acids into glucose/glycogen for energy.

NUTRITION

Complete protein sources area must for all, and even more so for those seeking increased mass and strength and fewer injuries. Good examples are lean red meat, lamb, fish, poultry, cheese, eggs, and milk. A mixture of complete sources is best. This is simple logic. Earlier I said a complete protein contains at least the "minimal" amount of amino acids to sustain life. The operative word is "minimal" here. If your amino acid pool is short on any one essential amino acid, then the whole muscle building process is compromised. This is why total veggie diets make no sense for athletes. Vegetable sources of protein are not complete, though various combinations do make up complete sources. Still, for serious muscle mass, the necessary volume of food with a veggie diet would be far too much for most to consume daily.

How much protein? The American recommended daily intake for protein is for couch potatoes. They really do not tear down enough protein based tissue to need much more than 60 grams daily. But really, you probably do not care about couch jockey facts if you are reading this book! With most of my clients, I have utilized a minimum of 1 GM of protein per LB of bodyweight per day. Note I said "minimum". Muscle is protein, training and stress breaks it down, supraphysiological levels of protein repair and increase growth of muscle tissue. Simple. If you have read a muscle magazine in the last decade, you have read about nitrogen balance. If you are in negative nitrogen balance, you are catabolizing muscle; if you are in positive nitrogen balance, you are in an anabolic state, or tissue growth state. Protein supplies nitrogen. Any mystery so far? More protein, means more nitrogen retention, means more muscle… to a point. New clients are required to write down everything they eat and drink for 10 days. Their protein sources, amounts, and timing is evaluated. Also carbs and fats to the same extent of course. More on that later. Once a base line is established, I begin increasing only protein intake about 50 GM per day until they begin to add adipose (fat) tissue. Then re-evaluate carb and fat sources. For "most" serious athletes, this is somewhere around 1.5-2.5 GMS of protein per LB of bodyweight with a total calorie intake of 18-20 calories per LB of bodyweight. This calorie count (18-20 calories per LB of bodyweight) is for adding mass.

There is a truism athletes face often without realizing it. You are what you absorb, not just what you eat. When you eat whole /complete protein source food such as round steak, your teeth grind up the fibers into smaller pieces. If you do not chew your food, digestive enzymes /juices fail to access enough area of these fibers to fully break them down. Less area exposed, less digestion, less amino acids to supply growth and repair.

Since one of the functions of protein synthesis is to manufacture digestive enzymes, unchewed food causes a drop in protein digestion and ultimately….retardation of growth.

I experienced difficulty eating enough whole/complete protein foods some years back simply because I felt full too easily when eating large amounts day in and day out. Speaking to clients and answering letters, I found many hard gainers shared this growth limiting problem. High tech solution! Small fibers digest easier than large. Enter "The

NUTRITION

Blender Solution". Try: 6 oz tuna, 1 oz whey protein, 8 oz diet coke. Ya, it sounds bad but actually they taste pretty good and it supplies 60 GMS of protein.

Our bodies utilize proteins in many ways. Repair, a source of energy, and even as raw materials for hormones and anti-oxidants. With all this going on, it's no wonder why hard training athletes need more protein than the average couch potato.

Most lean meats such as round and flank beef steak, fish, lamb, and pork, supply 6-7 G of complete protein per ounce. A 200 LB bodybuilder consuming 2G of protein per pound of bodyweight daily would therefore need to eat about 4 pounds of lean meats daily. Wow! That is a lot of chewing and a nice chunk of change. Enter protein powders.

When it comes to protein supplements, there is a great deal of confusion. This is mostly due to muscle magazine articles that are actually ads to sell specific brands, and high tech terms leading to misdirection and profit. The ads all sound scientific and even include medical references. However, many are misleading.

(BV) Biological Value is a common term. It is actually an attempt to measure how efficiently the body utilizes a certain protein. BV is a scientific method that measures nitrogen uptake - vs.- nitrogen excretion from a given amount/type of protein. I realize this is simplified to many researchers, but I am writing practical info not a research paper. The BV of whey protein is commonly listed as 104. This is off actually because 100 is the maximum BV possible. The extra 4% is a calculation that represents a margin of error. BV is not a universally accepted measure for protein quality. This is mostly due to the fact that BV tests are always performed on subjects in a fasted state. This affects nitrogen uptake differently than if subjects were in a fed state (Like most bodybuilders don't eat constantly?). Simply stated, not eating significantly alters the way the body absorbs nitrogen from protein. How often have you seen a BV of 159? This was an author who confused the difference between BV and chemical score. Chemical score involves measuring amino acid activity in the body, not retention and loss. Again, since the highest BV score is 100, the 159 BV is a bit stretched. But hey, it sounds good huh?

Ultrafiltration is a French originated process that uses a membrane filtering system. In its raw form, whey contains protein, lactose, ash, and some minerals. This should not surprise anyone since whey is the bi-product of cheese or casein production from milk. The original ultrafiltration method separated the ash and lactose from the whey protein resulting in a product providing about 35-70% protein. As the process improved the protein, content was elevated to up to 80% -86.5% protein content. Ultrafiltration provides a decent product with
many useful protein fractions. Though ultrafiltration produces a lower protein content compared to ion-exchange and contains slightly higher fat and lactose levels, it is usually the better way. It contains more lactoferrin, proteasepeptone, and glyromacropeptides.

Ion-exchange revolves around ion properties. (What?) Simply put, ions have positive and negative charges. The process involves a resin that isolates the protein material from whey, and adjustments in PH (acidity level), initially. Then the use of ultrafiltration methods that further concenttrated the protein were included. Bipro patented this process and called it whey protein isolate. This new technique has the unique quality of providing 90% protein and less than 1% lactose. Later Davisco bought and continued to produce Bipro. Sounds great but there are some problems with whey isolates. Whey isolate contains as much as 70% beta-lactabumin which is a much higher percentage than found naturally in cows milk and significantly different than the alfa-lactabumin. The reason this is significant is due to the fact that beta-lactoglobulin is much more allergenic to humans than alfa- lactoglobulin. Another problem with ion-exchange whey isolate is that the process does not favor the retention of vital smaller whey protein factions such as lactoferrin that have considerable health benefits. Human milk contains up to 17% lactoferrin, where as cows milk contains about 1%. It seems obvious nature intended lactoferrin to be high for human needs. However, the good news is that several companies are now happy to sell to you whey protein isolates that have had the original lactoferrin mixed back into their product (for another fee of course).

Lactalbumin is an often misused synonym for whey protein. In the supplemental protein industry, lactalbumin is a reference to whey protein that has been manufactured by a heat and acid process. Since heat and acid both denature vital protein fractions (broken a part = denature), and lactalbumin is a high heat process, the product retains few of its original bodybuilding qualities. It also contains above normal levels of beta-lactoglobulin. Biological activity sucks.

Fat content in whey protein products is quite deceptive. What is listed on the label is only free fat. This is fat that is not bound to the whey protein structure. The reason for this is simple. To test whey for total fat content, acid hydrolysis would be necessary. Normally whey protein fat content is tested utilizing an ether extract method. This results in a much lower fat content that "sounds" great. The fat bound in the whey protein structure is higher in cholesterol and saturated fat than normal cows milk. But in truth, for every 50 G of milk derived protein the cholesterol content will usually be 50-75 milligrams. In 20 G of whey protein concentrate, the cholesterol level will most likely be 50 MG or higher. Sad since the lie is actually a benefit. You see, included in the fat globule membrane of whey or milk are growth factors such as IGF-1. Take out the fat and lose the growth factors.

Mother's milk is an often coined term for products that mimic the natural mother's milk contents. Actual human mother's milk contains about 40-50% casein and 50-60% whey, and about 17% lactoferrin with no beta-lactoglobulin. As I said earlier, mother's milk contains alfa lactoglobulin. This is very different from cow's milk which contains about 80% casein and 20% whey with 1% lactoferrin being average. Lactoferrin has anti-viral activity, and is a potent immune system booster. Obviously this is an advantage for new born human (rug rats) since they lack complete immune system functions. Remember the fact that human mother's milk dominant protein fraction is alfa-lactalbumin? Well, there is a research project on going which claims acid folded alfa-lactabumin and lactoferrin have the ability to kill all cancer cells. Gee, wonder where my next research project might be? Anyway, lactoferrin has been shown in some studies to speed healthy tissue re-growth. Yes, anabolic. For the reason of high expense for purified lactoferrin and the high beta-lactoglobulin content in cows milk, a mother's milk supplement is just not possible for commercial sales. But the ratios of casein and whey can be duplicated. Since cows milk is 20% whey and 80% casein and commercial milk protein contains this ratio, the additional whey protein is simply mixed either by a manufacturer or by you at home. For those of you who hate math, simply mix 1 pound of casein protein with 1 pound whey protein to achieve the basic 50/50 ratio of mother's milk.

Glutamine makes up about half of the body's amino acid pool. Gee, do you think this amino acid maybe important? Hard training athletes should consume 15-25 G of glutamine daily in 3-8 divided dosages. Can you get enough glutamine from protein powders? That depends. I am looking at a bottle of whey protein while I write this. On the front label it states (proudly) "over 2 grams of glutamine per 50 gram serving", like they did some high tech mixture. Whey protein naturally contains about 6% peptide bonded glutamine. So about 6 G per 100 G of protein. Where did my other gram of glutamine go? The other milk protein, casein, contains 8-10 percent glutamine. Peptide bonded glutamine refers to glutamine that is bonded to at least one other amino acid by a peptide bond (ya, protein s & m) which is also referred to as a peptide chain. Bonded amino acids are always superior to free of "L" forms since free or "L" are very unstable in the presence of heat, water, or PH changes. Since peptide glutamine is much more stable, it is more resistant to hostile environments such as the stomach. Peptide amino acids are also absorbed much more efficiently. For example, peptide glutamine is absorbed as much as 10 times more efficiently than L-Glutamine. Beware when a product label reads 5 or 10 G of peptide bonded glutamine per serving. Since the weight of a peptide differs depending on how many other amino acids are in each peptide chain. So yes, if you ingest enough protein powder daily, you could get enough glutamine. Just drink a pound of whey concentrate daily like I do. Or not!

Micellar casein is native milk casein protein. It differs from caseinate in that it is not made by adjusting the acidic PH value more toward neutral by using an alkali. Native micellar casein contains several biologically active peptide sequences that are health and growth promoting for athletes. Casein protein is digested and absorbed more slowly than whey proteins. In fact plasma amino acid levels are prolonged from casein ingestion resulting in a distinct anti-catabolic effect. Whereas whey protein is quickly digested and can cause a supraphysiological plasma amino acid level (anabolic), casein can protect against muscle protein loss. The main problem with whey protein being so rapidly absorbed is that much of it can be shuttled to the liver where the amino acids can be oxidized for energy needs rather than muscle proteins synthesis. This would be advantages during dieting phases, but not during mass gaining protocols. So do you buy whey, casein, both, or what? Quick absorption can be a problem with hydrolyzed (pre-digested) proteins as well since they rapidly pass through the stomach into the intestines.

NUTRITION

Protein sources really are not that hard to deal with. Assuming you are a serious athlete, you ingest 1-2 G of protein daily per pound of bodyweight. If you weigh 200 LBS, that would be 200-400 G daily. The best protocol would utilize breaking this into at least 4 meals, with 6-8 being better. This allows for a continuous supply of amino acids from protein to sustain growth and repair while reducing catabolism. Using 400 G of protein daily as an example, 200 G would come from lean meats, fish, eggs, and dairy products. The other 200 G would come from a good quality protein powder. If you are eating all these slow digesting whole complete proteins from meat, fish, eggs, and dairy products, casein just is not as good as whey, nor is it necessary. If you ingest better than 60% of your daily protein from protein powders, a mixture of 50% casein and 50% whey concentrate would be best. Mixing one ounce of whey with 16 oz. of low fat milk works pretty well also. Tuna milk shakes are still the better choice if you have the stomach for them. Really! Each meal or shake should provide 30-60 G of protein. As to the body not being able to handle more than 30 G of protein at one time? I searched everywhere for any legit research to support this skinny persons belief. Nope, none, no where. I will keep looking!

CARBOHYDRATES

As a bodybuilder or serious athlete, you already know the importance of adequate carbohydrate intake to fuel glucose and glycogen production for intense work-outs and recovery. You also already know carbs, like fats, are anti-catabolic in that they aid in preventing the break down of muscle proteins (amino acids) for use as an alternative fuel source. But did you know carbohydrates aid in Insulin release manipulation? Of course you did. You can't pick up a muscle magazine today without being bombarded with ads stating "glucose aids in creatine storage in muscle cells by increasing Insulin release" or "our protein contains "0" carbs so you won't get fat". Kind of confusing, isn't it? My goal in this section is to simplify the issue with actual facts, not advertising ploys.

Carbs really are easy to understand. All carbs are converted into a blood sugar called glucose due to digestion processes. Depending on the glycemic rating of any given carb, from a scale of 0-100 (100 being the highest Insulin release stimulation) Insulin is released by the pancreas.

As an example, pure dextrose rates 100 on the glycemic index rating system, while pure starch would rate 0. As a rule of thumb, the lower the glycemic index score, or rating, the slower the digestion process and circulatory uptake. Therefore, the longer the carbohydrate fuel source will last for energy expenditure due to the slowed digestion/absorption factor. Also, since a lower glycemic index scoring carb causes less Insulin release, there is less fat storage "possible". Before going on, there is a newer supplement and food industry rating system for carbohydrates called a Dextrose Equivalence or D.E. Value. It utilizes the same scoring system as the glycemic index scoring method and often refers to maltodextrins, which we will discuss in awhile.

NUTRITION

When eating for mass gain, fat deposits can become a problem if too many high glycemic carbs are ingested. But it is paramount for athletes to store enough glycogen, derived from carbohydrates, for recovery and intense workouts. High intensity work-outs aid in altering fat conversion and storage by effecting enzymes and hormones if favor of muscle growth and fuel.

There are many dietary strategies that also aid in altering the ratio in favor glycogen storage. First, lower glycemic index carbs will cause a lower Insulin release by avoiding a supraphysiological blood circulatory level of glucose. This is turn allows the body to slowly convert glucose into glycogen allowing muscle tissue to absorb a higher amount of glycogen. Carbohydrates that are below 50 in glycemic index rating are best. Potatoes, yams, sweet potatoes, brown rice, pasta's made of whole wheat flour, oats, whole grain breads and vegetables are the best natural choices for most athletes. A good strategy for reducing fat deposits is to eat carbs from veggie sources on one day and a mixture of the rest listed above on the next. By alternating the two basic sources, the body gains an advantage by action/reaction simply because it does not become over loaded. Simple but it works quite well.

It can be difficult to consume enough low glycemic carbohydrates daily. Since the body will utilize amino acids as a fuel source in times of low glycogen stores (yes, carbs are anti-carbolic in this sense) it is necessary though. Assuming a hard training bodybuilder will need to ingest as much as 3.5 grams of carbohydrates daily per pound of bodyweight. This can mean major jaw action and too much time. The use of maltodextrin supplements can make this so much easier. I use D.E. 20 mixed with protein powders or even in blender solution shakes. D.E. 20 is a maltodextrin powder with a glycemic index rating of (surprise) 20. It is not only cheaper gram for gram than whole foods, the nutrient is much better absorbed and less time consuming.

As a rule, hard training bodybuilders will need to ingest 2-3 grams of carbohydrates per pound of body weight daily. Complex carbs from grains, potatoes, yams, sweet potatoes, and veggies are best. Simple carbs such as sucrose (table sugar) and glucose can be serious fat causing goodies, if miss timed or ingested too often.

In future articles and books, I will write in depth on diet strategies. Since this book is about reported chemical enhancing techniques, I will stop at the basics, merely to give the reader an idea of necessary diet needs. Simply stated, if a bodybuilder wants to be huge, major carbohydrate ingestion is necessary to prevent catabolism and fuel intensity training.

(Unless the athlete learns the dietary techniques and strategies that are coming in future books in this series too)

"LOSING BODY FAT WAS EASY"

I know a very intelligent and attractive lady from southern California who told my spouse and I that she paid a personal trainer about $700.00 - $900.00 per month. Upon asking about her progress several months later, she replied "he told me it will take time". What? My job as a professional trainer and consultant is to produce the greatest results in the shortest period of time. If I can not cause significant changes in a client's muscular structure within 60 days, I am nothing more than a thief. I hate these people who take a few Internet classes, take some ridiculous personal trainers certification test, and charge their even less knowledgeable clients for what they themselves do not know. But I see it every day. Results of course are dependent upon clients not making phone calls during work-outs, but few people have difficulty giving up their undivided attention for 45-60 minutes 3-5 times per week. Those that cannot, no one can help. The lady has major potential by the way.

Losing bodyfat or gaining muscle mass (even altering genetic shapes and sizes) is not all that difficult. I constantly read or hear about trainers and athletes who do unhealthy things simply because it works in "appearance". An example is dozens of bodybuilders who diet for 2-4 months on nothing but turkey, chicken, or tuna, and brown rice. Give me a break! Where are the life preserving (not to mention muscle mass, tendon and joint health supporting and fat burning essential fatty acids (okay, go read Prostaglandins one more time) and proper ratio of amino acids? These diets can cause a great lean appearance, but they can also cause permanent damage. And it just is not necessary. But, in truth there are many unhealthy things done in the name of aesthetics by many.

The following is a list of items that were reported to significantly have altered fat to muscle ratios quickly. Any one or combination of these items has been successfully utilized to reduce fat stores. All of these are explained within this book to some extent or boringly in depth. I plan to write an update in the future on training /diet/supplemental strategies that shredded most anyone in 28-42 day unless they were a blimp.

1. Any IGF-1 producing androgen such as Testosterone Propionate.
2. Any Testosterone stacked with any anti-estrogen (some added Primobolan Depot for more kick).
3. 200 MCG of T-4 or 50 MCG of T-3 Two-days on-Two days off.
4. Clenbuterol 80-120 MCG daily, 2 days on alternated with 50 MG of Ephedrine /350 MG of Caffeine.
5. 6 MG of DNP per KG of bodyweight daily for 5-10 days.
6. 6 G of Linoleic Acid and 2 G of Linolenic Acid daily (Flax Seed Oil).
7. 1 teaspoon of Virgin Olive Oil daily.
8. 2 I.U. of GH 2-4 times daily.
9. Replace equal amount of carbohydrate calories with MCT oil (Up to 3 TBS daily).
10. Ingest 2 G of protein per pound of bodyweight daily.
11. Eat broccoli 5-6 times daily.
12. Eat 4-5 OZ. Of salmon every 3rd day.
13. Take 4 G of Glutamine per 25 LB of bodyweight daily.
14. Drink 2 gallons of water daily.

15. Take 5 G of Vitamin-C in the morning.
16. Take 20 G of Amino Acid tablets per 100 LBS of bodyweight daily
    (A 250 LB bodybuilder ingested 50G daily)
17. Eat only what is on this list.
18. Have lots of sex, the best cardio there is.
19. 1 MG or Arimidex and 40 MG of Nolvadex daily, 2 days on-2 days off.
20. Smile more.
21. 250 MG of Cytadren 2 x d, 2 days on-2 days off.
22. (Drop water weight) 25-50 MG of Spironothiazid daily for 3 days.
23. 25 ML of Glycerin in 8 OZ water in AM and before bed.
24. Trade carbohydrate calories for protein calories gram for gram.

SUPPLEMENTAL CREATINE
(Methylgluanido-Acetic Acid)

Creatine is a nitrogenic compound naturally manufactured in the liver from the three amino acids Methionine, Arginine, and Glycine and is transported to the muscles via the circulatory system. Creatine is transformed into phosphocreatine and is stored in the muscle. (Also called Creatine Phosphate or CP) The conversion of Creatine to C.P. is aided by the enzyme Creatine Kinase (CK) in bonding the Creatine to a high energy phosphate group. Once C.P. is stored in a cell, it remains until it is used as a high energy source called Adenosine Triphosphate (ATP). Normally the body produces about 1-2 grams of Creatine daily, and of course, metabolizes about 2 grams daily also. The average person stores over 100 grams of Creatine in muscle tissue and in the liver. When C.P. is utilized in natural ATP regeneration, one of the by-products is called Creatinine which is then removed by the kidneys and eliminated in urine. Since Creatinine levels are checked as an indicator of proper kidney function (and as a stress indicator for the heart) one might assume supplemental Creatine would place undue stress on the kidneys. This just is not the case. In fact, a 5 year study showed no negative side effects from continuous Creatine supplementation. Pretty cool, huh? Creatine is also absorbed form animal and fish protein. In fact, I pound of red meat contains about 2 grams.

Loading phases (contrary to the belief of some half-experts) are very important to bodybuilders and strength athletes when using any supplemental creatine product. The goal is to raise muscle creatine concentrations to a supraphysiological level as quickly as possible. If the creatine product is simply ingested at a daily so-called maintenance dosage the result will be an action/reaction type response in which the body down-regulates CP storage enzyme secretion thus limiting the actual possible muscle cell CP hyper-concentration (total muscle cell CP content). Since ATP is the basis of all growth, and CP is the basis of ATP regeneration, does the elimination of a loading-phase seem maximum progress goal oriented? This increases nitrogen retention and creates an osmotic effect within muscle cells. You have often read about cell volumization in every creatine ad. If a bodybuilder is using creatine stores as fast as they come in, how can a supraphysiological (above normal concentration) saturation exist? Duh! Load first.

All AAS increase nitrogen retention and testosterone tends to notably create an even greater osmotic effect. Both facets increase protein synthesis and strength. Nitrogen retention is anabolic simply because amino acids are not exiting muscle cells. They therefore are available for repair and growth instead of exiting or becoming an energy source.

Osmotic reactions simply mean there is an elevated level of intracellular nutrients, including water, available. The way an osmotic response effects or induces an elevation in strength is basic physics. Try benching on a waterbed. (No, I mean weights) There is little in the way of structural integrity. Now, if you filled that waterbed with much more water, thus creating a firmer structure, the ability of it and you to support and leverage a higher weight load will improve. The osmotic effect is not simply water retention. It is an increase intracellularly (inside muscle cells) of growth nutrients, including C.P., for increased cellular repair and growth. If it were outside of the cells, you would be very smooth, but this is not the case. Strength increases from proper Creatine supplementation range from 5-10% and body weight increases (over a 2 month cycle) range from 3-10%. This means a bodybuilder that weighs 200 LBS and bench presses 200 LBS for 10 reps max can realistically expect to weigh 206-220 LBS and bench press 210-220 LBS for 10 reps by the end of a 2 month cycle. Results from any following Creatine cycles tend not to be as impressive as first time cycles. Unfortunately about 20% of Creatine users do not respond to Creatine. This is usually due to an inability to get the Creatine into muscle cells. But there is a solution.....Read on.

CREATINE SUPPLEMENTS

Creatine Monohydrate (CM)

This is the most common form of Creatine in the supplement industry. CM contains about 850-880 MG of free Creatine per 1000 MG of weight. When loading on C.M., daily intake will total .3 grams per kilo of bodyweight (a 220 LB bodybuilder would need 30 G per day for 5 days -100 KG x 0.3 =30 G) divided into 3-5 daily dosages, followed by a daily maintenance dosage of 5-15 GMS. C.M. dissolves much better in warn water and about 16 OZ per 5 GMS is a must. Simple fact is if it does not dissolve, it does not absorb. Undissolved C.M. crystals tend to cause intestinal irritations, and in some cases, the runs. This is due to the body's need to flood the intestinal tract with excess water to flush out the irritant. Try that on a heavy squat day!

The highest purity is a must when buying creatine products. Many brands utilize SKW Creatine (now Tracolabs), which is manufactured in Germany. When tested by HPLC (high pressure liquid chromatography) method, SKW creatine usually ranges between 99.5-99.8% pure Creatine Monohydrate. The by-product content is usually Dieyandiamide-20ppm, Creatinine-50 ppm, and Dihydrotriazine-n.d. (none detected). Ppm stands for parts per million. USA produced Creatine normally ranges in purity from 80-95% pure Creatine with by-product contents of Dicyandianmide 300-400-ppm, Creatinine 190-2500-ppm, and Dihydroltriazinde 90-410-ppm. Don't even think about China's Nanjing or Jeangsu produced Creatine. Purity ranges from 50-70% pure Creatine with other interesting things. Look for the Creapure R registered trade mark on Creatine Products. It means SKW manufactured Creatine.

There are other forms of Creatine. Creatine Citrate is very water soluble but requires twice the amount to equal the same amount of Creatine Monohydrate. Creatine Phosphate is another option but cost to effectiveness makes the product less effective than Creatine Monohydrate.

Many people have tried the second generation creatine products. These are products containing other nutrients to increase muscle cell absorption of C.P. There is a direct correlation between the amount of Creatine absorbed (not merely ingested) and results. At one time, the market was flooded with products containing Dextrose (glucose) and Creatine. They did improve cellular absorption to some extent. The reason is Insulin.

213

(Yes, go back and read the whole section on Insulin again) Okay, Insulin is a storage hormone. When the body senses excess blood sugar (Glucose), the pancreas releases Insulin to force it into cells including muscle tissue. So by utilizing a high glycemic carb such as Dextrose, an Insulin spike is created and more carbs and amino acids enter cells. Oh, did I mention Creatine is an amino acid? The idea helped, but the problem is timing. After ingesting Creatine, blood circulatory levels peak at about 90 minutes. So what? After ingesting Dextrose, circulatory levels peak and cause an Insulin spike after about 30 minutes, and is on the down side when the peak levels of Creatine arrive.

The third generation of Creatine products employed natural Insulin optimizers (they make Insulin receptors more sensitive in muscle tissue) and mimickers. The first real break through was the Insulin mimicker… ALFA LIPOIC ACID.

Alfa Lipoic Acid? Without writing an ad for anybody, let me simply say that Lipoic Acid increases receptor site sensitivity while also mimicking Insulin's actions. Though my choice for micro-nutrient of the year award for maximum creatine transport without an increase in bodyfat synthesis would be 4-hydroxy- Isoleucine. Major potential here!

For Creatine supplementation to result in an increase in strength and protein synthesis, the cellular concentration level must reach 20 MMOL/KG DM. During a 5 day loading periods with a high glycemic carbohydrate such as Dextrose and Creatine, the level reaches MMOL/KG DM. When Creatine levels increase in muscle cells, the active Creatine transporters are down-regulated, so less Creatine is transported. This could be avoided if the Creatine is fortified with the Creatine substrate 3-guanidinopropionate. Second, Creatine cannot be diffused across the muscle cell membrane without the co-transports of sodium and chloride ions to cause enough electrical charge to transport the Creatine. (Table salt) Other up-regulators of Creatine transport are Clenbuterol and Ephedrine as well as T-3 thyroid hormone. These are quite potent transporters to say the least. Of course, Insulin (Humulin) and IGF-1 are very effective Creatine transporters. Though Dextrose is an excellent trigger for Insulin release there is a higher glycemic carbohydrate. Malt extracts contain a mixture of maltodextrins, glucose, and dextrose which are made of glucose chains of 3-7 gycosyl units. And guess what? The small intestines absorb glucose chains containing 3-7 gycosyl units much faster than dextrose. This means a higher and stronger Insulin spike. So barley malt extract or maltodextrin is a better carb choice and can be utilized in lower levels than 75 GMs per dose. Whey protein also creates an Insulin spike which can prolong the spike from high glycemic carbs. By the way, caffeine intake over 400 MG daily, as well as the isoflavone genistein in soy protein inhibit creatine transport. Genistein inhibits tyrosine kinases which is necessary for nutrient transport.

The body has 3 periods when creatine uptake is highest: After a nights sleep, the body is in a fasted stated due to a period of natural GH pulses (about half of your daily total GH production is released during the first 4 hours of sleep) and a prolonged period without nutrients. This results in an up-regulation of nutrient transporters and enzymes which favor intramuscular uptake of nutrients, including Creatine.

When Creatine is ingested 45-90 minutes before a work-out, an athlete can take advantage of the training induced increases in blood flow to muscle tissue to transport essential nutrients across muscle cell membranes. (This also acts as a buffer to lactic acid) Since high intensity work-outs trigger the release of adrenal hormones such as Epinephrine and Norepinephrine, the cellular uptake of nutrients is improved. Remember, Ephedrine increases cellular uptake? Well Ephedrine is an Epinephrine Mimicker.

Within the first 45-90 minutes following an intense work-out, the body is in a very nutrient receptive state. Heavy training reduces muscle glycogen stores (glycogen comes from blood sugars such as carbs) and receptor-sites for nutrients become sensitive. This means the body is in a catabolic state requiring nutrient supply. Several storage enzymes are up- regulated and creatine (CP) levels are lower which of course means intramuscular nutrient storage ability is at a high level. It also means the muscle cells need ATP regeneration.

So what was the best Creatine mixture currently available?

16-32 OZ of water	300 MG of Lipoic Acid and/or 50 MG of D-Pinitol
5-10 G of Creatine	A source of 3-guanidinopropionate
250-500 MG of salt	4-25 G of Glutamine
50 G of Malt Extract	30 G-50 G of whey protein
25 MG of Ephedrine	1 MG of Triacana

CREATINE AND MUSCLE HYPERPLASIA

How many times have you heard some gym supplement expert say that the weight gained from creatine is just water? Well, researchers wrote an interesting paper concerning creatine called: **Dangott, B. Schulz, E. Mozdziak, P.E. "Dietary Creatine Monohydrate supplementation increases satellite cell mitotic activity during compensatory hypertrophy" in International Journal of Sports Medicine 21:13-16,2000.** What the heck is that, huh?

Satellite-cells are the "stem cells" of skeletal muscle which the body utilizes to produce or add new cells and fibers to existing cells. This means satellite-cells are used to: (1) Repair damaged muscle fibers from training (2) To add cells to existing fibers to make them larger (3) To form new muscle fibers through an action called muscle fiber hyperplasia. These researchers cut off the soleus and gastrocnemius (calve) muscle on a bunch of rats, then split them into two groups.

One group received a creatine/glucose/water mixture and the other did not. Then they exercised the poor rodents in a manner that the plantaris leg muscles had to compensate for the missing calve muscles. In both groups, the plantaris showed significant hypertrophy (growth). But the creatine/dextrose supplemental group showed much higher satellite-cell activity. In simple terms, the creatine appears to have increased hyperplasia and total muscle cell numbers. So what? Okay, go read "Growth Hormone" and come back. So, this supports idea that Creatine Supplementation increased the actual muscle mass on a very important level. More cells, more fibers, bigger muscles.

If you have been reading so far with a close eye upon anabolism (muscle growth) you will already realize the connection between CP, ATP, Anabolic/Androgenic steroids, Growth Hormone, Insulin, thyroid hormones, IGF-1, prohormones, and Creatine. Each is tied to the other by the actions of ATP and cellular CP levels. When a bodybuilder does a heavy set, intracellular ATP levels decrease. (Remember, muscle contractions depend on available ATP) As the work-out continues, ATP is further depleted. Another adaptive response to training is the up-regulation of androgen receptors. Simply stated, for several hours after training, your muscle cells have more androgen receptors than they did before training. This allows a greater amount of androgens, (whether naturally produced endogenously, or provided from exogenous sources such as steroids and prohormones) to enter the cell and signal anabolism. Unfortunately due to depleted ATP levels, the cell lacks the "energy" to do its thing. This results in low anabolism, or at least much less than would occur with higher ATP stores. This in part explains why Methyltestosterone and Oxandrolone made any reported AAS cycle much more effective. Methyltestosterone increases 3-guanidinopropionate and Oxandrolone increases CP synthesis.

Another example is GH and IGF-1. When GH finds a GH receptor-site on a muscle cell, it triggers IGF-1 release within the cell (or from the liver if the GH activates IGF-1 production there) and a high level of anabolism results. But not if ATP/CP levels are low. This is one of the reasons why, during dieting, it is difficult to increase muscle anabolism. GH works anabolically, only with high calories because high calories increase ATP production, and anabolism depends on ATP for an energy source. Anabolism is hard work. Again, this is why most anabolic/androgenic steroids work only in an environment of high calories. Every muscle fiber contains satellite-cells just waiting to join the fibers so the fibers can grow thicker and stronger. More cells, more fibers and thicker fibers, means more cell/fibers to grow. Creatine Monohydrate is an exogenous source of CP which increases ATP production.

I have noted that dieting bodybuilders not using Creatine lose bodyweight more quickly. Yet they also lose much more lean muscle mass as well. Those who used a T-3 thyroid hormone also had higher creatine stores, and those using Creatine supplementation with T-3 had the highest creatine stores. I have also noted that those using a fast acting glycemic carb, whey protein, creatine drink only after training and during diet phases lost more bodyfat yet actually gained lean muscle mass. Those who used the mixture of whey, Creatine, D-Pinitol, Triacana, Ephedrine, and Maltodextrin, looked much harder and fuller. So what do you think of Creatine now? There are several good creatine forms such as effervescent and those providing transporters and Insulin mimickers. But this is a book about hormones.

A great deal of personal experience and research went into this project, the latter often being refereed to as "available literature" or "commonly noted".

References and available literature

Effects of nandrolone on recovery in horses...
Author/s: Hyypp, S. Volume: 48 Issue: 6 Page: 343-352 Year: 2001
Source: *JOURNAL OF VETERINARY MEDICINE - SERIES A -*

A comparison of megastrol acetate, nandrolone decanoate...
Author/s: Batterham MJ Volume: 24 Issue: 4 Page: 232-240 Year: 2001
Source: *INTERNATIONAL JOURNAL OF ANDROLOGY*

Body composition and anthrometry in bodybuilders...
Author/s: Hartgens, F. Volume: 22 Issue: 3 Page: 235-241 Year: 2001
Source: *INTERNATIONAL JOURNAL OF SPORTS MEDICINE*

Liver-derived IGF-1 regulates hGH secretion at pituitary Level...
Author/s: K Wallenius Volume: 142 Issue: 11 Page: 4762-4770 Year: 2001
Source: *ENDOCRINOLOGY*

Biochemical of individual response to growth hormone...
Author/s: J.P. Monson Volume: 55 Page: 49-54 Year: 2001
Source: *HORMONE RESEARCH*

Relationship of physical exercise and aging to growth hormones...
Author/s: S J Hurel Volume: 51 Issue: 6 Page: 687-691 Year: 2000
Source: *CLINICAL ENDOCRINOLOGY*

Bush baby growth hormone is much more similar to nonprimate growth hormone...
Author/s: R M Adkins Volume: 18 Issue: 1 Page: 55-60 Year: 2000
Source: *MOLECULAR BIOLOGY AND EVOLUTION*

Growth hormone does not attenuate the inhibitory effects of...
Author/s: J Stamm Volume: 8 Issue: 2 Page: 103-109 Year: 2000
Source: *WOUND REPAIR AND REGENERATION*

The inhibitory effects of (gamma)-aminobutyric acid (GABA) on growth hormone...
Author/s: V L Trudeau Volume: 203 Pt 9 Page: 1477-1485 Year: 2000

Possible role of human growth hormone in penile erection.
Author/s: Scheller, Friedemann Volume: 164 Issue: 6 Page: 2138-2142 Year: 2000
Source: *JOURNAL OF UROLOGY*

Effects of physiological growth hormone therapy...
Author/s: Baum, H. B. A. Volume: 125 Issue: 11 Page: 883-890 Year: 1996
Source: *ANNALS OF INTERNAL MEDICINE*

Cellular localization of growth hormone receptors/binding protein…
Author/s: Hull_K_L Volume: 286 Issue: 1 Page: 69-80 Year: 1996
Source: *CELL AND TISSUE RESEARCH*

Effects of epoxyeicosatrienoic acids on growth hormone release…
Author/s: G D Snyder Volume: 256 Issue: 2 Pt 1 Page: E221-E226 Year: 1989
Source: *AMERICAN JOURNAL OF PHYSIOLOGY*

Drugs in sports-the role of the physician
Author/s: Dawson, R. T. Volume: 170 Issue: 1 Page: 55-61 Year: 2001
Source: *JOURNAL OF ENDOCRINOLOGY*

The effects of anabolic steroids on the distribution of muscles fibers…
Author/s: M Konishi Volume: 106 Issue: 2--1 Page: 175-183 Year: 2001
Source: *Italian journal of anatomy and embryology = Archivio it*

Anabolic steroid misuse: How much should we know?
Author/s: Gonzalez, Alejandro Volume: 5 Issue: 3 Page: 159-167 Year: 2001
Source: *INTERNATIONAL JOURNAL OF PSYCHIATRY IN CLINICAL PRACTIC*

Doping: effectiveness, consequences, prevention,…
Author/s: C Y Guezennec Volume: 62 Issue: 1-1 Page: 33-41 Year: 2001
Source: *ANNALES D ENDOCRINOLOGIE*

Insulin secretory response is positively associated with…
Author/s: T Akune Volume: 83-A Issue: 10 Page: 1537-1544 Year: 2001
Source: *JOURNAL OF BONE AND JOINT SURGERY (AMERICAN VOLUME)*

Insulin resistance and insulin Sensitizers
Author/s: M. Stumvoll Volume: 55 Page: 3-13 Year: 2001
Source: *HORMONE RESEARCH*

Graphical human insulin time-activity profiles using standardized…
Author/s: Frohnauer, Mary Volume: 3 Issue: 3 Page: 419-429 Year: 2001
Source: *DIABETES TECHNOLOGY & THERAPEUTICS*

Regulation of insulin/insulin-like growth factor-1 signaling…
Author/s: L Rui Volume: 276 Issue: 43 Page: 40362-40367 Year: 2001
Source: *JOURNAL OF BIOLOGICAL CHEMISTRY*

Rosiglitazone treatment of patients with extreme insulin resistance…
Author/s: Vestergaard, H. Volume: 250 Issue: 5 Page: 406-414 Year: 2001
Source: *JOURNAL OF INTERNAL MEDICINE*

Co-administration of etomoxir and RU-486 mitigates insulin resistance…
Author/s: M S Bitar Volume: 33 Issue: 10 Page: 577-584 Year: 2001
Source: *Hormone and metabolic research = Hormon- und Stoffwechs*

Insulin and IGF-1 induce different patterns of gene expression...
Author/s: J Dupont Volume: 142 Issue: 11 Page: 4969-4975 Year: 2001
Source: *ENDOCRINOLOGY*

Effects of transdermal testosterone treatment on serum lipid and...
Author/s: PJ Snyder Volume: 111 Issue: 4 Page: 255-260 Year: 2001
Source: *AMERICAN JOURNAL OF MEDICINE*

Randomized placebo-controlled trial of testosterone replacement...
Author/s: Howell, S. J. Volume: 55 Issue: 3 Page: 315-324 Year: 2001
Source: *CLINICAL ENDOCRINOLOGY*

Metabolism of orally administered androstenedione in young men...
Author/s: B Z Leder Volume: 86 Issue: 8 Page: 3654-3658 Year: 2001
Source: *JOURNAL OF CLINICAL ENDOCRINOLOGY AND METABOLISM*

Nongenomic effect of testosterone on chloride secretion...
Author/s: Leung, G. P. H. Volume: 280 Issue: 5-2 Page: C1160-C1167 Year: 2001
Source: *AMERICAN JOURNAL OF PHYSIOLOGY*

Testosterone replacement therapy for hypogonadal men...
Author/s: Seidman SN Volume: 62 Issue: 6 Page: 406-412 Year: 2001
Source: *JOURNAL OF CLINICAL PSYCHIATRY*

Effects of 8-epi-PGF-2 on isolated bronchial smooth muscle...
Author/s: Art Volume: 24 Issue: 3 Page: 215-221 Year: 2001
Source: *JOURNAL OF VETERINARY PHARMACOLOGY AND THERAPEUTICS*

Oxytocin stimulates prostaglandin F2a secretion from...
Volume: 65 Issue: 2-3 Page: 85-102 Year: 2001
Source: *Prostaglandins & other lipid mediators*

Analysis of meloncyte precursors in Nf1 mutants reveals that MGF...
Author/s: Meller, Margaret Volume: 232 Issue: 2 Page: 471-483 Year: 2001
Source: *DEVELOPMENTAL BIOLOGY*

Review of oxymetholone: a 17alpha-alkylated anabolic-androgenic steroid
Author/s: Pharmd Volume: 23 Issue: 6 Page: 789-801 Year: 2001
Source: *CLINICAL THERAPEUTICS*

Randomized phase III trial of oxymetholone for the treatment of ...
Author/s: Hengge, U. R. Volume: 6 Issue: 4 Page: 70 Year: 2001
Source: *ANTIVIRAL THERAPY*

Anabolic effects of oxandrolone after severe burn
Author/s: Ramzy, P. I. Volume: 233 Issue: 4 Page: 556-564 Year: 2001
Source: *ANNALS OF SURGERY*

Oxandrolone in trauma patients
Author/s: J M Gervasio Volume: 20 Issue: 11 Page: 1328-1334 Year: 2001
Source: *PHARMACOTHERAPY*

The anabolic steroid oxandrolone increases muscle mass in prepubescent...
Author/s: A Papadimitriou Volume: 14 Issue: 6 Page: 725-727 Year: 2001
Source: *Service Today*

Long term results of growth hormone therapy in Turner syndrome...
Author/s: JH Bramswig Volume: 15 Issue: 1 Page: 5-13 Year: 2001
Source: *ENDOCRINE JOURNAL.*
Comparison of the effects of 17alpha-methyltestosterone, methandrostenolone,...
Author/s: Clark, A. S. Volume: 110 Issue: 6 Page: 1478-1486 Year: 1996
Source: *BEHAVIORAL NEUROSCIENCE*

The effects of 17alpha-methyltestosterone, methandrostenolone and...
Author/s: M E Blasberg Volume: 61 Issue: 2 Page: 265-272 Year: 1997
Source: *PHYSIOLOGY AND BEHAVIOR*

Anabolic-androgenic steroid and adrenal steroid effects on...
Author/s: Clark_A_S Volume: 679 Issue: 1 Page: 64 Year: 1995
Source: *BRAIN RESEARCH*

Studies on anabolic steroids 11. 18-hydroxylated metabolites of...
Author/s: MASSE R Volume: 42 Issue: 3-4 Page: 399-410 Year: 1992
Source: *JOURNAL OF STEROID BIOCHEMISTRY AND MOLECULAR BIOLOGY*

[The outlook for hormonal therapy in nutrition]
Author/s: A Sanz Pars Volume: 9 Issue: 5 Page: 295-303 Year: 1994
Source: *Nutr Hosp*

Effect of estradiol dipropionate on the rate of protein synthesis...
Author/s: Varaksina, G. S. Volume: 27 Issue: 2 Page: 117-120 Year: 2001
Source: *BIOLOGIA MORA*

Characterisation of the affinity of different anabolics and synthetic...
Author/s: H Sauerwein Issue: 103 Page: S452-60 Year: 2001
Source: *APMIS. ACTA PATHOLOGICA, MICROBIOLOGICA ET IMMUNOLOGICA*

The fate of trenbolone acetate and melengestrol acetate after...
Author/s: B Schiffer Volume: 109 Issue: 11 Page: 1145-1151 Year: 2001
Source: *ENVIRONMENTAL HEALTH PERSPECTIVES*

Assessment of oestrogenic of chemicals used as growth promoters...
Author/s: R Le Guevel Issue: 103 Page: S473-9 Year: 2001
Source: *APMIS. ACTA PATHOLOGICA, MICROBIOLOGICA ET IMMUNOLOGICA*

Growth promoters and their effects on beef production
Author/s: Choi, S. H. Volume: 14 Issue: 1 Page: 123-135 Year: 2001
Source: *ASIAN AUSTRALASIAN JOURNAL OF ANIMAL SCIENCES*

Thyroxine treatment in patients with symptoms of hypothyroidism…
Author/s: M A Pollock Volume: 323 Issue: 7318 Page: 891-895 Year: 2001
Source: *BRITISH MEDICAL JOURNAL*

What is the optimal treatment for hypothyroidism?
Author/s: Walsh, J. P. Volume: 174 Issue: 3 Page: 141-143 Year: 2001
Source: *MEDICAL JOURNAL OF AUSTRALIA*

11beta-hydroxysteroid dehydrogenase bioactivity is increased in…
Author/s: Ruszymah, B. H. Volume: 109 Issue: 4 Page: 227-230 Year: 2001
Source: *Experimental and clinical endocrinology & diabetes : of*

Constitutive and interleukin-7 and interleukin-15 stimulated DNA…
Author/s: JZ Qin Volume: 117 Issue: 3 Page: 583-589 Year: 2001
Source: *JOURNAL OF INVESTIGATIVE DERMATOLOGY SYMPOSIUM PROCEEDI*

Interleukin-15 is the main mediator of lymphocyte proliferation…
Author/s: E Lewis Volume: 72 Issue: 5 Page: 886-890 Year: 2001
Source: *TRANSPLANTATION –BALTIMORE*

Production and distribution of interleukin-15 and its receptors…
Author/s: Saeed Volume: 82 Issue: 3 Page: 201-209 Year: 2001
Source: *INTERNATIONAL JOURNAL OF EXPERIMENTAL PATHOLOGY*
Effects of anti-TGF-II receptor antibody on experimental…
Author/s: Ito, Yasuhiko Volume: 60 Issue: 5 Page: 1745-1755 Year: 2001
Source: *KIDNEY INTERNATIONAL*
Effect of the beta (2) agonist clenbuterol on the locomotor activity…
Author/s: L Stevens Volume: 122 Issue: 1 Page: 103-112 Year: 2001
Source: *BEHAVIOURAL BRAIN RESEARCH*

Clenbuterol ingestion causing prolonged tachycardia, hypokalemia,…
Author/s: RJ Hoffman Volume: 39 Issue: 4 Page: 339-344 Year: 2001
Source: *JOURNAL OF TOXICOLOGY: CLINICAL TOXICOLOGY (1981-)*

Clenbuterol in the prevention of muscle atrophy: A study of…
Author/s: N M Herrera Volume: 82 Issue: 7 Page: 930-934 Year: 2001
Source: *ARCHIVES OF PHYSICAL MEDICINE AND REHABILITATION*

Effects of clenbuterol on insulin resistance in conscious obese…
Author/s: Z Ding Volume: 280 Issue: 4 Page: E554-E561 Year: 2001
Source: *American journal of physiology. Endocrinology and metab*

Influence of clenbuterol treatment during 6 weeks of chronic...
Author/s: M H Yacoub Volume: 122 Issue: 4 Page: 767-774 Year: 2001
Source: *JOURNAL OF THORACIC AND CARDIOVASCULAR SURGERY*

Lack of efficacy of finasteride in post-menopausal women with androgen...
Author/s: V Fiedler Volume: 43 Issue: 5-1 Page: 768-776 Year: 2001
Source: *JOURNAL OF THE AMERICAN ACADEMY OF DERMATOLOGY*

Finasteride cream in hirsutism
Author/s: K J Lucas Volume: 7 Issue: 1 Page: 5-10 Year: 2001
Source: *ENDOCRINE PRACTICE*

Aromatase, aromatase inhibitors, and breast cancer
Author/s: RW Brueggemeier Volume: 8 Issue: 5 Page: 333-344 Year: 2001
Source: *AMERICAN JOURNAL OF THERAPEUTICS*

Aminoglutethimide, a steroidogenesis inhibitor, abolishes hormonal...
Author/s: Bastida, C. M. Volume: 281 Issue: 1 Page: 244-248 Year: 2001
Source: *BIOCHEMICAL AND BIOPHYSICAL RESEARCH COMMUNICATIONS*

Sequential tamoxifen and aminoglutethimide vs tamoxifen alone...
Author/s: F Boccardo Volume: 19 Issue: 22 Page: 4209-4215 Year: 2001
Source: *JOURNAL OF CLINICAL ONCOLOGY*

Expression of messenger RNA for gonadotropin receptor in the...
Author/s: Yamamura, N. Volume: 129A Issue: 2-3 Page: 327-337 Year: 2001
Source: *Comparative biochemistry and physiology. Part A, Molecu*
Lipoproteins regulate the expression of the steroidogenic acute...
Author/s: M E Reyland Volume: 275 Issue: 47 Page: 36637-36644 Year: 2001
Source: *JOURNAL OF BIOLOGICAL CHEMISTRY*

Excretion of the anabolic steroid boldenone by racing pigeons
Author/s: Hagedorn, H.-W. Volume: 58 Issue: 3 Page: 224-227 Year: 1997
Source: *AMERICAN JOURNAL OF VETERINARY RESEARCH*

Stanozolol in chronic uticaria : A double blind placebo controlled...
Author/s: D Parsad Volume: 28 Issue: 6 Page: 299-302 Year: 2001
Source: *JOURNAL OF DERMATOLOGY*

Hepatic lipase activity influences high density lipoprotein...
Author/s: S M Grundy Volume: 40 Issue: 2 Page: 229-234 Year: 2001
Source: *JOURNAL OF LIPID RESEARCH*

Anabolic steroid abuse and cardiac sudden death...
Author/s: Baroldi, Giorgio Volume: 125 Issue: 2 Page: 253-255 Year: 2001
Source: *ARCHIVES OF PATHOLOGY AND LABORATORY MEDICINE*

On the role of human chorionic gonadotropin (hCG) in the embryo-...
Author/s: P Licht Volume: 19 Issue: 1 Page: 37-47 Year: 2001
Source: *Nephrology nursing journal : journal of the American Ne*

Periovulatory serum human chorionic gonadotropin (hCG)...
Author/s: Sills, E Scott Volume: 76 Issue: 2 Page: 397-399 Year: 2001
Source: *FERTILITY AND STERILITY -INTERNATIONAL EDITION-*

Recombinant human chorionic gonadotropin (rhCG) in assisted...
Author/s: P Chang Volume: 76 Issue: 1 Page: 67-74 Year: 2001
Source: *FERTILITY AND STERILITY -INTERNATIONAL EDITION*

Pharmacokinetics and pharmacodynamics of nandrolone esters in oil
Author/s: Minto, C. F. Volume: 281 Issue: 1 Page: 93-102 Year: 1997
Source: *JOURNAL OF PHARMACOLOGY AND EXPERIMENTAL THERAPEUTICS*

Effects of the anabolic steroid nandrolone decanoate on plasma...
Author/s: Obasanjo, Iyabo Volume: 45 Issue: 4 Page: 463-468 Year: 1996
Source: *METABOLISM, CLINICAL AND EXPERIMENTAL*

The androgenic anabolic steroid nandrolone decanoate prevents...
Author/s: Jerome, C. P. Volume: 20 Issue: 4 Page: 355-364 Year: 1997
Source: *Bone (New York, N.Y.)*

Effect of anabolic/androgenic steroids on myosin heavy chain expression...
Author/s: Noirez, Philippe Volume: 81 Issue: 1-2 Page: 155-158 Year: 2000
Source: *EUROPEAN JOURNAL OF APPLIED PHYSIOLOGY*

Trace contamination of over the counter androstenedione and positive...
Author/s: Green, G. A. Volume: 284 Issue: 20 Page: 2618-2621 Year: 2000
Source: *JUNKJAMA*

Safety and efficacy of nandrolone decanoate for treatment of...
Author/s: J Gold Volume: 10 Issue: 7 Page: 745-752 Year: 1996
Source: *AIDS*

Androgen therapy for anemia of chronic renal failure...
Author/s: Teruel, Jose L. Volume: 30 Issue: 5 Page: 403-408. Year: 1996
Source: *SCANDINAVIAN JOURNAL OF UROLOGY AND NEPHROLOGY*

IGF status is altered by tamoxifen in patient with breast cancer
Author/s: MJ Campbell Volume: 54 Issue: 5 Page: 307-310 Year: 2001
Source: *Molecular pathology : MP*

Possible roles of insulin-like growth factor in regulation of...
Author/s: Skrtic, Stanko Volume: 55 Issue: Suppl-1 Page: 1-6 Year: 2001
Source: *HORMONE RESEARCH*

Insulin-like growth factor 1 (IGF-1) induced twist expression is...
Author/s: J Dupont Volume: 276 Issue: 28 Page: 26699-26707 Year: 2001
Source: *JOURNAL OF BIOLOGICAL CHEMISTRY*